# Friends Forever
## Quilting Together

*by Nancy Smith*
*and*
*Lynda Milligan*

**POSSIBILITIES**®

...Publishers of DreamSpinners® patterns, I'll Teach
Myself™ sewing products, and Possibilities® books...

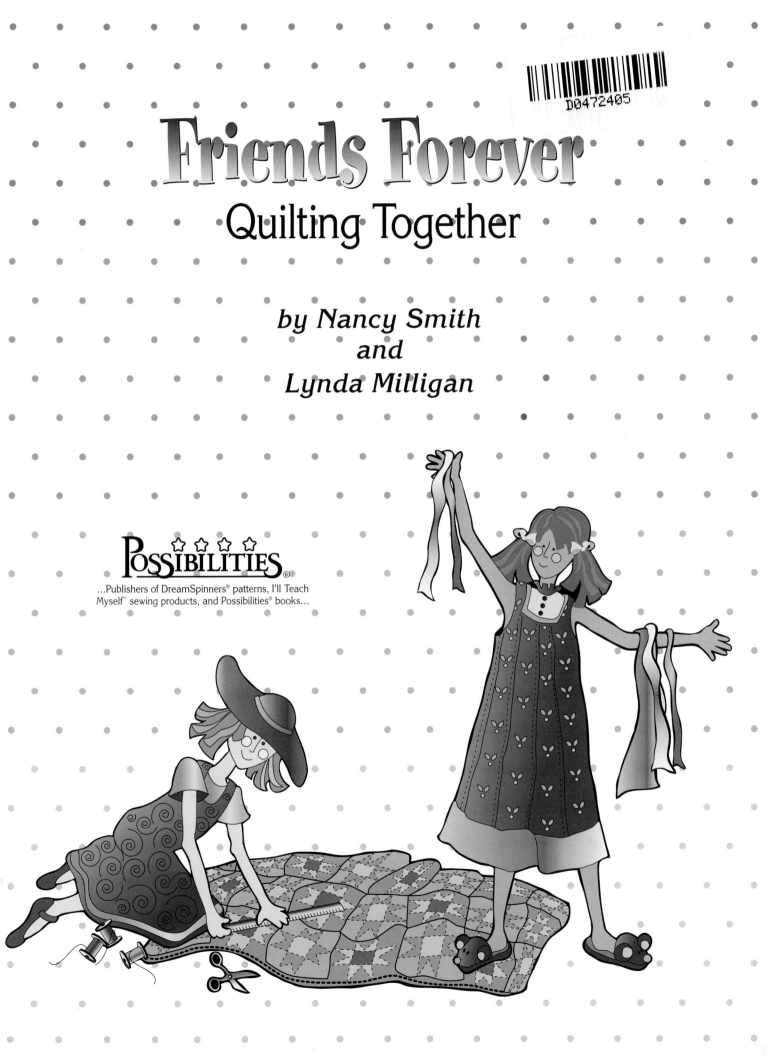

## Acknowledgements

Years ago, Ruth, one of our employees, forgot to imprint a customer's credit card number after a purchase. Ruth called every Malone in the phone book from Denver to Colorado Springs trying to find a Joanne Malone. A few weeks after she had given up hope, a customer came in, purchased something, and signed her charge receipt Joanne Malone. Ruth could hardly contain her excitement. She explained to Joanne what had happened, and they carried on a conversation that lasted for a couple of hours. By the end of the evening they had become good friends, and by the end of the week Joanne was working for us. We didn't know at that time how lucky we were to have hired her.

Joanne worked in the store for several years and now works with us in design. She is tops at machine applique, and when given a sewing challenge doesn't stop until she has it conquered. Joanne teaches classes, gives shop tours, lectures to women's groups, and inspires everyone she meets to start quilting.

Joanne punctuates every day with humor! She has the incredible ability to laugh at herself as well as others, oh, sorry, make *others* laugh. Her life away from the store includes time shared with her two daughters, Karen and Kathy, their husbands, and her four wonderful grandchildren. When she is not at work or with her family, she is usually piecing and quilting on her own machine at home.

It is with genuine friendship, caring, and laughter that we dedicate this book to Joanne.

**By the way, Joanne, where did you find your watch?**

## Special Thanks

Jane Dumler, Joanne Malone, Jan Hagan, Ann Petersen, Michielle Schlichenmayer, Laura Smith, Barbara O'Melia, Katie Wells, Susan Auskaps, Courtenay Hughes, Eileen Lingen, Sue Williams – for stitching, binding, and quilting.

Sandi Fruehling, Susan F. Geddes, Carolyn Schmitt – for long-arm machine quilting.

Sara Felton and Ashley Lawler for promotion and planning.

Crate & Barrel – for photography in their store.

Susan Johnson – for photography in her home and yard.

## Credits

Sharon Holmes – Editor, Technical Illustrator
Susan Johnson – Design, Graphics, Photo Stylist
Lexie Foster – Design, Graphics, Photo Stylist
Chris Scott – Editorial Assistant
Sandi Fruehling – Copy Reader
Brian Birlauf – Photography
Lee Milne – Digital Photography

Every effort has been made to ensure that the information in this book is accurate. Due to individual skills, conditions, and tools, we cannot be responsible for any losses, injuries, or other damages that may result from its use.

...Publishers of DreamSpinners® patterns, I'll Teach Myself™ sewing products, and Possibilities® books...

## Friends Forever Quilting Together
©2001 by Nancy Smith & Lynda Milligan

All rights reserved. No part of this book may be reproduced in any form without permission of the authors. The written instructions, photographs, patterns, and designs are intended for the retail purchaser and are protected under federal copyright laws. Projects may not be manufactured for commercial sale.

Published in the United States of America by Possibilities®, Denver, Colorado
Library of Congress Catalog Card Number: 2001095506
ISBN: 1-880972-45-X

# Photo Index

Treasure the heart of a FRIEND!

# Friends Forever

A special friend deserves a special quilt. This one is small enough to fit one of those nooks and crannies that all houses have and quick enough to make on your day off. Use your own alphabet to change the wording at the bottom of the wall hanging to fit any friendship, from gardening to cooking to playing tennis! Or leave the wording off entirely.

*It takes a long time to grow an old friend.*

Kathy Davis

Photo on front cover

Approximate size 24 x 28″

Use 42-45″-wide fabric. When strips appear in the cutting list, cut crossgrain strips (selvage to selvage).

Patterns are given for fusible web applique, reversed and ready to be traced. Be sure to have plenty of fusible web on hand if using this method. Reverse patterns and add seam allowance if doing hand applique.

## YARDAGE

| | |
|---|---|
| Sky | ⅔ yd blue |
| Grass | ⅛ yd green |
| Ground | ⅛ yd brown |
| Appliques | ¼ yd purple for dress |
| | ⅙ yd lavender for shirt |
| | ⅙ yd yellow for flower centers |
| | ⅙ yd orange for flower centers |
| | ⅙ yd purple for flower petals |
| | ⅛ yd each or scraps of other fabrics |
| Border 1 | ⅙ yd blue |
| Border 2 | ¼ yd each - lavender & purple |
| Binding | ⅜ yd blue |
| Backing | 1 yd |
| Batting | 28 x 32″ |

## CUTTING

*Cut these squares in HALF diagonally

| | |
|---|---|
| Sky | 1 rectangle 20½ x 19½″ |
| Grass | 1 rectangle 2½ x 19½″ |
| Ground | 1 rectangle 1½ x 19½″ |
| Appliques | 1 set - patterns on pages 34-37 |
| Border 1 | 3 strips 1″ wide |
| Border 2 | *22 squares 2⅞″ of each fabric |
| | 2 squares 2½″ of each fabric |
| Binding | 3-4 strips 2¼″ wide |

## DIRECTIONS

Use ¼" seam allowance unless otherwise noted.

1. Stitch grass and ground rectangles to bottom of sky rectangle. Press. Measure length and cut Border 1 side pieces that measurement. Stitch to quilt. Press. Measure width and cut Border 1 top/bottom pieces that measurement. Stitch to quilt. Press.

2. Applique center panel.

3. Border 2:

   a. Make 44 half-square triangle units as shown.

   b. Stitch half-square triangle units together for side borders. See diagram.

   c. Stitch side borders to quilt.

   d. Make top and bottom borders. Stitch corner squares to ends as shown.

   e. Stitch top and bottom borders to quilt. Press.

4. Cut backing to same size as batting. Layer and quilt as desired. Trim backing and batting even with top.

5. Stitch binding strips together end to end. Press in half lengthwise, wrong sides together. Bind quilt using ¼" seam allowance.

1.

3.  Make 44

Make 2 for sides

Make top & bottom

Flowers make us happy!

5

# True Blue

Keep this quilt in mind when you need a quick gift for a friend. We made this one in flannel with a wool batting—a great cuddleup quilt. Choose a color family, add an accent color, cut your squares, and start piecing. The simplicity of the pattern is repeated in the quilting design.

*There are those who pass like ships in the night, who meet for a moment then sail out of sight with never a backward glance of regret, folks we know briefly then quickly forget. Then there are friends who sail together through quiet waters and stormy weather, helping each other through joy and through strife, and they are the kind who give meaning to life.*

Unknown

Photo on page 20

Approximate size 60 x 84″

Use 42-45″-wide fabric. When strips appear in the cutting list, cut crossgrain strips (selvage to selvage).

## YARDAGE

| | |
|---|---|
| Squares | ¾ yd each of 6 blue flannels |
| Borders 1 & 2 including corner blocks | ¾ yd red |
| | 1½ yd blue |
| Binding | ⅔ yd blue |
| Backing | 5¼ yd |
| Batting | 66 x 90″ |

## CUTTING

*Cut these squares in HALF diagonally

| | |
|---|---|
| Squares | 96 squares 6½″ |
| Border 1 | *40 squares 3⅞″ of each fabric |
| Border 2 | 7 strips 3½″ wide - blue |
| Corner squares | 4 squares 3½″ - red |
| | 16 squares 2″ - blue |
| | *16 squares 2⅜″ of each fabric |
| Binding | 8 strips 2½″ wide |

# DIRECTIONS

Use ¼″ seam allowance unless otherwise noted.

1. Stitch squares into horizontal rows of 8. Stitch rows together. Press.

2. Corner Blocks: Make 4 blocks following diagram. Press.

3. Border 1: Make 80 half-square triangle units. Make 2 side borders of 24 units and 2 top/bottom borders of 16 units, rotating triangles as shown. Press. Check to see that borders fit quilt before proceeding.

4. Side Borders: Piece Border 2 strips to the length of long Border 1 units and stitch to blue sides of Border 1 units. Stitch side borders to quilt, rotating units as shown in whole-quilt diagram. Press.

5. Top/Bottom Borders: Piece Border 2 strips to the length of short Border 1 units and stitch to blue sides of Border 1 units. Stitch corner blocks to each end of top and bottom borders. Stitch borders to quilt. Press.

6. Piece backing vertically to same size as batting. Layer and quilt as desired. Our sample was quilted with heavy red thread like the whole-quilt diagram at left. Trim backing and batting even with top.

7. Stitch binding strips together end to end. Press in half lengthwise, wrong sides together. Bind quilt using ⅜″ seam allowance.

1.

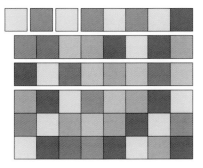

2.

■ Make 32

◤◥ Make 16

Make 4

3-5. ◨ Make 80

Make 2 - Sides

Make 2 - Top & Bottom

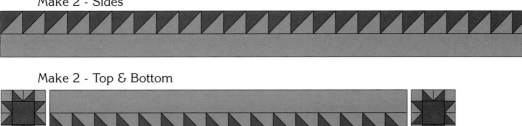

# Messages from the Heart

Give this envelope quilt to anyone who needs messages from your heart: a child on their birthday, a teenager going away to college, a grieving friend, an ill relative, or a neighbor who is moving away.

The envelopes can contain small treasures such as chocolates, small books, coupons to redeem for special favors, pens that light up when you write, special event tickets, pretty soaps, and anything else that will fit!

*Not what we give, but what we share, for the gift without the giver is bare.*

James Russell Lowell

Photo on page 52

Approximate size 34″      7″ block

Use 42-45″-wide fabric. When strips appear in the cutting list, cut crossgrain strips (selvage to selvage).

Patterns are given for fusible web applique, reversed and ready to be traced. Be sure to have plenty of fusible web on hand if using this method. Reverse patterns and add seam allowance if doing hand applique.

## YARDAGE

| | |
|---|---|
| Envelope blocks | ⅓ yd each of 7 or more bright prints |
| Appliques | ⅙ yd each of red & green |
| Sashing rectangles & Border 2 | ½ yd black |
| Sashing squares | ⅛ yd white |
| Border 1 | ⅓ yd green |
| Border 3 | ⅜ yd purple |
| Binding | ⅜ yd bright print |
| Backing | 1⅛ yd |
| Batting | 38x38″ |
| Snaps | 9 small to medium size |

## CUTTING

| | |
|---|---|
| Envelope blocks | 9 squares 7½″ for backs |
| | 18 squares 8″ for sides |
| | 9 rectangles 7½x4″ for flaps |
| Appliques | 9 sets - pattern on page 38 |
| Sashing rectangles | 24 rectangles 1½x7½″ |
| Sashing squares | 16 squares 1½″ |
| Border 1 | 4 strips 2″ wide |
| Border 2 | 4 strips 1½″ wide |
| Border 3 | 4 strips 2½″ wide |
| Binding | 4 strips 2½″ wide |

## DIRECTIONS

Use ¼″ seam allowance unless otherwise noted.

1. Envelope blocks - Make 9

   a. Press 2 side pieces in half diagonally, wrong sides together. Pin to right side of block back piece, bottom corners matching. Points will extend beyond back piece.

   b. Pin side pieces together at overlap. Remove sides from back and stitch close to edge along diagonal overlap.

   c. Applique flowers to left side of each envelope.

   d. Place sides on back piece again. Stitch side and bottom edges together ⅛″ from edge, as shown.

   e. Fold flap piece in half, right sides together, to a 3¾ x 4″ rectangle. Stitch one 3¾″ edge. See diagram. Trim point. Turn right side out and place seam in center as shown. Press.

   f. Pin flap to top edge of envelope block, raw edges even, and stitch ⅛″ from edge. Trim points.

   g. Stitch snap parts to point of flap and directly beneath.

2. Make 4 rows of sashing rectangles and sashing squares. Make 3 rows of blocks and sashing rectangles. See diagram.

3. Stitch rows of sashing and rows of blocks together. Press.

4. Border 1: Measure length of quilt. Cut border strips to the measured length and stitch to sides of quilt. Repeat at top and bottom. Press.

5. Borders 2 and 3: Repeat Step 4.

6. Cut backing to same size as batting. Layer and quilt as desired. Trim backing and batting even with top.

7. Stitch binding strips together end to end. Press in half lengthwise, wrong sides together. Bind quilt using ⅜″ seam allowance.

1.

Trim

Trim points

2.

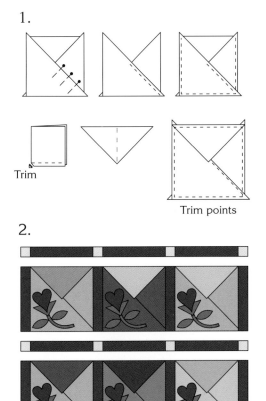

# Friendships Blossom

This quilt represents the neighborhood, the village, and the friendships that blossom there. When a friend or neighbor moves, get a group together to make a special good-bye gift. In fact, why wait until a friend relocates to get together and make a neighborhood quilt? If you need a smaller project, make just the center section, adding a border of squares instead of a border of houses.

*Friendship is a sheltering tree.*
Samuel Taylor Coleridge

Photo on page 21

Approximate size 58"    9½" House and Log Cabin Blocks

Use 42-45"-wide fabric. When strips appear in the cutting list, cut crossgrain strips (selvage to selvage).

Patterns are given for fusible web applique, reversed and ready to be traced. Be sure to have plenty of fusible web on hand if using this method. Reverse patterns and add seam allowance if doing hand applique.

## YARDAGE

| | |
|---|---|
| House blocks | ⅝ yd tan - background |
| | ¼ yd each of approximately 6 browns & 5 reds |
| | ⅛ yd each of approximately 6 blues |
| | ⅛ yd of 1 or more greens |
| | ⅛ yd each of approximately 4 yellows |
| Log Cabin blocks | ⅙ yd each of approximately 6 creams/tans |
| Center panel | ⅞ yd tan |
| Inner Border 1 | ⅙ yd medium blue |
| Inner Border 2 | ⅜ yd brown |
| Inner Border 3 | ⅙ yd dark blue |
| Appliques | ¼ yd tan - lower background |
| | ⅝ yd brown - tree |
| | ⅛ yd each of 2 greens - leaves |
| | ¼ yd dark blue - neighbors |
| | ¼ yd medium blue - lettering |
| | scraps from one of the house reds - hearts |
| Outer Border 1 | ⅓ yd green |
| Outer Border 2 | ⅓ yd each of 5 creams/tans |
| Binding | ⅝ yd green |
| Backing | 3⅞ yd |
| Batting | 64x64" |

## CUTTING

*Cut these squares in HALF diagonally

| House blocks | yellow | 12 rectangles 2½ x 2¾" - windows |
|---|---|---|
| | tan | *12 squares 2⅞" - background triangles |
| | tan | 36 squares 2½" - background squares |
| | tan | 24 rectangles 1¼ x 10" - background sides |
| | | 24 rectangles 1½ x 2¾" - shutters |
| | | 12 rectangles 1½ x 4½" - below roof (window side) |
| | | 24 rectangles 1⅝ x 4½" - above & below windows |
| | | 12 rectangles 2 x 5" - doors |
| | | 24 rectangles 1¾ x 5" - beside doors |
| | | 12 rectangles 1½ x 4½" - above doors |
| | | 12 each - patterns on pages 39 & 40 - roofs |
| | | 24 rectangles 1½ x 2½" - chimneys |

Continued on page 12

# DIRECTIONS

Use ¼″ seam allowance unless otherwise noted.

1. House Blocks: Make 12 following diagram. Press.

2. Log Cabin Blocks: Make 4 following diagram. Press.

3. Center Panel: Applique center panel, keeping your neighbor's fingers and toes out of the seam allowance.

4. Center Panel Border Units: Stitch one strip each of Inner Borders 1, 2, and 3 together for each side of quilt. Press. Cut each to 23″ length. Applique lettering to center strip for each side, being careful to rotate border units as needed.

5. Stitch Center Panel Border Units to sides of quilt. Applique hearts to corner squares, keeping them out of seam allowance. Stitch corner squares to ends of top and bottom borders, rotating as shown in whole-quilt diagram. Stitch top and bottom borders to quilt.

6. Stitch 3 house blocks together for sides, top, and bottom of quilt. Stitch one set to each side of quilt. Stitch Log Cabin blocks to each end of remaining border units. Stitch to top and bottom of quilt. Press.

7. Outer Border 1: Measure length of quilt. Piece outer border strips to the measured length and stitch to sides of quilt. Repeat at top and bottom. Press.

8. Outer Border 2: Make 3 strip sets using 1 strip of each of the five fabrics in each set. Press. Crosscut into 2½″ segments. Arrange segments as shown and stitch into 2 side borders and 2 top/bottom borders. Note that one square is removed from the length of the top/bottom border units. Press. Stitch side border units to sides of quilt. Stitch top and bottom border units to top and bottom of quilt. Press.

9. Piece backing to same size as batting. Layer and quilt as desired. Trim backing and batting even with top.

10. Stitch binding strips together end to end. Press in half lengthwise, wrong sides together. Bind quilt using ⅜″ seam allowance.

1.

Make 12

2.

Make 4

3-5.

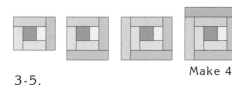

Diagrams continued on page 12

## Friendships Blossom Continued from pages 10 and 11

| | |
|---|---|
| Log Cabin blocks | 4 squares 3″ of darkest fabric |
| | 1-2 strips 2¼″ wide of each remaining fabric |
| Center panel | 1 square 23″ |
| Inner Border 1 | 4 strips 1″ wide |
| Inner Border 2 | 4 strips 2½″ wide |
| Inner Border 3 | 4 strips 1″ wide |
| Inner Border corner squares | 4 squares 3½″ |
| Appliques | patterns on pages 39-42 |
| Outer Border 1 | 5 strips 1¾″ wide |
| Outer Border 2 | 3 strips 2½″ wide of each fabric |
| Binding | 6 strips 2½″ wide |

6.

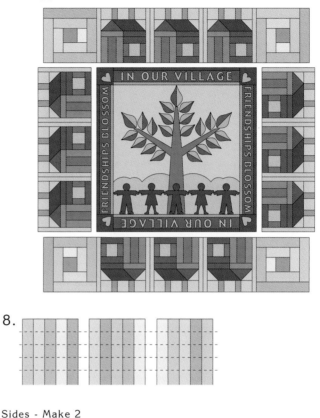

8.

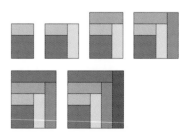

Sides - Make 2

Top & Bottom - Make 2

One square removed

# LOG CABIN PILLOW

Photo on page 21    20″ square

1. Cut corner squares 4½″. Cut 2½″ strips for logs. Stitch strips to center square as shown, trimming end of strip as you go. Make 4 blocks. Press. Stitch blocks together into 2 horizontal rows, rotating as shown. Stitch rows together. Press.

2. Optional: Layer with backing and batting. Quilt as desired. Trim backing and batting to same size as block.

3. Cut 2 envelope back pieces 15x20½″. Make 1″ double-fold hem on 20½″ side of each. Lay back pieces, wrong side down, on wrong side of block, raw edges matching, hemmed edges overlapping at center of pillow. Baste entire outside edge.

4. Stitch binding strips together end to end. Press in half lengthwise, wrong sides together. Bind pillow using ⅜″ seam allowance. Insert a 20″ pillow form.

# BREADCLOTHS

Photos on pages 56 & 60    20″ square

Use 42-45″-wide fabric. When strips appear in the cutting list, cut crossgrain strips (selvage to selvage).

Patterns are given for fusible web applique, reversed and ready to be traced. Be sure to have plenty of fusible web on hand if using this method. Reverse patterns and add seam allowance if doing hand applique.

## Yardage

**House**
| | |
|---|---|
| block | ⅛ yd each of 7 fabrics or scraps |
| border | ⅜ yd |
| backing | ⅛-⅙ yd each of 4-6 fabrics |

**Coffee Cup**
| | |
|---|---|
| block | ⅛ yd each of 8 fabrics or scraps |
| background | ⅛-⅙ yd each of 4-6 fabrics |
| backing | ⅔ yd |

**Sunflower**
| | |
|---|---|
| Log Cabins | ⅛-⅙ yd each of 4-8 fabrics |
| backing | ⅔ yd |

**Tulip**
| | |
|---|---|
| border | ½ yd |
| sashing rect. | ⅓ yd |
| sashing sq. | ⅙ yd |
| backing | ⅔ yd |

| | |
|---|---|
| Appliques | ⅛-⅙ yd pieces or scraps |
| Binding | ⅓ yd for each breadcloth |
| Flannel | 20½ x 20½″ for each breadcloth |

## Cutting

*Cut these squares in HALF diagonally

| Applique | patterns on pages: House block on 39-40 Coffee Cup block on 94 others on 44-45 |
|---|---|
| Binding | 2-3 strips 2½″ wide for each |

**House**
| | |
|---|---|
| border | 2 pieces 5¾ x 10″ |
| | 2 pieces 5¾ x 20½″ |
| backing | 3 strips 1½″ wide |
| | 4 strips 2½″ wide |
| | 3 strips 3½″ wide |

**Coffee Cup**
| | |
|---|---|
| background | same as backing for house breadcloth above |
| backing | 1 square 20½″ |

**Sunflower**
| | |
|---|---|
| Log Cabins | 4 squares 4½″ |
| | 1-2 strips 2½″ wide |
| backing | 1 square 20½″ |

**Tulip**
| | |
|---|---|
| background | 1 square 14½″ |
| border rect. | 4 rectangles 3½ x 14½″ |
| border sq. | 4 squares 3½″ |
| backing | 1 square 20½″ |

## Directions

Use ¼″ seam allowance unless otherwise noted.

Diagrams for breadcloths on pages 44-45.

### HOUSE BREADCLOTH

Make house block following directions on page 11 (divide numbers of pieces in cutting chart by 12). Stitch short border pieces to each side. Stitch long border pieces to top and bottom. Press. Cut backing strips to 24″ long and stitch together in any order desired. Press. Trim to 20½″ square. Applique apples to each corner, rotating as shown. Skip to Layer, Quilt, & Bind paragraph below.

### COFFEE CUP BREADCLOTH

Make coffee cup block following directions on page 59. Cut background strips to 24″ long and stitch together in desired order. Press. Trim to 20½″ square. Turn under block edges ¼″ and applique block to center of background square. Applique hearts to each corner of backing, rotating as shown. Skip to Layer, Quilt, & Bind paragraph below.

### SUNFLOWER BREADCLOTH

Make 4 log cabin blocks following diagrams at bottom of page 12. Stitch into 2 rows of 2 blocks, rotating as shown. Stitch rows together. Press. Applique sunflowers to each corner of backing. Skip to Layer, Quilt, & Bind paragraph below.

### TULIP BREADCLOTH

Stitch border rectangles to sides of background square. Stitch border squares to ends of remaining border rectangles. Stitch to top and bottom of block. Press. Applique tulips to center of block. Applique tulips to each corner of backing, rotating as shown. Skip to Layer, Quilt, & Bind paragraph below.

### LAYER, QUILT, & BIND

Layer top with flannel and backing. Baste edges. Quilt as desired. Stitch binding strips together end to end. Press in half lengthwise, wrong sides together. Bind quilt using ⅜″ seam allowance.

### MATCHING JAR LIDS

Cut 8″ fabric circles with pinking shears. Center and applique one of the patterns on pages 44-45. Tie on wide-mouth jars with ribbon or jute.

One of the nicest things you can do for a friend is teach her to quilt. If she likes fabric, sewing, color, pattern, texture, some of the above, or all of the above, chances are she will love to make quilts. There is something very comforting about handling beautiful fabrics and seeing a patchwork or applique pattern grow as you sew. Quilting nourishes the soul and warms the heart. It's been scientifically proven that blood pressure is lowered when stitching! Give the gift of quilting to a friend!

*He that does good to another does good also to himself.*

Seneca

Photo on page 17

Approximate size 33″    11″ blocks including frame

Use 42-45″-wide fabric. When strips appear in the cutting list, cut crossgrain strips (selvage to selvage).

Patterns are given for fusible web applique, reversed and ready to be traced. Be sure to have plenty of fusible web on hand if using this method. Reverse patterns and add seam allowance if doing hand applique.

## YARDAGE

| | |
|---|---|
| Cream - includes sashing | 1 yd |
| Dark red - includes Border 2 | ¾ yd |
| Dark blue - includes binding | ⅝ yd |
| Light red - includes Border 1 | ⅜ yd |
| Tan, medium red, medium blue, dark green, medium green | ¼ yd each |
| Light blue, light green, dark yellow, medium yellow #1, medium yellow #2, light yellow | ⅛ yd each |
| Backing | 1⅛ yd |
| Batting | 38x38″ |

## CUTTING

*Cut these squares in HALF diagonally

**Block 1**

| | |
|---|---|
| Cream | 1 square 3½″ |
| | 4 rectangles 2x3½″ |
| | *2 squares 3⅞″ |
| Dark red, medium red, dark green, medium blue | *1 square 3⅞″ from each fabric |
| Dark, med, & light yellows | 1 rectangle 2x3½″ from each of 4 fabrics |
| Dark green | 2 pieces 1½x9½″ - frame |
| | 2 pieces 1½x11½″ - frame |

**Block 2**

| | |
|---|---|
| Cream, tan | 2 squares 5″ from each fabric |
| Dark red, medium red | 2 tulips each - pattern on page 16 |
| Medium red, light red | 2 tulip centers each - pattern on page 16 |
| Dark green | 2 stems - pattern on page 16 |
| Medium green | 4 leaves - pattern on page 16 |
| Medium blue | 2 pieces 1½x9½″ - frame |
| | 2 pieces 1½x11½″ - frame |

**Block 3**

| | |
|---|---|
| Cream | 4 rectangles 2¾x5″ |
| | 4 squares 2″ |
| Tan | 4 squares 2¾″ |
| | 5 squares 2″ |

Continued on page 16

## DIRECTIONS

Use ¼″ seam allowance unless otherwise noted.

1. Make blocks following diagrams. Press.

2. Make 3 rows of sashing rectangles and sashing squares. Make 2 rows of blocks and sashing rectangles. See diagram.

3. Stitch rows of sashing and rows of blocks together. Press.

4. Border 1: Measure length of quilt. Cut border strips to the measured length and stitch to sides of quilt. Repeat at top and bottom. Press.

5. Border 2: Repeat Step 4.

6. Cut backing to same size as batting. Layer and quilt as desired. Trim backing and batting even with top.

7. Stitch binding strips together end to end. Press in half lengthwise, wrong sides together. Bind quilt using ⅜″ seam allowance.

1.

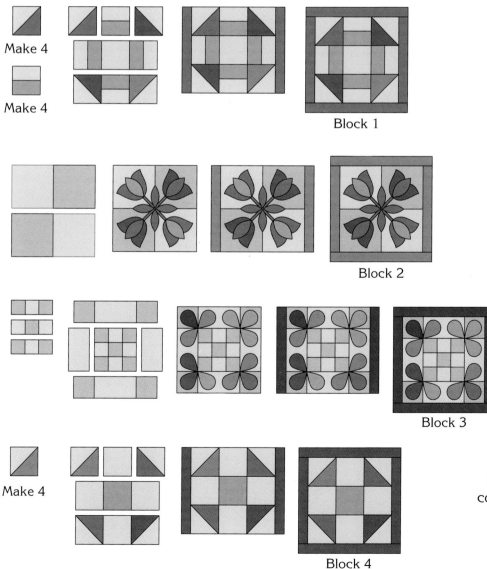

Make 4

Make 4

Block 1

Block 2

Make 4

Block 3

Block 4

Diagrams continued on page 16

# Teach a Friend to Quilt Quilt   Continued from pages 14 and 15

Dark, medium, & light
  red, blue, green & yellow    1 applique piece each - 12 total - pattern below
Dark blue    2 pieces 1½ x 9½″ - frame
   2 pieces 1½ x 11½″ - frame

**Block 4**

Cream    4 squares 3½″
   *2 squares 3⅞″

Medium yellow    1 square 3½″
Medium red, green & blue,
  dark green    *1 square 3⅞″ from each fabric
Dark red    2 pieces 1½ x 9½″ - frame
   2 pieces 1½ x 11½″ - frame

Sashing rectangles    12 rectangles 2 x 11½″ - cream
Sashing squares    9 squares 2″ - dark green, dark blue
Border 1    4 strips 1½″ - light red
Border 2    4 strips 3″ - dark red
Binding    4 strips 2½″ - dark blue

2.

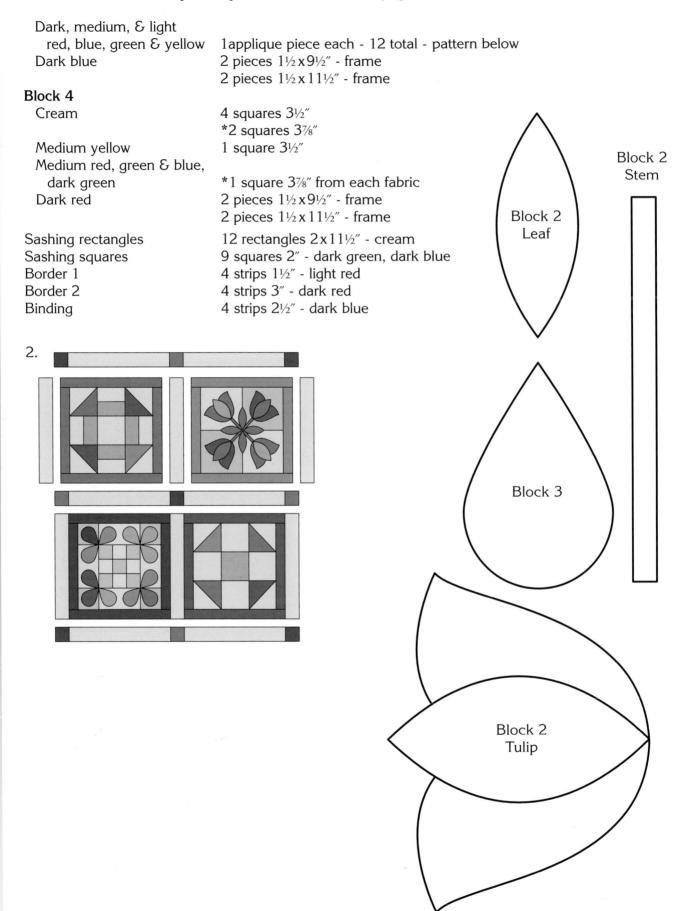

16

Teach a Friend to Quilt Quilt – Page 14

# Best Buds

This would be a fun quilt for a fabric exchange. Have your friends bring the fabrics for their appliqued girls to fit their unique personality, or choose the fabrics yourself and make a game of trying to guess which friend each figure represents.

*Don't walk before me. I may not follow. Don't walk behind me. I may not lead. Just walk beside me and be my friend.*

Albert Camus

Photo on page 28

Approximate size 59x59″      12″ block

Use 42-45″-wide fabric. When strips appear in the cutting list, cut crossgrain strips (selvage to selvage).

Patterns are given for fusible web applique, reversed and ready to be traced. Be sure to have plenty of fusible web on hand if using this method. Reverse patterns and add seam allowance if doing hand applique.

**NOTE:** The pieced border in this quilt necessitates the exact piecing of all elements prior to it, so exact lengths for all pieces for the quilt, except Border 3, are given in the cutting chart or in the directions.

## YARDAGE

| | |
|---|---|
| Block background | 1⅜ yd black print |
| Appliques | ⅙ yd each - or scraps at least 6x8″ - of 9 or more fabrics - dresses |
| | ⅛ yd each - or small scraps - faces, hands, hair, hearts, stockings |
| Sashing, corner squares | ¾ yd fuchsia |
| Border 1 | ½ yd teal |
| Border 2 | ¾ yd purple |
| Borders 2 & 3 | 1⅝ yd black |
| Binding | ⅝ yd fuchsia |
| Backing | 3⅞ yd |
| Batting | 65x65″ |

## CUTTING

*Cut these squares in HALF diagonally

| | |
|---|---|
| Block background | 9 squares 12½″ |
| Appliques | 9 sets - patterns on pages 43-44 |
| Sashing | 8-9 strips 2″ wide |
| Border 1 | 5 strips 2″ wide |
| Border 2 | *120 squares 2⅜″ - purple |
| | *120 squares 2⅜″ - black |
| | 4 squares 3½″ - fuchsia |
| Border 3 | 6 strips 4½″ wide |
| Binding | 6-7 strips 2½″ wide |

1-3.

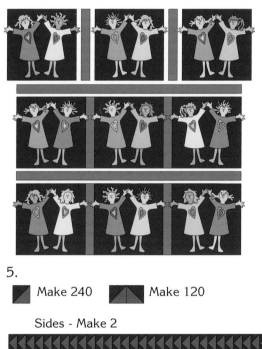

5.

Make 240    Make 120

Sides - Make 2

Top & Bottom - Make 2

# DIRECTIONS

Use ¼″ seam allowance unless otherwise noted.

1. Applique 9 blocks as shown, leaving hands unstitched until after blocks are stitched to sashing. Use permanent marker for eyes and nose, blush makeup for cheeks.

2. Sashing: Cut 6 pieces of sashing 12½″ long. Cut remaining sashing strips into 4 pieces 39½″ long and 2 pieces 42½″ long, piecing if necessary.

3. Make 3 rows of 3 blocks and two 12½″ sashing pieces, keeping hands out of seam allowances. Stitch rows together with 39½″ pieces of sashing between them. See diagram. Stitch 39½″ pieces of sashing to sides. Stitch 42½″ pieces of sashing to top and bottom. Press. Finish appliqueing hands.

4. Border 1: Stitch border pieces end to end. Press. Cut 2 pieces 42½″ long. Stitch to sides of quilt. Cut 2 pieces 45½″ long. Stitch to top and bottom. Press.

5. Border 2: Make 240 half-square triangle units. Stitch together in pairs as shown. Stitch units together into 4 borders of 30 units each. Press. Stitch one to each side of quilt, purple triangles pointing as shown in whole-quilt diagram. Stitch 3½″ fuchsia squares to ends of remaining borders. Stitch to top and bottom of quilt, purple triangles pointing as shown. Press.

6. Border 3: Measure length of quilt. Piece border strips to the measured length and stitch to sides of quilt. Repeat at top and bottom. Press.

7. Piece backing to same size as batting. Layer and quilt as desired. Trim backing and batting even with top.

8. Stitch binding strips together end to end. Press in half lengthwise, wrong sides together. Bind quilt using ⅜″ seam allowance.

True Blue – Page 6

Friendships Blossom – Page 10     Log Cabin Pillow – Page 12

# Grandmother's Garden

Most of us know an avid gardener who always has the prettiest flowers whether it is spring, summer, or fall. Often they are willing to share either the blossoms or the plants so that the rest of us can enjoy them in our own homes and yards. Quilters too, are quick to share their beautiful fabrics. Plan a get-together with your gardening and quilting friends and trade pastel scraps to get the largest variety possible for this easy-to-make quilt.

*Go oft' to the house of thy friend. For weeds choke up the unused path.*

Shakespeare

Photo on page 25

Approximate size 61x76″     9″ block

Use 42-45″-wide fabric. When strips appear in the cutting list, cut crossgrain strips (selvage to selvage).

## YARDAGE

Note: Choose pairs of bright pastels for each block (2 blues, 2 pinks, etc.)

Brights & bright pastels
| | |
|---|---|
| blocks, Border 2, binding | ⅓ each of 30 or more fabrics |
| Block centers, sashing squares | ⅙ yd each of 5 greens |
| Sashing rectangles | 1 yd light green |

White
| | |
|---|---|
| Borders | 2 yd |
| Backing | 4⅞ yd |
| Batting | 67x82″ |

## CUTTING

*Cut these squares in HALF diagonally

Brights & bright pastels
| | |
|---|---|
| each block | 4 squares, 4 squares - 3½″ - use 2 shades of 1 color |
| each half-block | 3 squares, 2 squares - 3½″ - use 2 shades of 1 color |
| Border 2 | *37 squares 3⅞″ |
| binding | strips 2½″ wide by varying lengths should be approx. 300″ long once pieced |

| | |
|---|---|
| Block centers | 31 squares 3½″ - greens |
| Sashing squares | 32 squares 2″ - greens |
| Sashing rectangles | 48 rectangles 2 x9½″ |

White
| | |
|---|---|
| Border 1 | 6 strips 2¼″ wide |
| Border 2 | *37 squares 3⅞″ |
| | 4 squares 3½″ |
| Border 3 | 7 strips 4″ wide |

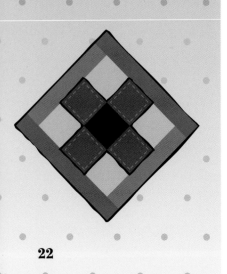

## DIRECTIONS

Use ¼" seam allowance unless otherwise noted.

1. Make 17 whole and 14 half blocks following diagram. Press.

2. Arrange blocks, half blocks, sashing squares, and sashing rectangles. Stitch rows of sashing squares and sashing rectangles. Stitch rows of blocks and sashing rectangles. Stitch rows together. Press. Trim outside edge of quilt, leaving ¼" seam allowance.

3. Border 1: Measure length of quilt. Piece border strips to the measured length and stitch to sides of quilt. Repeat at top and bottom.

4. Border 2: Make 74 half-square triangle units as shown. Stitch 21 units together for each side border. Stitch side borders to quilt. Stitch 16 units together for top and bottom borders. Stitch white squares to each end. Stitch top and bottom borders to quilt. Press.

5. Border 3: Repeat Step 3.

6. Piece backing vertically to same size as batting. Layer and quilt as desired. Trim backing and batting even with top.

7. Stitch binding strips together end to end. Press in half lengthwise, wrong sides together. Bind quilt using ⅜" seam allowance.

**1.**

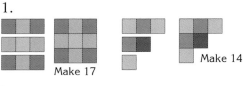

Make 17

Make 14

**2.**

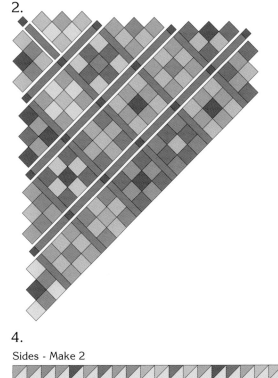

**4.**

Sides - Make 2

Top & Bottom- Make 2

*In my Grandmother's Garden, I planted my first rose. s.j.*

23

Heart in Hand – Page 70

Friends Are Like Flowers – Page 68     Grandmother's Garden – Page 22

# Remember When

This quilt could also be named A Picture Is Worth a Thousand Words. What better way to honor a friend than to make a quilt with photographs of special shared memories. If you can't decide on only five photos, make more five-photo blocks and sash them together. For a fun group project, get several friends to make five-photo blocks and join them together into one quilt.

*Treat your friends as you do your pictures, and place them in the best light.*

Jennie Churchill

Photo on page 49

Approximate size 26 x 26"      16" block

Use 42-45"-wide fabric. When strips appear in the cutting list, cut crossgrain strips (selvage to selvage).

## YARDAGE

| | |
|---|---|
| Photo transfers | 5 - each should have margin enough to cut 4½" square |
| Background | ⅛ yd each of 4 creams |
| Stars | ⅛ yd each - 4 blues, 4 greens, 4 purples, 4 rusts - OR scraps |
| Border 1 | ⅙ yd rust |
| Border 2 | ½ yd blue |
| Border 3 | ¼ yd cream |
| Binding | ⅓ yd purple |
| Backing | 1 yd |
| Batting | 30 x 30" |

## CUTTING

*Cut these squares in HALF diagonally

| | |
|---|---|
| Photo transfers | 5 squares 4½" |
| Background | 3 squares 2½" from each fabric |
| | *4 squares 2⅞" from each fabric |
| Stars | *1 square 2⅞" from each fabric |
| Border 1 | 2 strips 1½" |
| Border 2 | 4 strips 3½" |
| Border 3 | 4 strips 1½" |
| Binding | 3 strips 2½" wide |

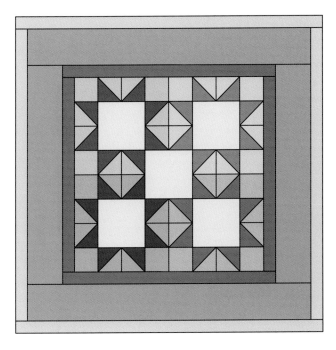

## DIRECTIONS

Use ¼″ seam allowance unless otherwise noted.

1. For each star, use one background fabric and one star color for the points. Make 8 half-square triangle units for each star (8 purple, 8 green, 8 blue, 8 rust). Stitch units into pairs. See diagram.

2. Arrange star parts and photo transfers according to diagram. Stitch into rows. Stitch rows together. Press carefully following photo transfer maker's guidelines.

3. Border 1: Measure length of quilt. Cut border strips to the measured length and stitch to sides of quilt. Repeat at top and bottom.

4. Borders 2 and 3: Repeat Step 3.

5. Cut backing to same size as batting. Layer and quilt as desired. Trim backing and batting even with top.

6. Stitch binding strips together end to end. Press in half lengthwise, wrong sides together. Bind quilt using ⅜″ seam allowance.

1.

Make 8 with each star color    Make 4 with each star color

2.

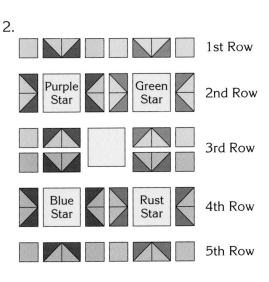

1st Row
2nd Row — Purple Star, Green Star
3rd Row
4th Row — Blue Star, Rust Star
5th Row

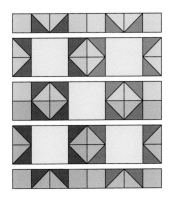

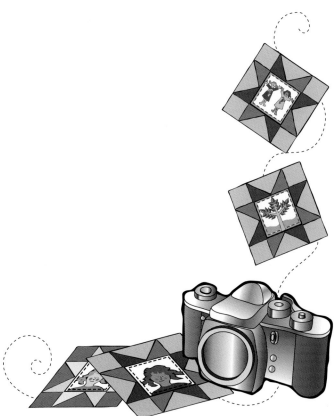

Best Buds – Page 18    Knock Three Times – Page 54

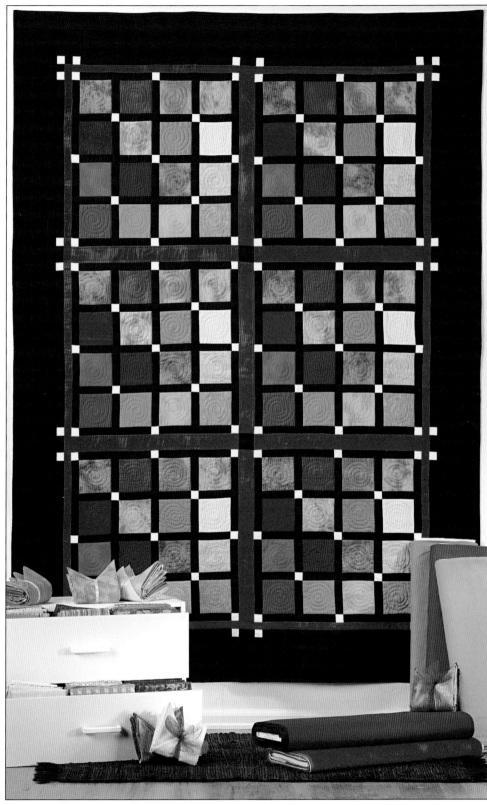

Simply Charming – Page 46

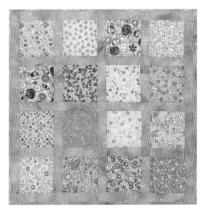

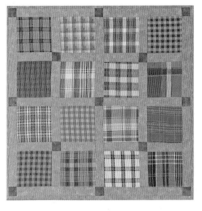

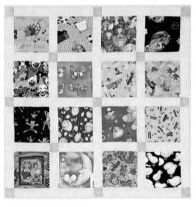

Exchange fabric squares with members of your quilting group.
Anything from novelty fabrics to plaids to florals would be
delightful for creating your own Simply Charming quilt.

# Milky Way

A great quilt for a batik fat quarter exchange! Get a group of your quilting friends together to exchange fat quarters so you can all make this gorgeous twinkling star quilt. We chose a dark purple background to set off the bright batiks used for the stars.

*Friendship cheers like a sunbeam; charms like a good story; inspires like a brave leader; binds like a golden chain; guides like a heavenly vision.*

Newell D. Hillis

Photo on page 32

Approximate size 64 x 76"      6" units

Use 42-45"-wide fabric. When strips appear in the cutting list, cut crossgrain strips (selvage to selvage).

## YARDAGE

| | |
|---|---|
| Stars | 3 blues, 3 greens, 3 purples, 3 reds, 3 teals, 3 light oranges, 3 yellows - fat quarters or ¼ yd each - batiks |
| Background, Borders 2 & 4 | 3½ yd dark purple |
| Borders 1 & 3 | ¼ yd each of 8 batiks |
| Binding | ⅔ yd purple |
| Backing | 4⅞ yd |
| Batting | 70 x 82" |

## CUTTING

**NOTE:** For each star, cut 2 squares for the center from the first fabric, 2 squares for the center from the second fabric, and all the star points from the third fabric. Alternate fabrics for each star made from the same set of 3 fabrics. There are 32 stars.

*Cut these squares in HALF diagonally

| | |
|---|---|
| Stars - for each | 4 squares 2½" - center |
| | *2 squares 2⅞" - short star points |
| | 4 long star points - pattern on page 38 - NOTE: Cut all points with template & right side of fabric facing up |
| Background | 32 squares 4½" |
| | 80 squares 2½" |
| | *64 squares 2⅞" |
| | 128 long star points - pattern on page 38 |
| | 8 squares 2½" - border corners |
| | 13-14 strips 2½" wide - Borders 2 & 4 |
| Borders 1 & 3 | 2 strips 2½" wide from each of 8 fabrics |
| Border corners | 8 squares 2½" from star fabrics |
| Binding | 7-8 strips 2½" wide |

## DIRECTIONS

Use ¼″ seam allowance unless otherwise noted.

1. Use coloring diagram on page 33 to plan the placement of color. Coloring two diagrams and cutting one apart into units may help you to see how units will sew together into interlocked stars. Refer also to upper left section diagram below which shows 5 of the interlocked stars.

2. Make units using coloring diagram and piecing directions in diagram below. Lay units out on floor or pin to design wall as you make them to avoid confusion with color placement.

   Hint: For accurate stitching of spiky triangle units, mark seamlines on wrong side of each triangle. Pin pieces together through corner seam intersections before stitching.

3. Stitch units into horizontal rows. Stitch rows together. Press.

4. Border 1: Measure length and width of quilt. Piece border strips to the measured length for sides of quilt. Stitch side borders to quilt. Piece border strips to the measured width for top and bottom of quilt. Stitch corner squares to top and bottom borders. Stitch borders to quilt.

5. Borders 2, 3, and 4: Repeat Step 4.

6. Piece backing vertically to same size as batting. Layer and quilt as desired. Trim backing and batting even with top.

7. Stitch binding strips together end to end. Press in half lengthwise, wrong sides together. Bind quilt using ⅜″ seam allowance.

1.  Upper Left Section

2.  For 1 Center Unit:

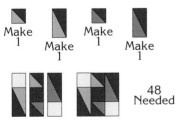

For 1 Side or Corner Unit:

Milky Way – Page 30

**Friends Forever**

Match to dotted line below for full pattern

Match to dotted line above for full pattern

34

**Friends Forever**

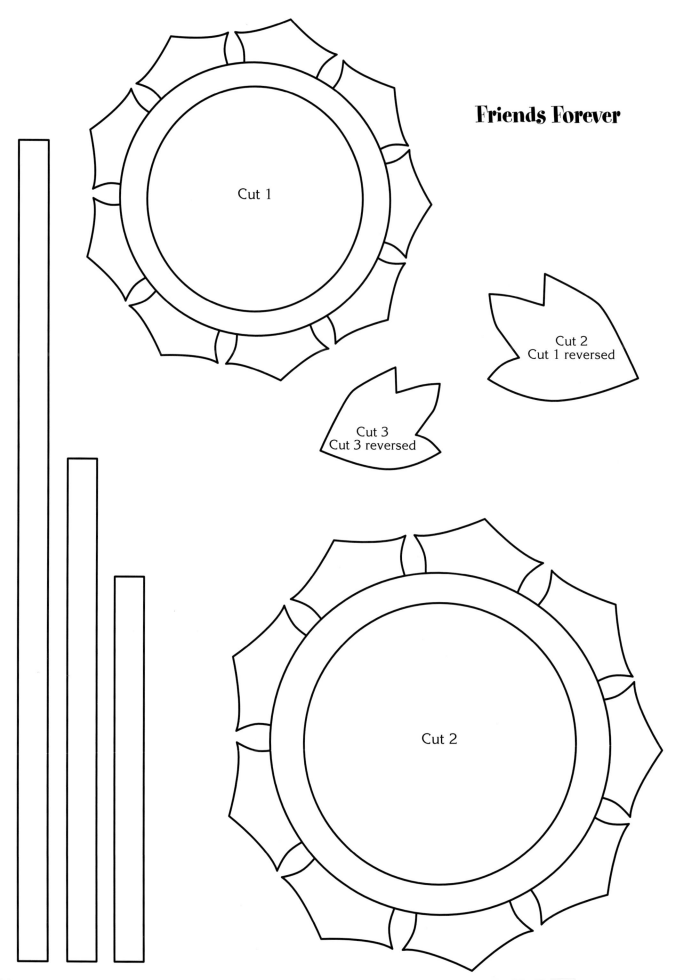

Friends Forever

Cut 1

Cut 2
Cut 1 reversed

Cut 3
Cut 3 reversed

Cut 2

**Friends Forever**

Messages from the Heart

Milky Way

Place right side up on right side of fabric for cutting all pieces

PLEAS

Knock Three Times     House Blend

ABCDEFGH
IJKLMNOPQR
STUVWXYZ.

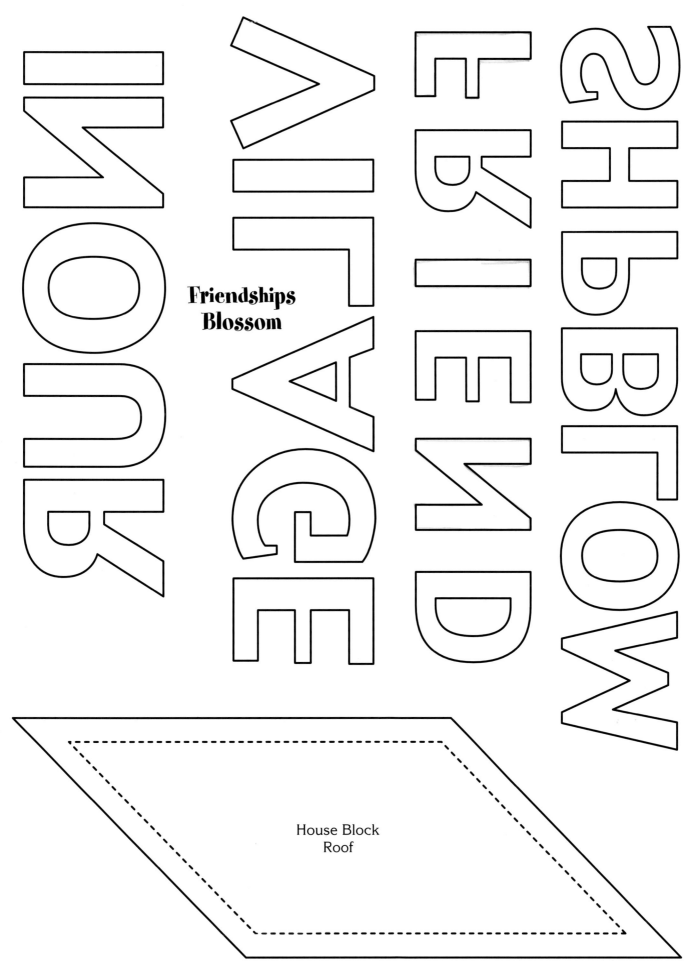

SHRUB GROW

FRIEND

VILLAGE

YOUR

Friendships
Blossom

House Block
Roof

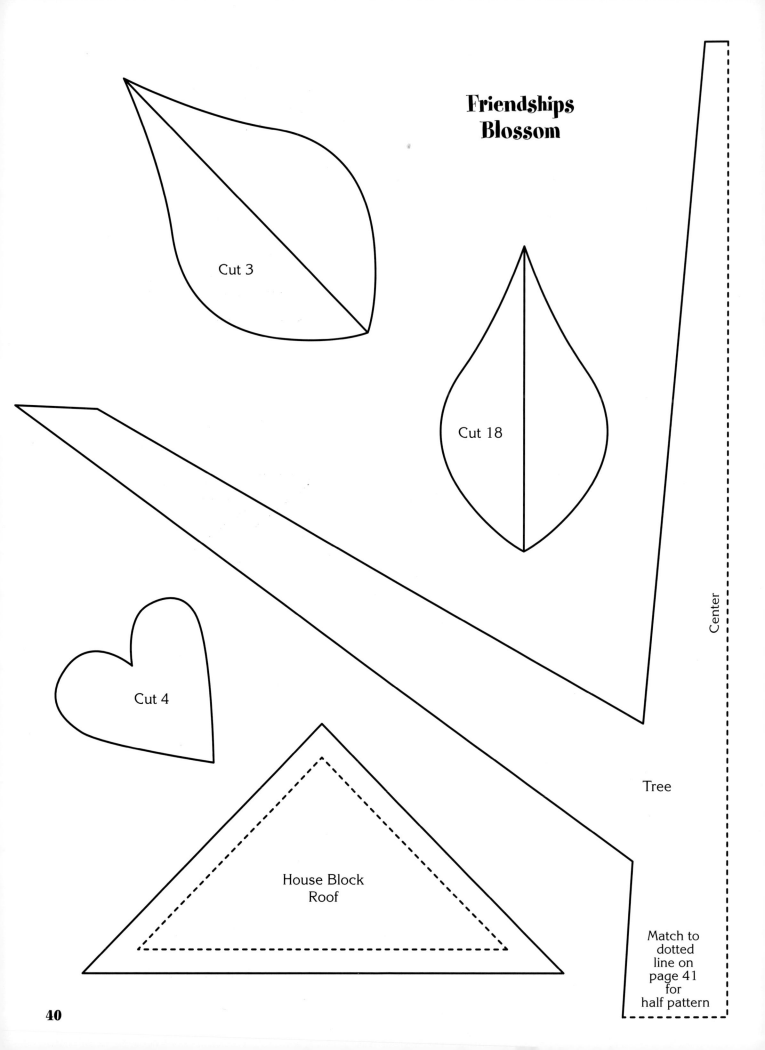

**Friendships Blossom**

Cut 3

Cut 18

Cut 4

Center

Tree

House Block Roof

Match to dotted line on page 41 for half pattern

40

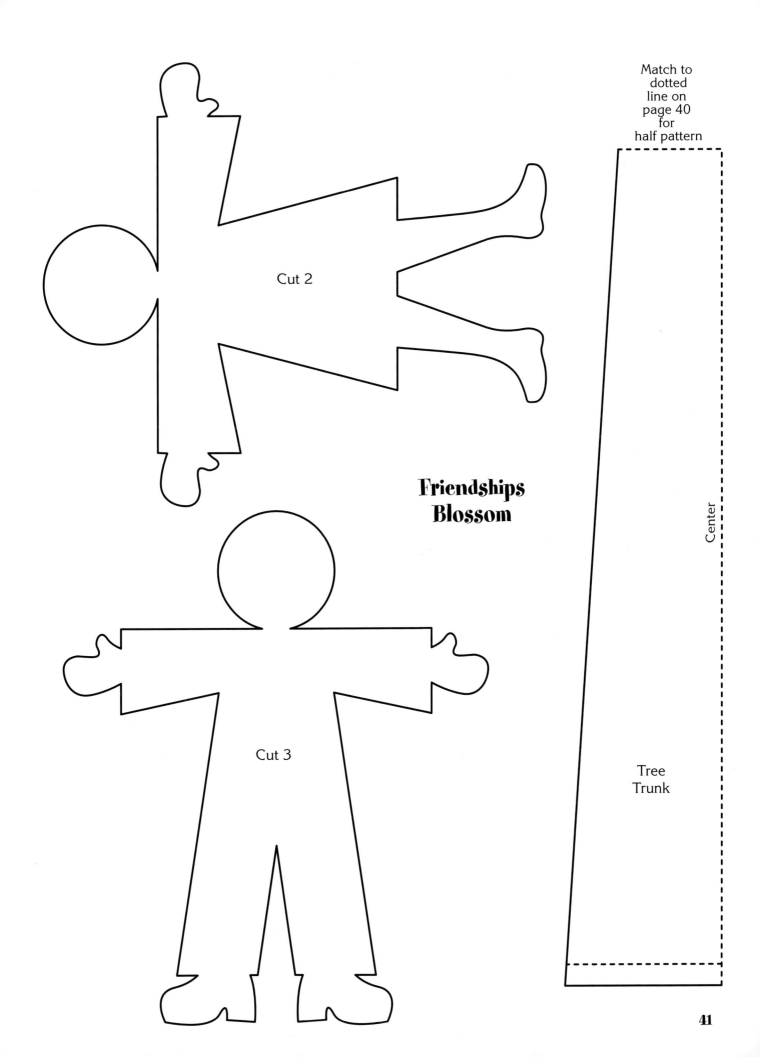

Cut 2

**Friendships Blossom**

Cut 3

Match to dotted line on page 40 for half pattern

Center

Tree Trunk

41

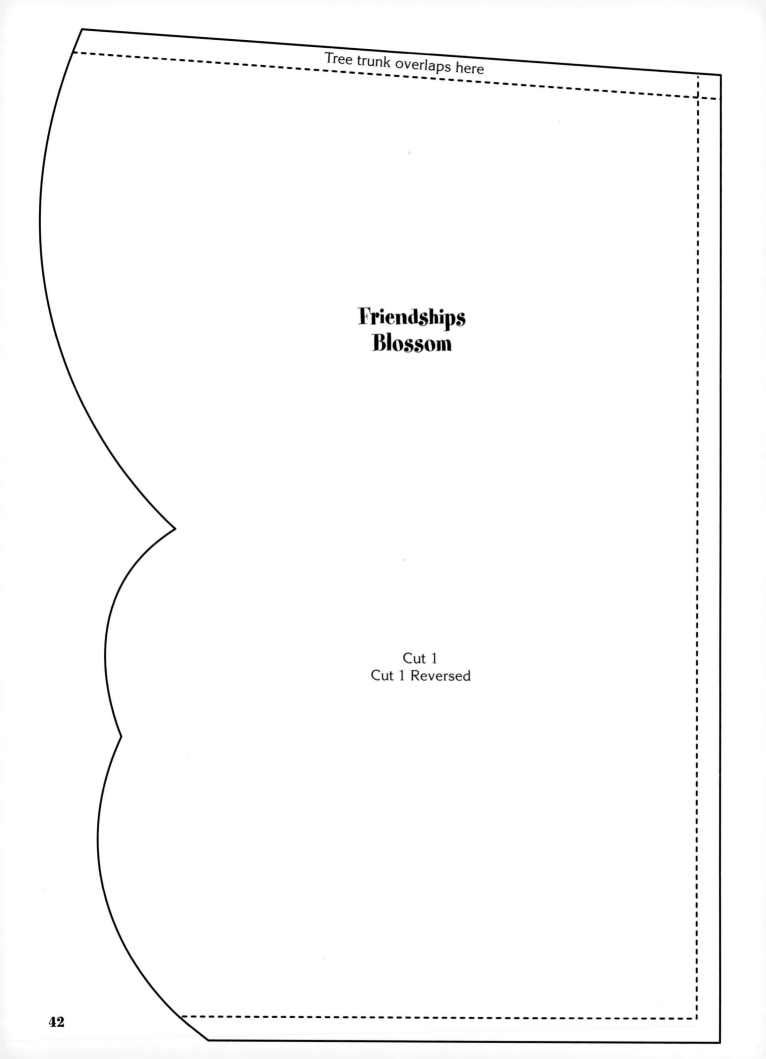

Tree trunk overlaps here

**Friendships Blossom**

Cut 1
Cut 1 Reversed

Use blush makeup for cheeks

Use permanent marker for nose & eyes

**Best Buds**

Cut 3, reversing as needed

Cut 9
Cut 9 reversed

Cut 3, reversing as needed

43

# Best Buds

Cut 3, reversing as needed

Cut 3, reversing as needed

Cut 3, reversing as needed

Cut 3, reversing as needed

# Breadcloths

# Jar Lids

Cut 4 for Breadcloth
Cut 1 for Jar Lid

Cut 4 for Breadcloth
Cut 1 for Jar Lid

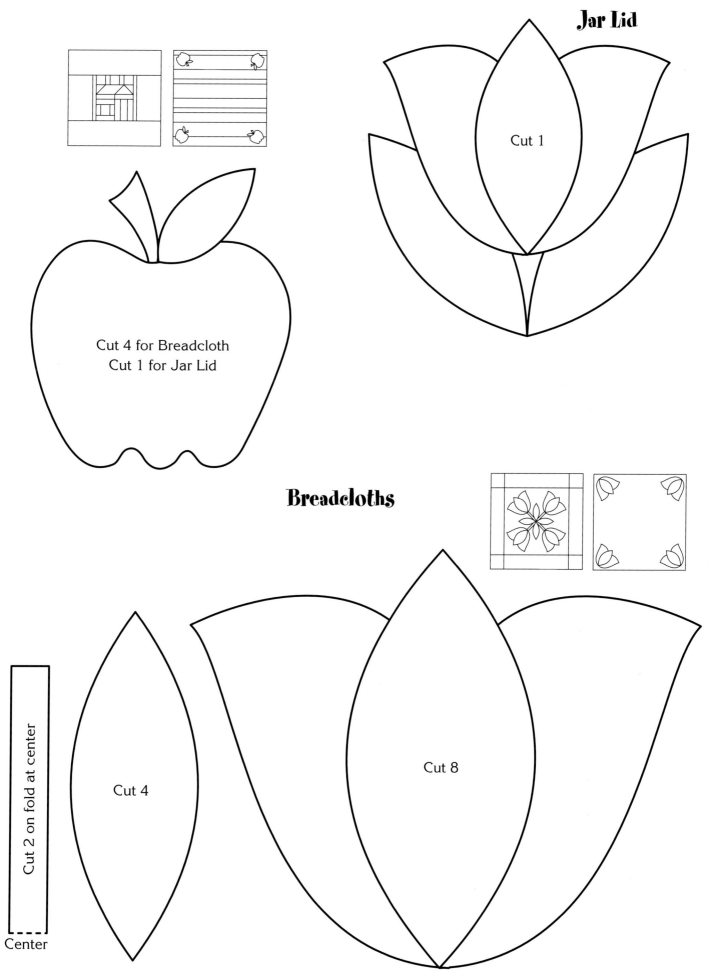

**Jar Lid**

Cut 1

Cut 4 for Breadcloth
Cut 1 for Jar Lid

**Breadcloths**

Cut 2 on fold at center

Center

Cut 4

Cut 8

45

# Simply Charming

Six large blocks of colored squares are all that are needed to make this colorful quilt, but it makes a great friendship quilt when you solicit 4½"-cut squares from your friends and make every patch different. See our alternate combinations to find just the right assortment for your friends.

*A true friend laughs at your stories even when they're not so good, and sympathizes with your troubles even when they're not so bad.*

Proverb

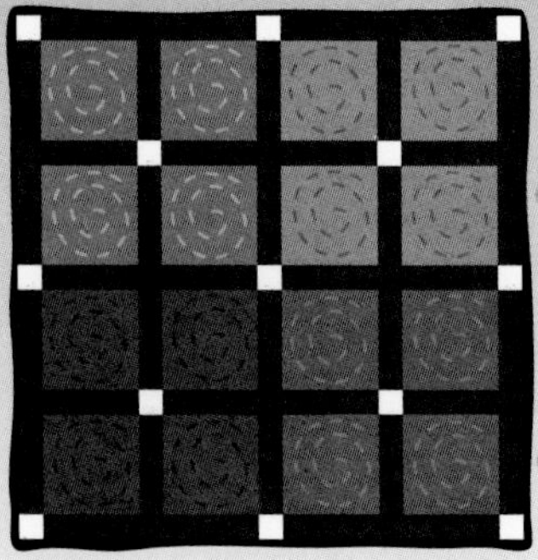

Photo on page 29

Approximate size 58 x 81"    21" block

Use 42-45"-wide fabric. When strips appear in the cutting list, cut crossgrain strips (selvage to selvage).

**NOTE:** The pieced black and white border in this quilt necessitates the exact piecing of all elements prior to it, so exact lengths for all pieces for the quilt, except the outer border, are given either in the cutting chart or in the directions.

## YARDAGE

| | |
|---|---|
| Squares | ⅙ yd each of 16 fabrics |
| | 4 red, 4 orange, 4 green, 4 purple |
| Setting squares, setting rectangles, Border 2, Border 3 | 3 yd black |
| Setting squares | ¼ yd white |
| Sashing, Border 1 | 1 yd red |
| Binding | ⅔ yd black |
| Backing | 5⅛ yd |
| Batting | 64 x 87" |

## CUTTING

| | |
|---|---|
| Squares | 6 squares 4½" of each of the 16 fabrics |
| Setting squares | 8 squares 1½" - black |
| | 2 squares 2½" - black |
| | 102 squares 1½" - white |
| Setting rectangles | 6 rectangles 1½ x 2½" |
| | 96 rectangles 1½ x 4½" |
| | 72 rectangles 1½ x 9½" |
| | 10 rectangles 1½ x 19½" |
| Sashing | 7 rectangles 2½ x 21½" |
| Border 1 | 6 strips 1½" wide |
| Border 3 | 7 strips 5½" wide |
| Binding | 8 strips 2½" wide |

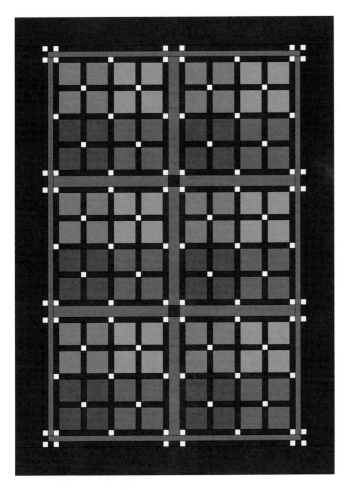

# DIRECTIONS

Use ¼" seam allowance unless otherwise noted.

1. For each block make 4 "color units", each with fabrics from one color family. See diagram. Use 1½" white setting squares and 1½ x 4½" black setting rectangles. Press.

2. Stitch "color units" into blocks as shown, using 1½" white setting squares and 1½ x 9½" black setting rectangles. Press.

3. Make 3 rows of 2 blocks joined by one 2½ x 21½" red sashing rectangle. Make 2 rows of sashing using 2½" black setting squares and 2½ x 21½" red sashing rectangles. Stitch rows of sashing and rows of blocks together. Press.

4. Border 1: Stitch 1½" red border strips together end to end. Press. Cut into 2 pieces 67½" long and 2 pieces 46½" long. Stitch long pieces to sides of quilt. Stitch short pieces to top and bottom. Press.

5. Border 2: Following diagram, stitch border pieces together as shown for sides of quilt. Stitch to quilt. Stitch border pieces together as shown for top and bottom of quilt. Stitch to quilt. Press.

6. Border 3: Measure length of quilt. Piece border strips to the measured length and stitch to sides of quilt. Measure width of quilt. Repeat at top and bottom. Press.

7. Piece backing vertically to same size as batting. Layer and quilt as desired. Trim backing and batting even with top.

8. Stitch binding strips together end to end. Press in half lengthwise, wrong sides together. Bind quilt using ⅜" seam allowance.

1.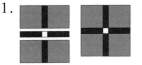
For each block, make 1 "color unit" with 4 red squares, 1 with 4 orange squares, 1 with 4 green squares, and 1 with 4 purple squares.

2.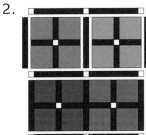
Make 6

3.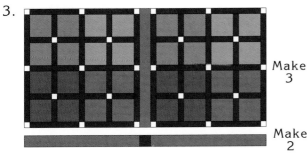
Make 3

Make 2

5.
Make 2 - Sides

Make 2 - Top & Bottom

# Quilt Labels

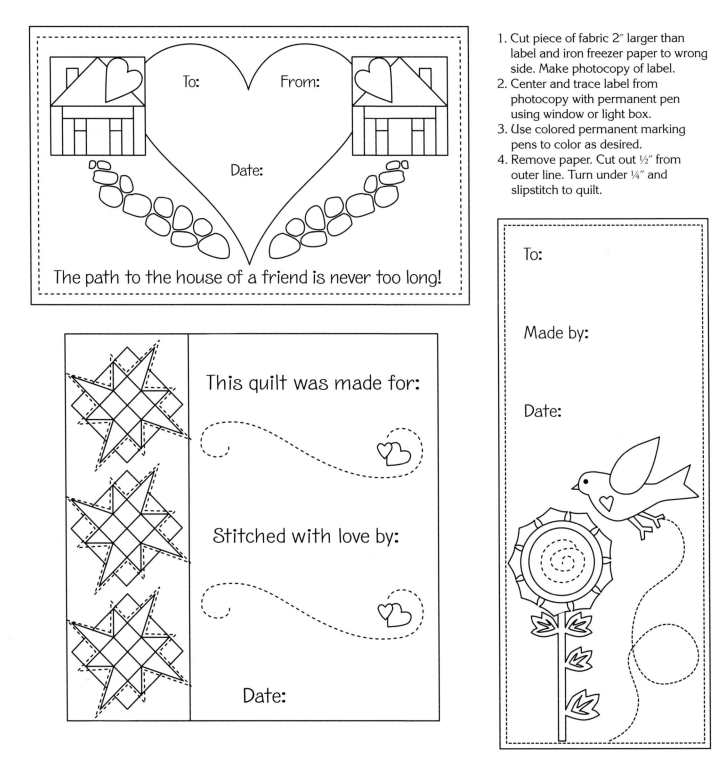

To:

From:

Date:

The path to the house of a friend is never too long!

1. Cut piece of fabric 2″ larger than label and iron freezer paper to wrong side. Make photocopy of label.
2. Center and trace label from photocopy with permanent pen using window or light box.
3. Use colored permanent marking pens to color as desired.
4. Remove paper. Cut out ½″ from outer line. Turn under ¼″ and slipstitch to quilt.

This quilt was made for:

Stitched with love by:

Date:

To:

Made by:

Date:

Join a neighborhood quilting bee, for many hands make light work. . . and bonds of truest friendship are formed with each stitch you take together.

Remember When – Page 26

# Signed With Love

We recently celebrated 20 years in business and wanted to involve our customers in some meaningful way. We made rail fence signature blocks and backed the white strips with freezer paper to make them easier to sign. We'll be making a couple more of these quilts with the rest of the signed blocks we collected. Keep Signed With Love in mind when you need a special quilt for a memorable occasion such as a graduation, wedding, or birthday.

*A true friend is the greatest of all blessings, and the one which we take the least thought to acquire.*
La Rochefoucauld

Photo on page 52

Approximate size 66 x 84"       16" block

Use 42-45"-wide fabric. When strips appear in the cutting list, cut crossgrain strips (selvage to selvage).

## YARDAGE

| | |
|---|---|
| Bright prints for blocks, Border 1, binding | ⅓ yd each of 20 fabrics OR ¼ yd each of 40 fabrics |
| White for blocks, tilting strips, Border 2 | 5¼ yd |
| Green for sashing | 1⅜ yd |
| Backing | 5¼ yd |
| Batting | 72 x 90" |

## CUTTING

| | |
|---|---|
| Bright prints | 40 strips 1½" wide - blocks |
| | 15-20 pieces 2½ x 14-24" - binding (approx. 320" long after seaming) |
| | 132 rectangles 1½ x 2½" - Border 1 |
| White | 20 strips 1¾" wide - blocks |
| | 24 strips 4½" wide - tilting strips |
| | Cut from each strip: |
| | 1 piece 13½" long & 1 piece 21½" long |
| | 8 strips 4½" wide - Border 2 |
| Green | 16 rectangles 2½ x 16½" - vertical sashing pieces |
| | 7-8 strips 2½" wide - horizontal sashing |

*Laura*

**1-2.**

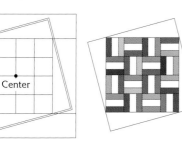

**3.**

**5.**

Center

**6.**

# DIRECTIONS

Use ¼″ seam allowance unless otherwise noted.

1. Cut all strips for blocks in half crosswise, to 20-22″ long. Make 40 strip sets by mixing colors randomly on either side of white strips. Press. Crosscut strip sets into 3¾″ segments (192 needed).

2. Have participants sign the squares and write short messages, keeping writing out of the seam allowances.

3. Make 16-square units as shown, rotating every other square. Press.

4. Stitch shorter 4½″ white strips to opposite sides of each block. Stitch longer 4½″ white strips to remaining sides of each block. Press.

5. Make a plastic template 16½″ square. Mark center of template. Mark a seamline on each side of template ¼″ in from edge. Place template on right side of block, matching centers, and rotate counter-clockwise as shown in diagram. Rotate until marked seamline touches corner of 16-square unit. Mark around template and cut out block. Repeat with remaining blocks.

6. Make 4 rows of vertical sashing rectangles and blocks. Measure width of rows. Piece sashing strips to the measured length. Make 5. Stitch horizontal rows of sashing and rows of blocks together. Press.

7. Border 1: Stitch border rectangles together end to end to fit sides of quilt. Stitch side borders to quilt. Repeat at top and bottom. Press.

8. Border 2: Measure length of quilt. Piece border strips to the measured length and stitch to sides of quilt. Repeat at top and bottom. Press.

9. Piece backing vertically to same size as batting. Layer and quilt as desired. Trim backing and batting even with top.

10. Stitch binding strips together end to end. Press in half lengthwise, wrong sides together. Bind quilt using ⅜″ seam allowance.

Messages from the Heart – Page 8    Signed with Love – Page 50

Starring My Friends – Page 72

# Knock Three Times

Perfect for bedroom doors in college dorms, by the phone in a busy kitchen, or near back doors in friendly neighborhoods, this "message board" quilt is sure to delight any friend. Keep the pencil sharp and the pocket filled with notepaper.

*But every house where Love abides and Friendship is a guest, is surely home, and home, sweet home; for there the heart can rest.*

Henry Van Dyke

Photo on page 28

Approximate size 23x23″

Use 42-45″-wide fabric. When strips appear in the cutting list, cut crossgrain strips (selvage to selvage).

Patterns are given for fusible web applique, reversed and ready to be traced. Be sure to have plenty of fusible web on hand if using this method. Reverse patterns and add seam allowance if doing hand applique.

## YARDAGE

| | |
|---|---|
| Background | ½ yd black |
| Envelopes, lettering, pencil pocket, notepad pocket flap | ¼ yd each of 8 brights |
| Notepad pocket | ¼ yd |
| Horizontal borders | ⅛ yd each of 2 fabrics |
| Binding | ⅓ yd black |
| Backing | ⅞ yd |
| Batting | 27x27″ |

## CUTTING

| | |
|---|---|
| Background | 1 rectangle 23½x8½″ for top |
| | 1 rectangle 7½x12½″ for left side |
| | 6 rectangles 1½x5″ for sashing |
| | 3 rectangles 1½x16½″ for sashing |
| Name envelopes | 4 rectangles 5x7″ for backs |
| | 8 squares 5½″ for sides |
| | 4 rectangles 3¾x7″ for flaps |
| | letters for names - patterns on page 38 |
| Notepad & pencil pockets | 1 rectangle 5½x15″ for notepad pocket |
| | 1 rectangle 5½x3″ for flap |
| | 1 rectangle 3½x4½″ for pencil pocket |
| Horizontal borders | 35 squares 1½″ of each fabric |
| Binding | 3 strips 2½″ wide |

# DIRECTIONS

Use ¼″ seam allowance unless otherwise noted.

1. Name envelopes - Make 4

   a. Press 2 side pieces in half diagonally, wrong sides together. Pin to right side of back piece, bottom corners matching. Points extend at top. See diagram.

   b. Pin side pieces together at overlap. Remove sides from back and stitch close to edge along diagonal overlap. Place sides on back piece again. Stitch side and bottom edges together ⅛″ from edge, as shown.

   c. Fold flap piece in half, right sides together, to a 3½x3¾″ rectangle. Stitch one 3½″ edge. See diagram. Trim point. Turn right side out and place seam in center as shown. Press. Applique names to flaps. Pin flap to top edge of envelope block, raw edges even, and stitch ⅛″ from edge. Trim points.

2. Notepad & pencil pockets: Fold pencil pocket piece in half, right sides together, to 1¾x4½″. Stitch 3 open sides, leaving an opening on the long side for turning. Clip, turn, and press. Fold flap piece in half, right sides together, to 2¾x3″. Stitch one 2¾″ side. Trim point. Turn right side out, place seam in center, and press. Place flap, right sides together, at one end of notepad pocket piece as shown. Fold notepad pocket piece in half, right sides together, to 5½x7½″. Stitch 3 open sides, catching flap in seam and leaving an opening on the side for turning. Trim corners, turn, and press.

3. Make 2 rows of envelope blocks as shown. Stitch rows together with sashing strips between as shown. Press. Stitch notepad pocket background piece to left of envelope blocks section. Stitch pencil pocket to notepad pocket. Stitch notepad pocket to notepad pocket background.

4. Stitch 1½″ squares into 3 rows of 23. Stitch one to top and one to bottom of envelope row. Stitch 8½x23½″ background piece to top. Stitch remaining row of squares to top. Press. Applique lettering to top background.

5. Cut backing to same size as batting. Layer and quilt as desired. Trim backing and batting even with top.

6. Stitch binding strips together end to end. Press in half lengthwise, wrong sides together. Bind quilt using ⅜″ seam allowance.

1 a-b.

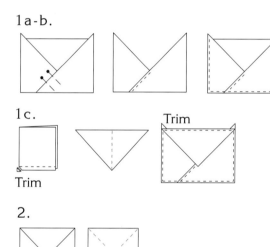

1 c.

Trim

Trim

2.

3-4.

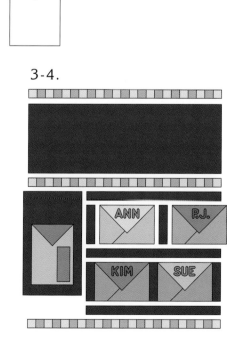

Kitchen Chicks – Page 82    Breadcloths & Jar Lids – Page 13

Sister's Choice – Pages 76 & 78

# House Blend

What better way to start your day than meeting a friend for coffee or tea. This quilt would be a special treat for that friend. It also would make a great gift for several friends to make for someone who is moving away or going through hard times.

*We cannot tell the precise moment when friendship is formed. As in filling a vessel drop by drop, there is at last a drop which makes it run over; so in a series of kindnesses there is a last one which makes the heart run over.*

James Boswell

Photo on page 60

Approximate size 36 x 50″      12¾″ blocks

Use 42-45″-wide fabric. When strips appear in the cutting list, cut crossgrain strips (selvage to selvage).

Patterns are given for fusible web applique, reversed and ready to be traced. Be sure to have plenty of fusible web on hand if using this method. Reverse patterns and add seam allowance if doing hand applique.

## YARDAGE

| | | |
|---|---|---|
| Blocks | background | ¾ yd tan |
| | coffee cups | ⅙ yd each of 6 - brown, rust |
| | handles, saucers | ⅛ yd each of 6 or more - purple, green, blue |
| | steam | ⅛ yd cream |
| | hearts | ⅛ yd each of 2 reds |
| Block frames | | ⅛ yd each of 4 medium blues |
| Block setting triangles | | ¼ yd each of 4-6 medium browns |
| Sashing | | ⅙ yd each of 6 or more dark blues |
| Sashing squares | | ⅛ yd tan |
| Sashing appliques | | ⅛ yd tan |
| Flat piping | | ⅙ yd brown |
| Border | | ½ yd blue |
| Binding | | ½ yd dark blue |
| Backing | | 1¾ yd - must have 42″ usable width |
| Batting | | 42 x 56″ |

## CUTTING

*Cut these squares in HALF diagonally

| | |
|---|---|
| Appliques | patterns on page 38 & 94 |
| Block frames | 12 rectangles 1½ x 7½″ |
| | 12 rectangles 1½ x 9½″ |
| Setting triangles | *12 squares 7¼″ |
| Sashing | 17 rectangles 2½ x 13¼″ |
| Sashing squares | 12 squares 2½″ |
| Flat piping | 4 strips 1″ wide |
| Border | 4-5 strips 2½″ wide |
| Binding | 5 strips 2½″ wide |

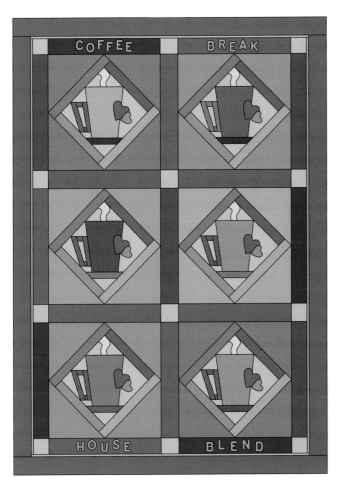

## DIRECTIONS

Use ¼″ seam allowance unless otherwise noted.

1. Make 6 photocopies of paper piecing pattern on page 94. Paper piece 6 coffee cup blocks.

2. Applique steam and hearts to blocks.

3. Stitch short frame rectangles to opposite sides of blocks as shown. Stitch long frame rectangles to remaining sides. Press. Remove paper. Stitch setting triangles to blocks. See diagram.

4. Make 4 rows of sashing rectangles and sashing squares. Make three rows of blocks and sashing rectangles. See diagram.

5. Stitch rows of sashing and rows of blocks together.

6. Applique words on sashing at top and bottom of quilt. Keep applique ½″ from outside edges of quilt to avoid having flat piping overlap it.

7. Flat Piping: Stitch strips end to end. Fold in half, wrong sides together. Press. Measure length of quilt. Cut two pieces that measurement and baste to sides of quilt, folded edge toward center of quilt, raw edges even. Measure width of quilt. Cut two pieces that measurement and baste to top and bottom of quilt.

8. Border: Measure length of quilt. Piece border strips to the measured length for sides of quilt. Stitch side borders to quilt, including piping in seam. Measure width of quilt. Cut border strips to that measurement for top and bottom borders. Stitch top and bottom borders to quilt, including flat piping in seam. Press.

9. Cut backing to same size as batting. Layer and quilt as desired. Trim backing and batting even with top.

10. Stitch binding strips together end to end. Press in half lengthwise, wrong sides together. Bind quilt using ⅜″ seam allowance.

3.

4-5.

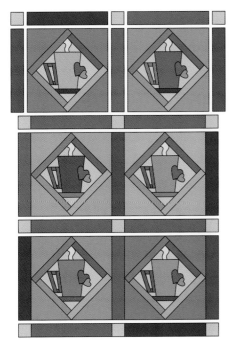

House Blend – Page 58     Breadcloths & Jar Lids – Page 13

Fireside Comfort – Page 66

# Block Party

Do you have a special neighbor who is a really good friend? You might want to make this special quilt for her. Block Party would also be fun for a group exchange in which each friend makes her house block to represent her own personality. Personalize by writing the block giver's name and address on the grass below each house.

*Happy is the house that shelters a friend.*
Ralph Waldo Emerson

Photo on page 64

Approximate size 30″      8″ block, 11″ when tilted

Use 42-45″-wide fabric. When strips appear in the cutting list, cut crossgrain strips (selvage to selvage).

Patterns are given for fusible web applique, reversed and ready to be traced. Be sure to have plenty of fusible web on hand if using this method. Reverse patterns and add seam allowance if doing hand applique.

## YARDAGE

| | |
|---|---|
| Houses | ¼ yd black - background |
| | ¼ yd each of 6 brights |
| |     orange, red, pink, purple, 2 blues |
| | ½ yd each of 1 medium & 1 light green - tilting strips |
| Appliques | included in brights above |
| Sashing | ¼ yd each - black & white |
| Border 1 | ⅙ yd bright green |
| Border 2 | ⅜ yd black |
| | ½ yd red |
| Border 2 Corners | ⅛ yd black print |
| Binding | ⅜ yd black |
| Backing | 1⅛ yd |
| Batting | 34 x 34″ |

## CUTTING

*Cut these squares in HALF diagonally

| | | |
|---|---|---|
| Houses | black | *4 squares 4⅞″ |
| | | 8 rectangles 1½ x 4½″ |
| | brights | 4 triangles - pattern on page 88 - roofs |
| | | 4 rectangles 2½ x 3½″ - center walls |
| | | 4 rectangles 1½ x 6½″ - top walls |
| | | 8 rectangles 1½ x 3½″ - side walls |
| | | 8 squares 1½″ - windows |
| | | 8 rectangles 1½ x 2½″ - below windows |
| | greens | 3 strips 3½″ wide of each fabric |
| Appliques | | patterns on page 88 |
| Sashing | white | 72 squares 1½″ |
| | black | 69 squares 1½″ |
| Border 1 | | 4 strips 1″ wide |
| Border 2 | black | 104 rectangles 1½ x 2½″ |
| | red | 208 squares 1½″ |
| Border 2 Corners | | 4 squares 2½″ |
| Binding | | 4 strips 2¼″ wide |

# DIRECTIONS

Use ¼″ seam allowance unless otherwise noted.

1. Blocks: Applique chimneys to black triangles as shown. Make 2 blocks with chimney at right and 2 blocks with chimney at left, as shown. Applique hearts on opposite sides of roofs from chimneys, as shown, keeping applique out of seam allowance. Press.

2. Stitch medium green 3½″ strips to sides of each block with heart at left. Stitch light green 3½″ strips to sides of each block with heart at right. Press. Stitch light green 3½″ strips to top and bottom of each block with heart at left. Stitch medium green 3½″ strips to top and bottom of each block with heart at right. Press.

3. Make a plastic template 11½″ square. Mark center of template. On right side of block with heart at left, tilt template as shown in first diagram on page 65. Make sure center of template is on center of block. Mark around template and cut out block. Cut other block with heart at left in the same way. Repeat with remaining blocks, **tilting template the opposite way**.

4. Sashing: Make 6 sashing pieces with 5 black and 6 white squares. Make 3 sashing pieces with 13 black and 12 white squares.

5. Arrange blocks and sashing pieces as shown in diagram, page 65. Stitch blocks and short sashing strips into horizontal rows. Stitch rows together.

6. Border 1: Measure length of quilt. Cut border strips to the measured length and stitch to sides of quilt. Repeat at top and bottom. Press.

7. Flying Geese Border: Place red square on black rectangle, right sides together, as shown. Stitch across red square as shown. Trim, leaving ¼″ seam allowance. See diagram. Press. Repeat on other side of black rectangle. Make 104. Stitch together into 4 border units of 26 each. Press. Applique stars to corner squares, keeping applique out of seam allowance. Stitch corner squares to 2 of the border units.

8. Stitch Flying Geese Border units to sides of quilt, points of black triangles pointing as shown in diagram. Stitch border units with star corner squares to top and bottom

1.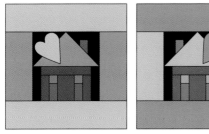

Make 2 with right chimney
Make 2 with left chimney

 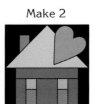

Make 2    Make 2

2.

Diagrams continued on page 65

Continued on page 65

**63**

Block Party – Page 62    Block Party Pillow – Page 65

3.

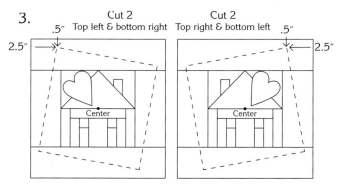

Cut 2
Top left & bottom right

Cut 2
Top right & bottom left

.5″  2.5″

2.5″  .5″

Center

Center

Continued from page 63

# Block Party

of quilt, points of black triangles pointing as shown in diagram. Press.

9. Cut backing to same size as batting. Layer and quilt as desired. Trim backing and batting even with top.

10. Stitch binding strips together end to end. Press in half lengthwise, wrong sides together. Bind quilt using ¼″ seam allowance.

4-5.

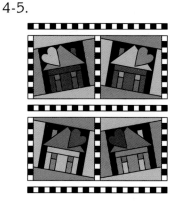

7.    Trim          Trim

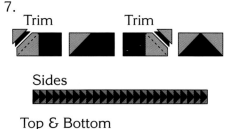

Sides

Top & Bottom

8.

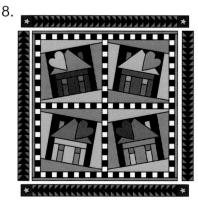

# BLOCK PARTY PILLOW

Photo on page 64      16″

1. Make 1 Block Party block.

2. Border 1: Cut 1″ strips and stitch to sides, then top and bottom.

3. Border 2: Make 48 Flying Geese units. Stitch into 4 border units of 12 each. Stitch one to each side of block. Stitch 2½″ corner squares to ends of remaining border units. Stitch border units to top and bottom of block. Applique stars to corner squares and heart to roof.

4. Optional: Layer with backing and batting. Quilt as desired. Trim backing and batting to same size as block.

5. Cut 2 envelope back pieces 16½ x 24″. Fold each in half lengthwise, wrong sides together, and press. Lay back pieces on wrong side of block, raw edges matching, folded edges overlapping at center of pillow. Baste entire outside edge.

6. Stitch binding strips together end to end. Press in half lengthwise, wrong sides together. Bind pillow using ⅜″ seam allowance. Insert a 16″ pillow form.

# Fireside Comfort

Two shades each of four colors and a background are all that are needed for this comfy quilt. What a wonderful quilt to make for a special male friend or relative. The fabrics we chose were flannel solids, but it would also be great in homespuns. Use wool batting to make this quilt extra cuddly.

*Love comforteth like sunshine after rain.*
William Shakespeare

Photo on page 61

Approximate size 58x76"     12x16" block

Use 42-45"-wide fabric. When strips appear in the cutting list, cut crossgrain strips (selvage to selvage).

## YARDAGE
Blocks

| | |
|---|---|
| Light rust | ¼ yd |
| Dark rust | ⅝ yd |
| Light green | ¼ yd |
| Dark green | ⅝ yd |
| Light gold | ⅛ yd |
| Dark gold | ⅝ yd |
| Light blue | ⅛ yd |
| Dark blue | ⅝ yd |
| Black | 2 yd |
| Border 1 | ⅝ yd black |
| Border 2 | ⅞ yd dark gold |
| Binding | ⅔ yd rust |
| Backing | 4⅞ yd |
| Batting | 64x82" |

## CUTTING
Blocks

| | |
|---|---|
| Light rust | 17 squares 2½" |
| Dark rust | 17 rectangles 2½x4½" |
| | 17 rectangles 2½x6½" |
| Light green | 17 squares 2½" |
| Dark green | 17 rectangles 2½x4½" |
| | 17 rectangles 2½x6½" |
| Light gold | 16 squares 2½" |
| Dark gold | 16 rectangles 2½x4½" |
| | 16 rectangles 2½x6½" |
| Light blue | 16 squares 2½" |
| Dark blue | 16 rectangles 2½x4½" |
| | 16 rectangles 2½x6½" |
| Black | 66 squares 2½" |
| | 66 rectangles 2½x4½" |
| | 66 rectangles 2½x6½" |
| Border 1 | 6-7 strips 2½" wide |
| Border 2 | 7 strips 3½" wide |
| Binding | 8 strips 2½" wide |

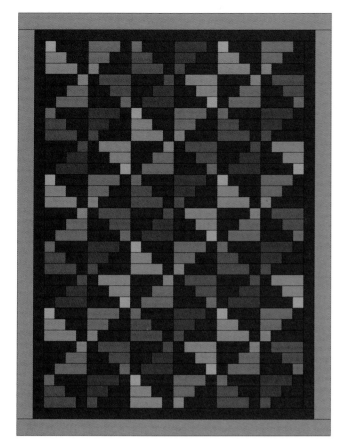

## DIRECTIONS

Use ¼″ seam allowance unless otherwise noted.

1. Make units as shown. Note that placement of pieces is the same for the gold and rust units and the opposite for the green and blue units. Press.

2. Make Blocks A, whole and half, and Blocks B, whole and half, as shown. Press.

3. Place blocks as shown, alternating A and B, and stitch into horizontal rows. Stitch rows together. Press.

4. Border 1: Measure length of quilt. Piece border strips to the measured length and stitch to sides of quilt. Repeat at top and bottom. Press.

5. Border 2: Repeat Step 4.

6. Piece backing vertically to same size as batting. Layer and quilt as desired. Trim backing and batting even with top.

7. Stitch binding strips together end to end. Press in half lengthwise, wrong sides together. Bind quilt using ⅜″ seam allowance.

1.
Layout for
Gold & Rust

Gold - Make 16  Rust - Make 17

Layout for
Green & Blue

Green - Make 17  Blue - Make 16

2.

Block A - Make 8

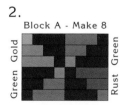

Half-Block A - Make 1

Block B - Make 7

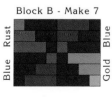

Half-Block B - Make 2

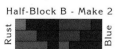

3.

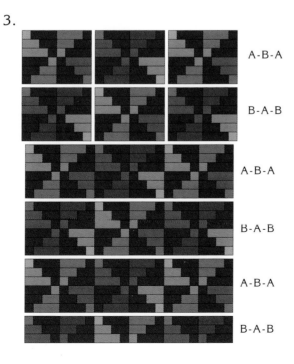

A-B-A

B-A-B

A-B-A

B-A-B

A-B-A

B-A-B

# Friends Are Like Flowers

Give a lasting bouquet to a friend you treasure. Many different color combinations would work for this pretty floral wall quilt, making it perfect for anyone's decor. It would also look lovely above a bench in a breakfast nook or as a topper on a simple squares quilt.

*Love is the only flower that grows and blossoms without the aid of seasons.*
Kahil Gibran

Photo on page 25

Approximate size 45x24″     6x12″ blocks

Use 42-45″-wide fabric. When strips appear in the cutting list, cut crossgrain strips (selvage to selvage).

Patterns are given for fusible web applique, reversed and ready to be traced. Be sure to have plenty of fusible web on hand if using this method. Reverse patterns and add seam allowance if doing hand applique.

## YARDAGE

| | |
|---|---|
| Background | 1¼ yd |
| Flower & lettering fabrics | ⅛ yd each of 2-3 purples, 2 pinks, 2 fuchsias, 2-3 yellows, 2 oranges, 6-8 greens |
| Sashing | ⅝ yd blue |
| Border      purple | ⅓ yd |
|             light blue | ⅓ yd |
|             yellow | ⅓ yd |
|             pink | ⅛ yd |
| Binding | ⅜ yd blue |
| Backing | 1½ yd |
| Batting | 49x28″ |

## CUTTING

*Cut these squares in HALF diagonally

| | |
|---|---|
| Lettering | patterns on pages 95-98 |
| Sashing | 6 rectangles 2x12½″ - verticals |
| | 2 rectangles 3½x39½″ - top and bottom |
| Border | 2 rectangles 2x12½″ - purple |
| | 2 rectangles 2x33½″ - purple |
| | 8 squares 2″ - pink |
| | 20 squares 2″ - light blue |
| | 16 squares 2″ - purple |
| | 4 squares 2″ - yellow |
| | *30 squares 2⅜″ - light blue |
| | *30 squares 2⅜″ - yellow |
| Binding | 4 strips 2½″ wide |

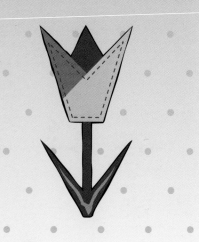

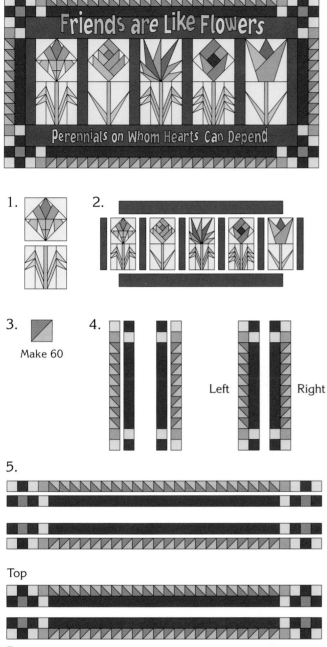

1.

2.

3.
Make 60

4.
Left    Right

5.

Top

Bottom

# DIRECTIONS

Use ¼″ seam allowance unless otherwise noted.

1. Photocopy paper piecing patterns on pages 96-103. Paper piece blossom and leaf sections of blocks. Stitch top and bottom sections of blocks together. Press.

2. Stitch blocks together with vertical sashing strips. Press. Stitch top and bottom sashing strips to row of blocks. Press.

3. Make 60 half-square triangle units with yellow and light blue triangles. Press.

4. Make side borders as shown. Stitch to quilt. Press.

5. Make top and bottom borders as shown. Stitch to quilt. Press.

6. Applique words to quilt.

7. Cut backing to same size as batting. Layer and quilt as desired. Trim backing and batting even with top.

8. Stitch binding strips together end to end. Press in half lengthwise, wrong sides together. Bind quilt using ⅜″ seam allowance.

# Heart in Hand

The heart in hand is a symbol of true friendship that is recognized throughout the world. This large medallion quilt can be made smaller by simply eliminating borders. Make a smaller quilt for a wall hanging or a bed topper.

*Of all the things a woman's hands have made, the quilt so lightly thrown across her bed— the quilt that keeps her loved ones warm—is woven of her love and dreams and thread.*

Carrie A. Hall

Photo on page 24

Approximate size 82x82″    9″ applique blocks, 5″ star blocks

Use 42-45″-wide fabric. When strips appear in the cutting list, cut crossgrain strips (selvage to selvage).

Patterns are given for fusible web applique, reversed and ready to be traced. Be sure to have plenty of fusible web on hand if using this method. Reverse patterns and add seam allowance if doing hand applique.

**NOTE:** The pieced borders in this quilt necessitate the exact piecing of all elements, so exact lengths for all pieces for the quilt, except Border 7, are given in the cutting chart or in the directions.

## YARDAGE

| | |
|---|---|
| Background, sashing, borders | 4½ yd black |
| Blocks, Border 4 | ⅜ yd each of 8 brights |
| Applique | ¼ yd each of 9 brights |
| Sashing | 1⅛ yd white |
| Borders 5 & 7 | 2⅝ yd purple |
| Binding | ¾ yd purple |
| Backing | 7⅝ yd |
| Batting | 88x88″ |

## CUTTING

*Cut these squares in HALF diagonally

| | |
|---|---|
| Blocks | 9 squares 9½″ - black |
| Applique | patterns on pages 87 & 88 |
| Sashing | 5 strips 1½″ wide - black & white |
| Border 1 | 4 strips 2½″ wide - black |
| Border 2 | 28 squares 3″ - brights |
| | 112 squares 1¾″ - black |
| | *112 squares 2⅛″ - brights |
| | *112 squares 2⅛″ - black |
| | 4 squares 5½″ - corners - black |
| Border 3 | 5 strips 2¾″ wide - black |
| Border 4 | 8 strips 2½″ wide - black |
| | 8 strips 4½″ wide - brights |
| | 4 squares 3¼″ - corners - black |
| Border 5 | 6 strips 3″ wide |
| Border 6 | *42 squares 3⅞″ - black & white |
| Border 7 | 8 strips 8½″ wide |
| Binding | 9 strips 2½″ wide |

# DIRECTIONS

Use ¼″ seam allowance unless otherwise noted.

1. **Blocks:** Applique hands and hearts to background squares, centered.

2. **Sashing:** Make a strip set with 4 black and 5 white strips. Press. Crosscut into 1½″ segments (24 needed). Cut 1½″ squares from remaining black strip (16 needed). Make 4 horizontal sashing rows with sashing units and black squares. Make 3 rows of blocks and sashing units. See diagram. Stitch rows of blocks and rows of sashing together. Press.

3. **Border 1:** Cut 2 border pieces 31½″ long and 2 pieces 35½″ long. Stitch short pieces to sides of quilt. Stitch long pieces to top and bottom. Press.

4. **Border 2:** Applique hearts to corner squares. Make 28 star blocks. For each block, use black as the background and 2 brights, one for the center, and one for the star points. Press. See diagram. Stitch 7 blocks together for each side border. These borders should be 35½″ long. Press. Stitch one border to each side of quilt. Stitch corner squares to each end of remaining borders, rotating as shown. Stitch to top and bottom of quilt. Press.

5. **Border 3:** Stitch border pieces end to end. Press. Cut 2 borders 45½″ long and 2 borders 50″ long. Stitch short pieces to sides of quilt. Stitch long pieces to top and bottom. Press.

6. **Border 4:** Make 8 strip sets, each with 1 black strip and 1 of the bright strips. **Press seams toward black.** Crosscut into 2½″ segments (76 needed—there will be waste). Alternating colors as desired, stitch into 4 borders of 19 segments, offsetting segments as shown. Trim long edges leaving ¼″ seam allowance on each side—width should be 3¼″. Trim ends as shown leaving ¼″ seam allowance. Borders should be 50″ long. Stitch one border to each side of quilt. Stitch corner squares to each end of remaining borders. Stitch to top and bottom of quilt. Press.

Continued on page 75

2.

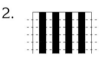

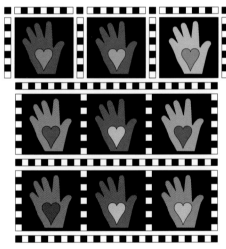

4. For each block

Make 8

Make 4

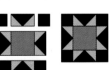

Diagrams continued on page 75

Sides - Make 2

Top & Bottom - Make 2

# Starring My Friends

This quilt is the result of a friendship block exchange. Ann Petersen, the lucky recipient of the blocks, added several others and came up with this lovely arrangement. In order to have more fabrics for the background without buying them all, exchange 9" squares with friends.

*A friend is someone who understands your past, believes in your future, and accepts you today just the way you are.*

Unknown

Photo on page 53

Approximate size 86x102"     2" units - 4", 6", 8", 10", & 12" blocks

Use 42-45"-wide fabric. When strips appear in the cutting list, cut crossgrain strips (selvage to selvage).

**NOTES:** The yardage for the background of this quilt is open to your interpretation. Ann used approximately 150 fabrics for her background squares. You could get by with a minimum of 60, but there will be less blending and less variety in the background. Using both sides of some fabrics will help extend your collection. Exchanging 9" squares with friends will also help! Each square yields 9 patches.

We have provided four paper piecing patterns and directions for six other pieced blocks. See pages 73-74 and 89-93. **You will need other star patterns in 4", 6", 8", 10", and 12" sizes.**

## YARDAGE

| | |
|---|---|
| Background, Border 2 | ⅛ yd each of 60-150 fabrics - whites, pastels, greens, blues, purples - ranging from light-light to dark-dark |
| Blocks | ⅛-¼ yd pieces as needed |
| Border 1 | ½ yd pink |
| Border 3, binding | 3⅛ yd blue |
| Backing | 8⅛ yd |
| Batting | 92x108" |

## CUTTING

| | |
|---|---|
| Background, Border 2 | 931 squares 2½" |
| Blocks | see patterns on pages 73-74 & 89-93 |
| Border 1 | 8 strips 1½" wide |
| Border 3 | 9 strips 8½" wide |
| Binding | 10 strips 2½" wide |

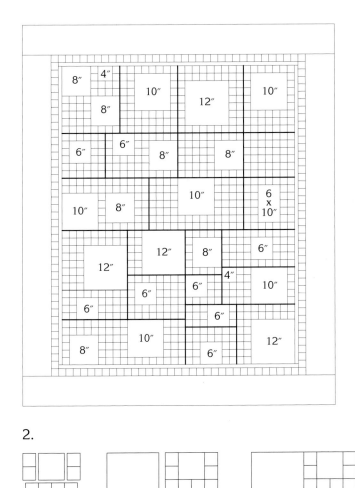

**2.**

## DIRECTIONS

Use ¼″ seam allowance unless otherwise noted.

1. Make 28 blocks in sizes shown at left. Press. Four paper piecing patterns are given on pages 89-93. Six additional patchwork blocks with cutting and piecing diagrams appear on pages 73-74.

2. Stitch blocks and background squares together in sections shown on diagrams at left. Stitch sections together. Press.

3. Border 1: Measure length of quilt. Piece border strips to the measured length and stitch to sides of quilt. Repeat at top and bottom. Press.

4. Border 2: Stitch 2 border units of 41 squares each for sides. Adjust length if necessary. Stitch to sides of quilt. Stitch 2 border units of 35 squares each. Adjust if needed. Stitch to top and bottom of quilt. Press.

5. Border 3: Repeat Step 3.

6. Piece backing horizontally to same size as batting. Layer and quilt as desired. Trim backing and batting even with top.

7. Stitch binding strips together end to end. Press in half lengthwise, wrong sides together. Bind quilt using ⅜″ seam allowance.

Top Left Section

Directions for more blocks are on page 74

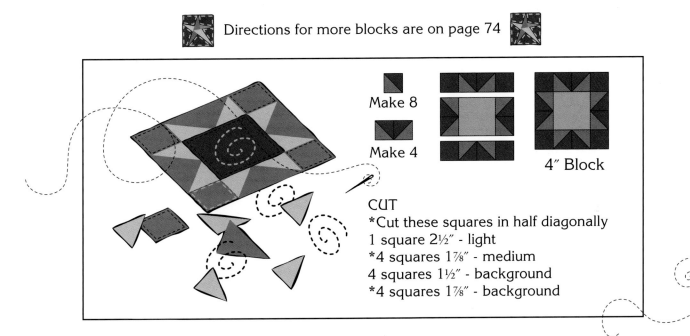

Make 8

Make 4

4″ Block

CUT
*Cut these squares in half diagonally
1 square 2½″ - light
*4 squares 1⅞″ - medium
4 squares 1½″ - background
*4 squares 1⅞″ - background

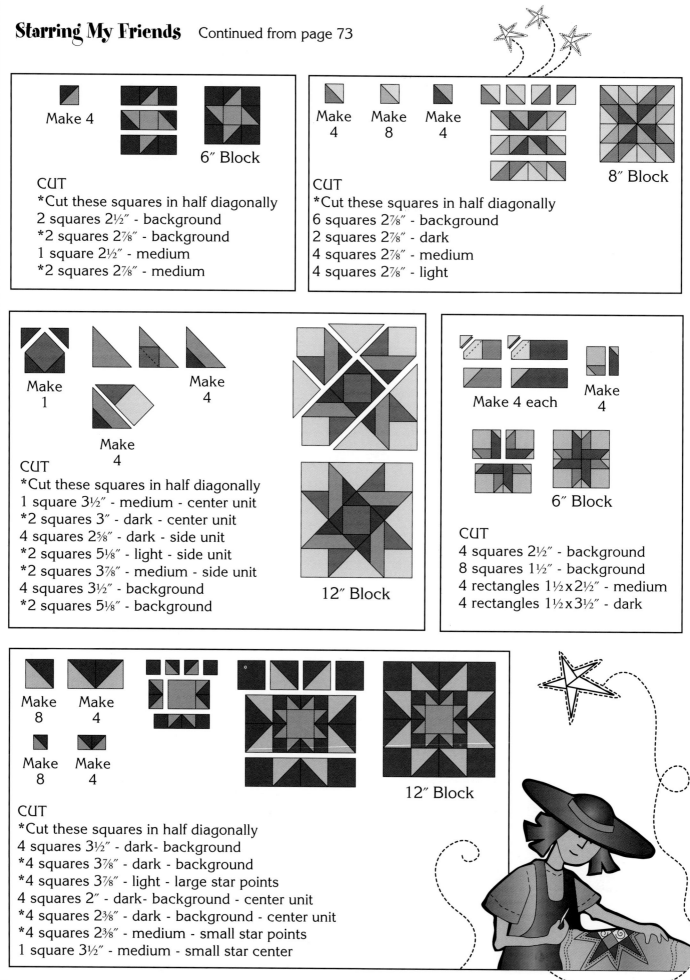

Make 4

6″ Block

CUT
*Cut these squares in half diagonally
2 squares 2½″ - background
*2 squares 2⅞″ - background
1 square 2½″ - medium
*2 squares 2⅞″ - medium

Make 4   Make 8   Make 4

8″ Block

CUT
*Cut these squares in half diagonally
6 squares 2⅞″ - background
2 squares 2⅞″ - dark
4 squares 2⅞″ - medium
4 squares 2⅞″ - light

Make 1   Make 4   Make 4

12″ Block

CUT
*Cut these squares in half diagonally
1 square 3½″ - medium - center unit
*2 squares 3″ - dark - center unit
4 squares 2⅝″ - dark - side unit
*2 squares 5⅛″ - light - side unit
*2 squares 3⅞″ - medium - side unit
4 squares 3½″ - background
*2 squares 5⅛″ - background

Make 4 each   Make 4

6″ Block

CUT
4 squares 2½″ - background
8 squares 1½″ - background
4 rectangles 1½ x 2½″ - medium
4 rectangles 1½ x 3½″ - dark

Make 8   Make 4

Make 8   Make 4

12″ Block

CUT
*Cut these squares in half diagonally
4 squares 3½″ - dark- background
*4 squares 3⅞″ - dark - background
*4 squares 3⅞″ - light - large star points
4 squares 2″ - dark- background - center unit
*4 squares 2⅜″ - dark - background - center unit
*4 squares 2⅜″ - medium - small star points
1 square 3½″ - medium - small star center

# Heart in Hand   Continued from page 71

7. Border 5: Stitch border pieces end to end. Press. Cut 2 borders 55½″ long and 2 borders 60½″ long. Stitch short pieces to sides of quilt. Stitch long pieces to top and bottom. Press.

8. Border 6: Make 84 half-square triangle units. Stitch 20 units together for each side border. These borders should be 60½″ long. Press. Stitch one border to each side of quilt. Stitch half-square triangle units to each end of remaining borders, rotating as shown. Stitch to top and bottom of quilt. Press.

9. Border 7: Measure length of quilt. Piece border strips to the measured length and stitch to sides of quilt. Repeat at top and bottom. Press.

10. Piece backing to same size as batting. Layer and quilt as desired. Trim backing and batting even with top.

11. Stitch binding strips together end to end. Press in half lengthwise, wrong sides together. Bind quilt using ⅜″ seam allowance.

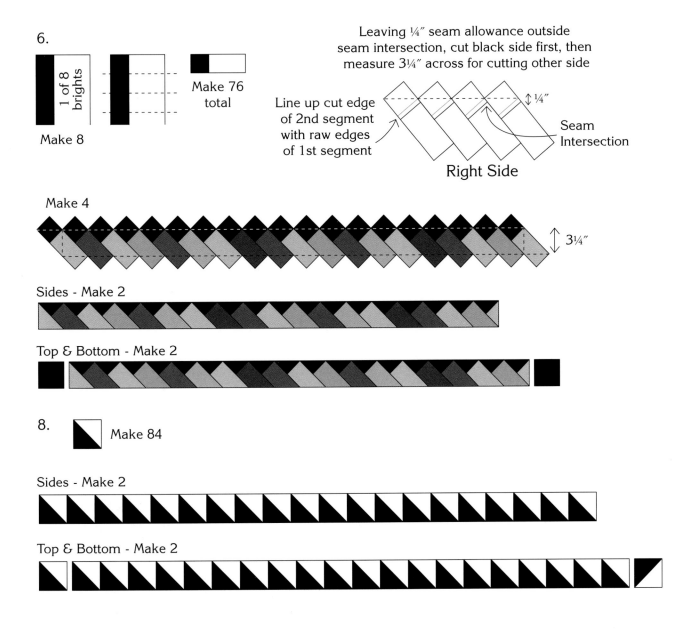

6.

1 of 8 brights

Make 8

Make 76 total

Leaving ¼″ seam allowance outside seam intersection, cut black side first, then measure 3¼″ across for cutting other side

Line up cut edge of 2nd segment with raw edges of 1st segment

Seam Intersection

¼″

Right Side

Make 4

3¼″

Sides - Make 2

Top & Bottom - Make 2

8.   Make 84

Sides - Make 2

Top & Bottom - Make 2

# Sister's Choice

**Three-Color Version**

We loved the simplicity of only having to choose three fabrics for this quilt. Make the crib size in pink or blue for a friend's new baby, or choose a more sophisticated color combination. Use the yardage chart on page 80 to make any size from small wall hanging to king.

*I breathed a song into the air. It fell to earth, I knew not where. And the song from beginning to end, I found again in the heart of a friend.*

Louisa May Alcott

Photo on page 57

Approximate size 48 x 62″     10″ block

Use 42-45″-wide fabric. When strips appear in the cutting list, cut crossgrain strips (selvage to selvage).

**NOTE:** Yardage and cutting chart for five other sizes of this quilt appears on page 80.

## YARDAGE

| | | |
|---|---|---|
| Color 1 - dark | 2¼ yd dark blue | |
| Color 2 - medium | 1¼ yd medium blue | |
| Color 3 - light | 1¼ yd light blue | |
| Binding | ⅝ yd dark blue | |
| Backing | 3¼ yd | |
| Batting | 54 x 68″ | |

## CUTTING

*Cut these squares in HALF diagonally

Blocks
| | | |
|---|---|---|
| Color 1 | 48 squares 2½″ | |
| | *48 squares 2⅞″ | |
| Color 2 | 12 squares 2½″ | |
| Color 3 | 144 squares 2½″ | |
| | *48 squares 2⅞″ | |

Sashing
| | | |
|---|---|---|
| Color 1 | 26 strips 2″ wide | |
| Color 2 | 16 strips 2″ wide | |
| Binding | 6 strips 2½″ wide | |

♥We Love To Quilt!♥

## DIRECTIONS

Use ¼″ seam allowance unless otherwise noted.

1. Make 12 blocks following diagram. Press.

2. Sashing: Make 2 Strip Set A and 12 Strip Set B. Crosscut 2 Strip Set A into forty 2″ segments. Crosscut 1 Strip Set B into twenty 2″ segments. Crosscut remaining Strip Set B into thirty-one 10½″ segments. Make nine-patch units from 2″ segments. See diagram. Press.

3. Make 5 rows of sashing rectangles and nine-patch units as shown. Make 4 rows of blocks and sashing rectangles as shown. Stitch rows together. Press.

4. Piece backing horizontally to same size as batting. Layer and quilt as desired. Trim backing and batting even with top.

5. Stitch binding strips together end to end. Press in half lengthwise, wrong sides together. Bind quilt using ⅜″ seam allowance.

1. For each block

Make 8

Make 4

Make 12

2.

A  B

Make 2  Make 12  Cut 40  Cut 20  Cut 31  Make 20

3.

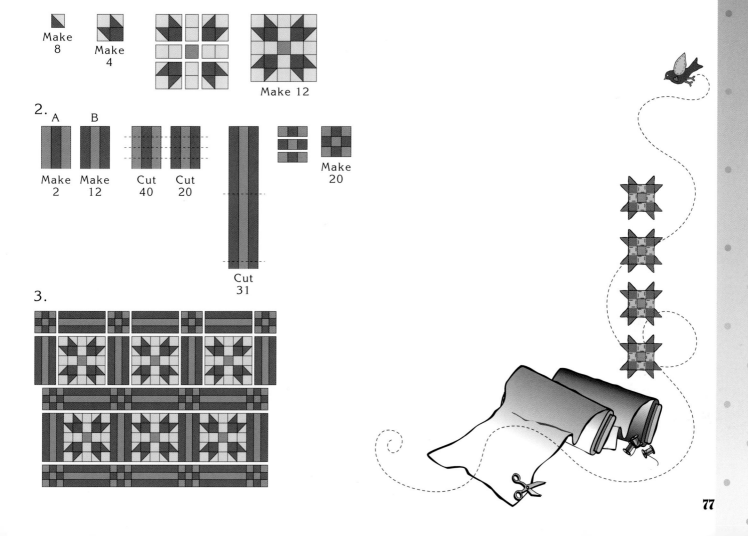

# Sister's Choice

**Scrap Version**

Study this quilt to see the subtle changes in the warm golden background. We used leftover squares from the quilt to make the three coordinated pillows seen in the photo. Use the yardage chart on page 81 to make any size from small wall hanging to king.

*For there is no friend like a sister in calm or stormy weather.*

Christina Rosetti

Photo on page 57

Approximate size 91x106″      10″ block

Use 42-45″-wide fabric. When strips appear in the cutting list, cut crossgrain strips (selvage to selvage).

**NOTE:** Yardage and cutting chart for five other sizes of this quilt appears on page 81.

## YARDAGE

| | |
|---|---|
| Background | 1⅛ yd each - peach - 2 light-light, 2 light-medium, 4 medium |
| Stars | ¼ yd each of 14 - pink, peach, purple, blue, green, fuchsia, rust |
| Sashing, binding | 3¾ yd medium green |
| Backing | 8½ yd |
| Batting | 97x112″ |

## CUTTING

*Cut these squares in HALF diagonally

| | |
|---|---|
| Background | 63 squares 2½″ of each fabric |
| | *21 squares 2⅞″ of each fabric |
| | 25 rectangles 2x10½″ of each fabric |
| | 28 squares 2″ of each fabric |
| Stars | 15 squares 2½″ of each fabric - makes 3 stars |
| | *12 squares 2⅞″ of each fabric - makes 3 stars |
| Sashing | 97 rectangles 2x10½″ |
| | 280 squares 2″ |
| Binding | 10-11 strips 2½″ wide |

FIND A TREASURE.
STORE IT HERE.
ALL LIFE LONG,
KEEP MEMORIES DEAR.

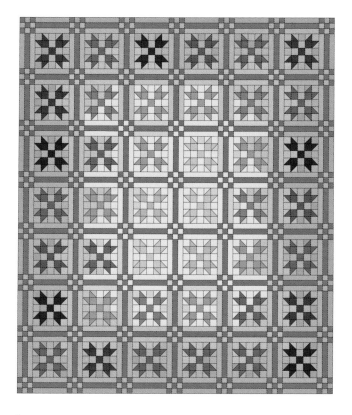

## DIRECTIONS

Use ¼″ seam allowance unless otherwise noted.

1. Make 42 blocks following diagram. The background should shade from darkest at the outside edge of the quilt to lightest at the center. As blocks are made, lay them out on the floor or pin them to a design wall in the position they will have in the finished quilt. This will make it easier to shade the background of the nearby blocks. Press.

2. Sashing: Make 56 nine-patch sashing units as shown, mixing background fabrics. Make 97 rectangular sashing units as shown, mixing background fabrics. See diagram. Press.

3. Make 8 rows of sashing rectangles and nine-patch units as shown. Make 7 rows of blocks and sashing rectangles as shown. Stitch rows together. Press.

4. Piece backing horizontally to same size as batting. Layer and quilt as desired. Trim backing and batting even with top.

5. Stitch binding strips together end to end. Press in half lengthwise, wrong sides together. Bind quilt using ⅜″ seam allowance.

1. Lay out each block separately to facilitate placing the different background colors

Make 8    Make 4    Make 42

2. Lay out each unit separately to facilitate placing the different background colors

Make 56    Make 97

3.

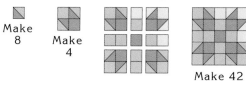

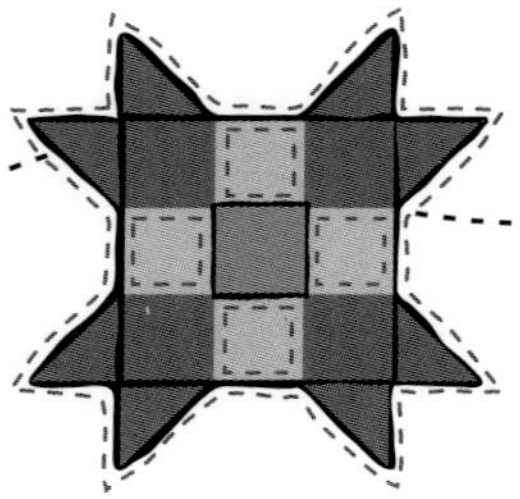

# Sister's Choice – Three-Color Version

| | Wall Hanging 48x48" 3x3 blocks | Baby 48x62½" 3x4 blocks | Lap 62½x77" 4x5 blocks | Twin 62½x91½" 4x6 blocks | Double/Queen 91½x106" 6x7 blocks | King 106x106" 7x7 blocks |
|---|---|---|---|---|---|---|
| # of blocks - 10" | 9 | 12 | 20 | 24 | 42 | 49 |
| # rectangular sashing units | 24 | 31 | 49 | 58 | 97 | 112 |
| # 9-patch sashing units | 16 | 20 | 30 | 35 | 56 | 64 |

## Yardage

| | Wall Hanging | Baby | Lap | Twin | Double/Queen | King |
|---|---|---|---|---|---|---|
| Light blue - background | 1 yd | 1¼ yd | 1⅞ yd | 2¼ yd | 3⅝ yd | 4¼ yd |
| Med. blue - stars, sashing | 1 yd | 1¼ yd | 1¾ yd | 2⅛ yd | 3⅛ yd | 3¾ yd |
| Dark blue - stars, sashing | 1⅞ yd | 2¼ yd | 3½ yd | 4 yd | 6½ yd | 7½ yd |
| Binding | ⅝ yd | ⅝ yd | ⅔ yd | ⅔ yd | 1 yd | 1 yd |
| Backing | 3¼ yd | 3¼ yd | 4⅞ yd | 5¾ yd | 8½ yd | 9¾ yd |
| Batting | 1 seam 54x54" | horiz seam 54x68" | vertical seam 68x83" | vertical seam 68x97" | 2 horiz seams 97x112" | 2 seams 112x112" |

## Cutting

*Cut these squares in HALF diagonally.

When strips appear in the cutting list, cut crossgrain strips (selvage to selvage).

| | Wall Hanging | Baby | Lap | Twin | Double/Queen | King |
|---|---|---|---|---|---|---|
| **Light blue** | | | | | | |
| 2½" squares | 108 | 144 | 240 | 288 | 504 | 588 |
| *2⅞" squares | 36 | 48 | 80 | 96 | 168 | 196 |
| **Medium blue** | | | | | | |
| 2½" squares | 9 | 12 | 20 | 24 | 42 | 49 |
| 2" strips | 13 | 16 | 25 | 30 | 48 | 56 |
| **Dark blue** | | | | | | |
| 2½" squares | 36 | 48 | 80 | 96 | 168 | 196 |
| *2⅞" squares | 36 | 48 | 80 | 96 | 168 | 196 |
| 2" strips | 20 | 26 | 41 | 48 | 78 | 91 |
| **Binding - dark blue** | | | | | | |
| 2½" strips | 5-6 | 6 | 7-8 | 8 | 10-11 | 11 |
| **# of strip sets for 9-patches** | | | | | | |
| Strip Set A - med/dk/med | 2 | 2 | 3 | 4 | 6 | 7 |
| Strip Set B - dk/med/dk | 9 | 12 | 19 | 22 | 36 | 42 |

# Sister's Choice – Scrap Version

| | Wall Hanging 48x48" 3x3 blocks | Baby 48x62½" 3x4 blocks | Lap 62½x77" 4x5 blocks | Twin 62½x91½" 4x6 blocks | Double/Queen 91½x106" 6x7 blocks | King 106x106" 7x7 blocks |
|---|---|---|---|---|---|---|
| # of blocks - 10" | 9 | 12 | 20 | 24 | 42 | 49 |
| # rectangular sashing units | 24 | 31 | 49 | 58 | 97 | 112 |
| # 9-patch sashing units | 16 | 20 | 30 | 35 | 56 | 64 |

## Yardage

| | Wall Hanging | Baby | Lap | Twin | Double/Queen | King |
|---|---|---|---|---|---|---|
| **Background - each fabric** | | | | | | |
| 2 light, 2 med, 4 dark med | 3/8 yd | 1/2 yd | 2/3 yd | 3/4 yd | 1⅛ yd | 1¼ yd |
| Star - ¼ each of | 3 | 4 | 7 | 8 | 14 | 17 |
| Sashing | 7/8 yd | 1 yd | 1⅝ yd | 1⅞ yd | 2⅞ yd | 3¼ yd |
| Binding | 5/8 yd | 5/8 yd | 2/3 yd | 2/3 yd | 1 yd | 1 yd |
| Backing | 3¼ yd | 3¼ yd | 4⅞ yd | 5¾ yd | 8½ yd | 9¾ yd |
| | 1 seam | horiz seam | vertical seam | vertical seam | 2 horiz seams | 2 seams |
| Batting | 54x54" | 54x68" | 68x83" | 68x97" | 97x112" | 112x112" |

## Cutting

*Cut these squares in HALF diagonally.
When strips appear in the cutting list, cut crossgrain strips (selvage to selvage).

| | Wall Hanging | Baby | Lap | Twin | Double/Queen | King |
|---|---|---|---|---|---|---|
| **Background - from each of 8** | | | | | | |
| 2½" squares | 14 | 18 | 30 | 36 | 63 | 74 |
| *2⅞" squares | 5 | 6 | 10 | 12 | 21 | 25 |
| 2x10½" | 6 | 8 | 13 | 15 | 25 | 28 |
| 2" squares | 8 | 10 | 15 | 18 | 28 | 32 |
| **Star - from each fabric (3 stars)** | | | | | | |
| 2½" squares | 15 | 15 | 15 | 15 | 15 | 15 |
| *2⅞" squares | 12 | 12 | 12 | 12 | 12 | 12 |
| **Sashing** | | | | | | |
| 2x10½" | 24 | 31 | 49 | 58 | 97 | 112 |
| 2" squares | 80 | 100 | 150 | 175 | 280 | 320 |
| **Binding** | | | | | | |
| 2½" strips | 5-6 | 6 | 7-8 | 8 | 10-11 | 11 |

# Kitchen Chicks

Nothing is more inviting than a brightly colored wall hanging that says Welcome to My Kitchen. make the projects that we have selected and then use your creativity to make other things like place mats or table runners.

*To invite a person into your house is to take charge of his happiness for as long as he is under your roof.*

A. Brillat-Savarin

Photo on page 56

Approximate size 27x57″

Use 42-45″-wide fabric. When strips appear in the cutting list, cut crossgrain strips (selvage to selvage).

Patterns are given for fusible web applique, reversed and ready to be traced. Be sure to have plenty of fusible web on hand if using this method. Reverse patterns and add seam allowance if doing hand applique.

## YARDAGE

| | |
|---|---|
| Background, checkerboard | ¾ yd white |
| Frame, star centers binding | ⅝ yd green |
| | ⅛ yd turquoise |
| Checkerboard corners | ⅛ yd yellow |
| Sashing | ⅜ yd red |
| Checkerboard, border | 1⅛ yd blue |
| Appliques | ¼ yd each of 1-2 greens or 6x7″ scraps - bird bodies |
| | ⅛ yd each of yellow, blue, red |
| Backing | 2 yd |
| Batting | 32x62″ |

## CUTTING

*Cut these squares in HALF diagonally

| | |
|---|---|
| Background | 3 squares 8½″ white |
| Frame | 6 rectangles 1x8½″ - turquoise |
| | 6 rectangles 1x9½″ - green |
| Checkerboard | 5 strips 1½″ wide - blue & white |
| | 12 squares 2½″ - corners - yellow |
| Star blocks | 4 squares 3″ - green |
| | 16 squares 1¾″ - white |
| | *16 squares 2⅛″ - white |
| | *16 squares 2⅛″ - blue |
| Appliques | patterns on pages 86-87 |
| Sashing | 4 strips 2½″ wide - red |
| Border | 4 strips 5½″ wide - blue |
| Binding | 5 strips 2¼″ wide - green |

## Potholder  8″ square

Make star block following directions on page 83. Add 1¼″ border (cut 1¾″). Layer and quilt. Bind, extending binding at one corner to make loop.

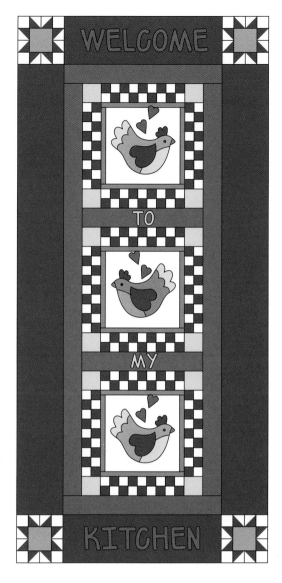

## DIRECTIONS

Use ¼″ seam allowance unless otherwise noted.

1. Stitch turquoise frame rectangles to sides of background squares. Stitch green frame rectangles to top and bottom. Press.

2. Checkerboards: Make 5 strip sets with blue and white strips as shown. Crosscut into 1½″ segments (108 needed). Make 12 border units as shown. Press.

3. Stitch border units to sides of blocks. Stitch yellow corner squares to ends of remaining border units. Stitch to top and bottom of each block. Press.

4. Applique chickens to blocks, overlapping hearts on frame pieces.

5. Measure width of blocks. Cut 2 red sashing pieces that length. Stitch blocks and red sashing pieces into a vertical row. See diagram. Press. Measure length of row. Cut (or piece, if necessary) 2 pieces of red sashing that length. Stitch to sides of quilt. Measure width. Cut sashing pieces and stitch to quilt. Press. Center and applique lettering to horizontal sashing strips between blocks.

6. Star Blocks: Make 4 blocks following diagram. Press.

7. Border: Measure width and length of quilt. Piece border strips to the measured length and stitch to sides of quilt. Cut border strips to the measured width and stitch star blocks to ends of each. Center and applique lettering to borders. Stitch borders to top and bottom of quilt. Press.

8. Cut backing to same size as batting. Layer and quilt as desired. Trim backing and batting even with top.

9. Stitch binding strips together end to end. Press in half lengthwise, wrong sides together. Bind quilt using ¼″ seam allowance.

1.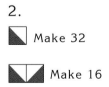

Make 12

2. Make 32

Make 16

Make 4

3.

## Chairback   16″ square

Use ¼″ seam allowance unless otherwise noted.

To chicken block, add 2″ sashing (cut 2½″) and corner squares (cut 2½″). Make 1″ checkerboard (cut 1½″) for border (2-3 strip sets and 56 crosscuts needed). Layer, quilt, and bind. Make 4 ties (cut 2½ x 30″, folded right sides together lengthwise, stitched, and turned right side out). Fold ties in half and stitch folds to corners of chairback.

Fill wide-mouth quart jars with these pretty gift mixes and top them with a fabric jar topper – directions on page 13. Copy the recipes onto your own cardstock and attach them to the jars. Share with old friends or new neighbors in baskets of goodies.

## BUSY DAY BROWNIES

Preheat oven to 350°.

Grease 9x9" square or 7x11" pan.

Mix contents of jar with:
1 tsp vanilla
2/3 cup vegetable oil
3 eggs

Bake 7x11" pan for 32-37 minutes, 9x9" pan 27-30 minutes.

Cool and enjoy!

### TO MAKE LAYERED BROWNIE MIX:

½ tsp salt
⅔ cup flour
⅓ cup cocoa powder
½ cup flour
⅔ cup brown sugar
½ cup chocolate chips
½ cup vanilla chips
½ cup chopped nuts

Layer ingredients in clear quart jar. Put metal lid on jar. Attach fabric jar topper and recipe to jar.

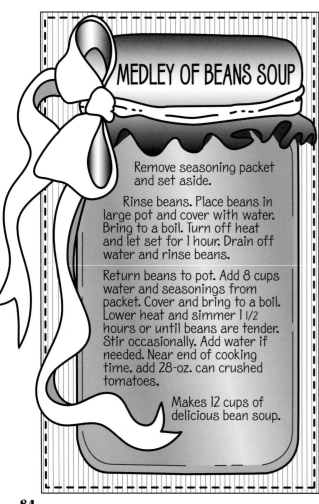

## MEDLEY OF BEANS SOUP

Remove seasoning packet and set aside.

Rinse beans. Place beans in large pot and cover with water. Bring to a boil. Turn off heat and let set for 1 hour. Drain off water and rinse beans.

Return beans to pot. Add 8 cups water and seasonings from packet. Cover and bring to a boil. Lower heat and simmer 1 1/2 hours or until beans are tender. Stir occasionally. Add water if needed. Near end of cooking time, add 28-oz. can crushed tomatoes.

Makes 12 cups of delicious bean soup.

### TO MAKE LAYERED BEAN MIX:

BEANS for LAYERS (keep separated until ready to fill jars)
3/4 cup each of several kinds of dried beans such as red, black, Great Northern, split peas, red or yellow lentils

SEASONING MIX
Mix and place in sandwich baggie:
2 tbsp dried minced onion
2 tbsp beef bouillon granules
2 tbsp dried parsley flakes
2 tsp dried basil
2 tsp powdered lemonade mix with sugar
1½ tsp chili powder
1 tsp garlic powder
1 tsp pepper
1 tsp dried oregano

Layer beans in clear quart jar. Top with seasoning baggie. Put metal lid on jar. Attach fabric jar topper and recipe to jar.

# BLUEBERRY-GINGER MUFFINS

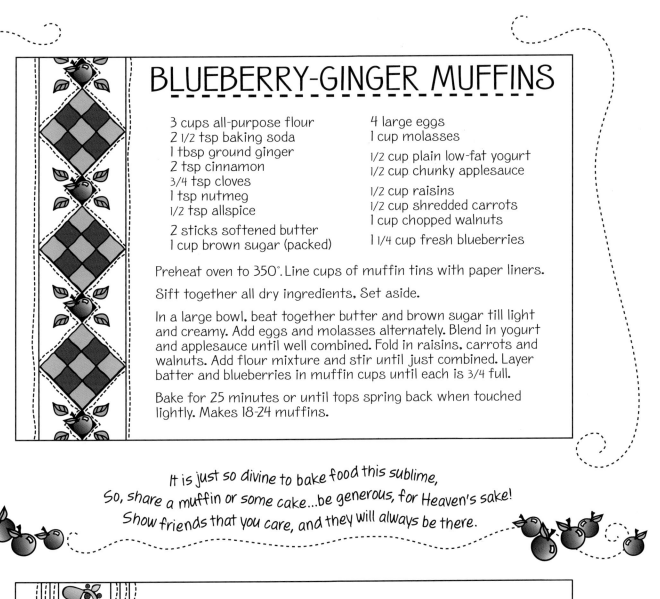

3 cups all-purpose flour
2 1/2 tsp baking soda
1 tbsp ground ginger
2 tsp cinnamon
3/4 tsp cloves
1 tsp nutmeg
1/2 tsp allspice

2 sticks softened butter
1 cup brown sugar (packed)

4 large eggs
1 cup molasses

1/2 cup plain low-fat yogurt
1/2 cup chunky applesauce

1/2 cup raisins
1/2 cup shredded carrots
1 cup chopped walnuts
1 1/4 cup fresh blueberries

Preheat oven to 350°. Line cups of muffin tins with paper liners.

Sift together all dry ingredients. Set aside.

In a large bowl, beat together butter and brown sugar till light and creamy. Add eggs and molasses alternately. Blend in yogurt and applesauce until well combined. Fold in raisins, carrots and walnuts. Add flour mixture and stir until just combined. Layer batter and blueberries in muffin cups until each is 3/4 full.

Bake for 25 minutes or until tops spring back when touched lightly. Makes 18-24 muffins.

*It is just so divine to bake food this sublime,*
*So, share a muffin or some cake...be generous, for Heaven's sake!*
*Show friends that you care, and they will always be there.*

# DELICIOUS DATE MUFFINS

1 cup All-Bran cereal
1/2 cup milk
2 3-oz pkg cream cheese

2 pkg Pillsbury Date Bread mix
1 cup sour cream
1 tbsp flour (+1 for high altitudes)

Preheat oven to 400°.

Soak cereal in milk for 10 minutes to soften it.

Cut each cream cheese block into 6-8 equal pieces. Set aside.

Add bread mix, sour cream, and flour to softened cereal and stir 50-75 strokes to moisten ingredients.

Fill greased muffin cups 7/8 full. Press one cube of cream cheese into each muffin. Spread batter to cover cream cheese completely.

Bake for 20-25 minutes.

Makes 12 large or 16 medium muffins.

Reheat wrapped in foil 15 minutes at 325°.

Kitchen Chicks

Cut 2
Cut 1 Reversed

Cut 6

86

Kitchen
Chicks

Heart in Hand

Cut 9

87

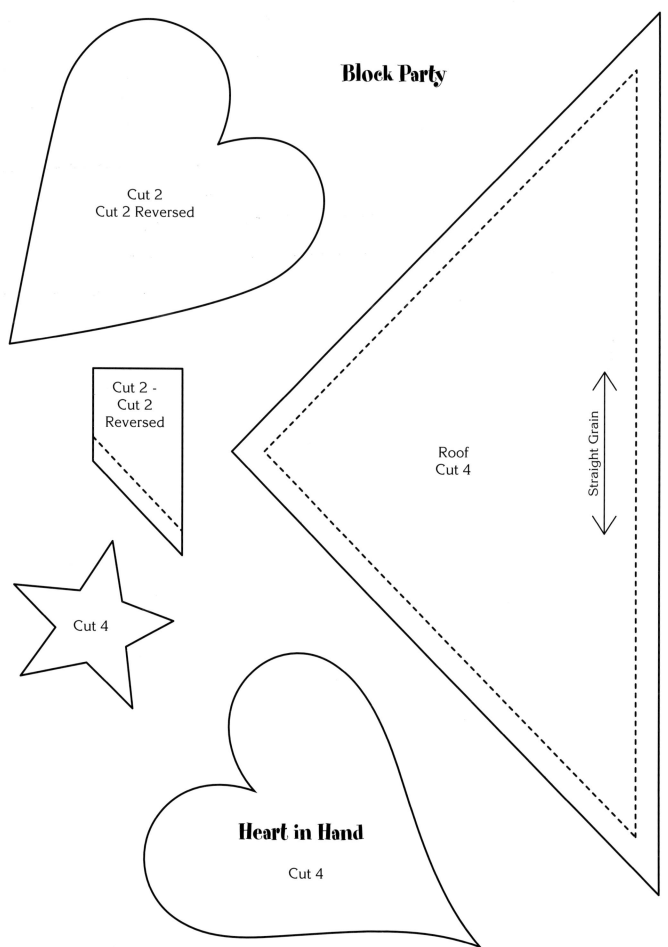

**Block Party**

Cut 2
Cut 2 Reversed

Cut 2 -
Cut 2
Reversed

Roof
Cut 4

Straight Grain

Cut 4

**Heart in Hand**

Cut 4

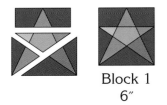

Block 1
6"

# Starring My Friends

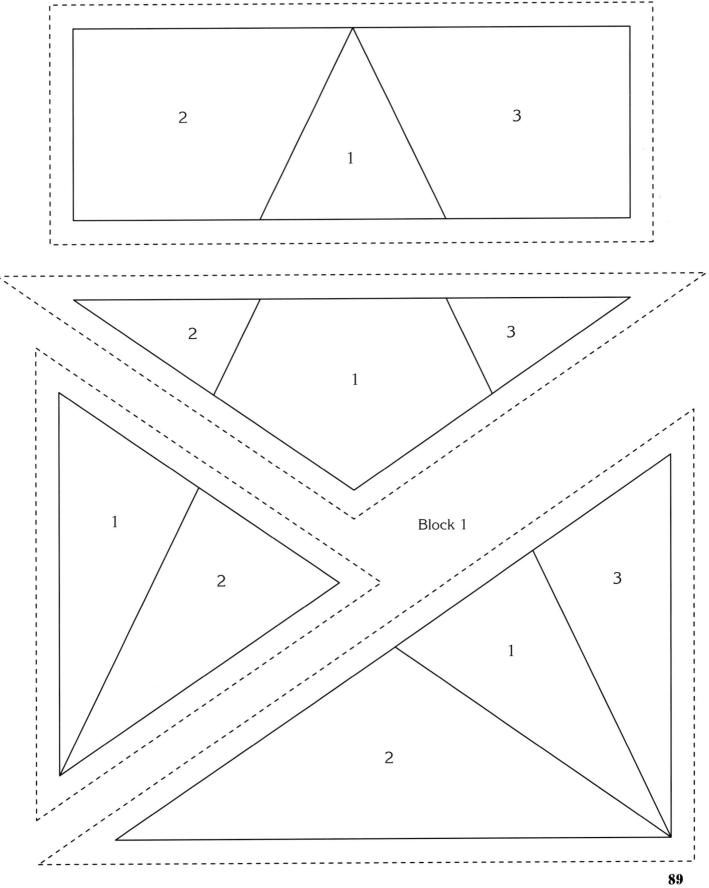

2

1

3

2

1

3

1

2

Block 1

3

1

2

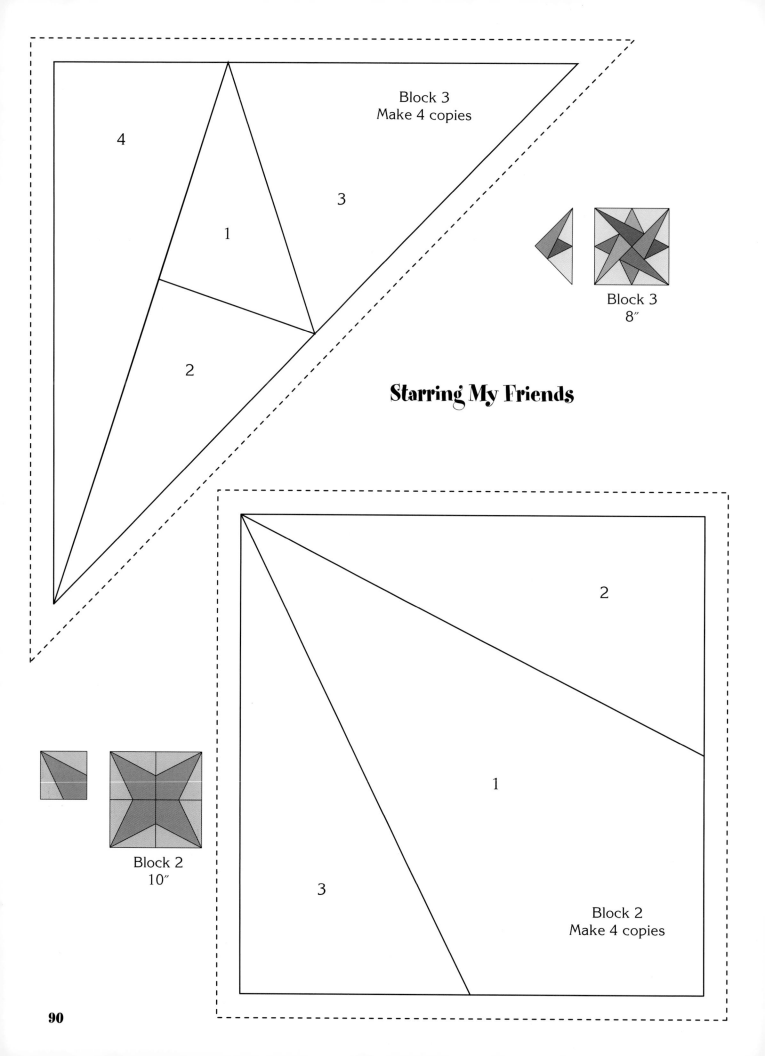

Block 3
Make 4 copies

4

3

1

2

Block 3
8″

**Starring My Friends**

2

1

3

Block 2
10″

Block 2
Make 4 copies

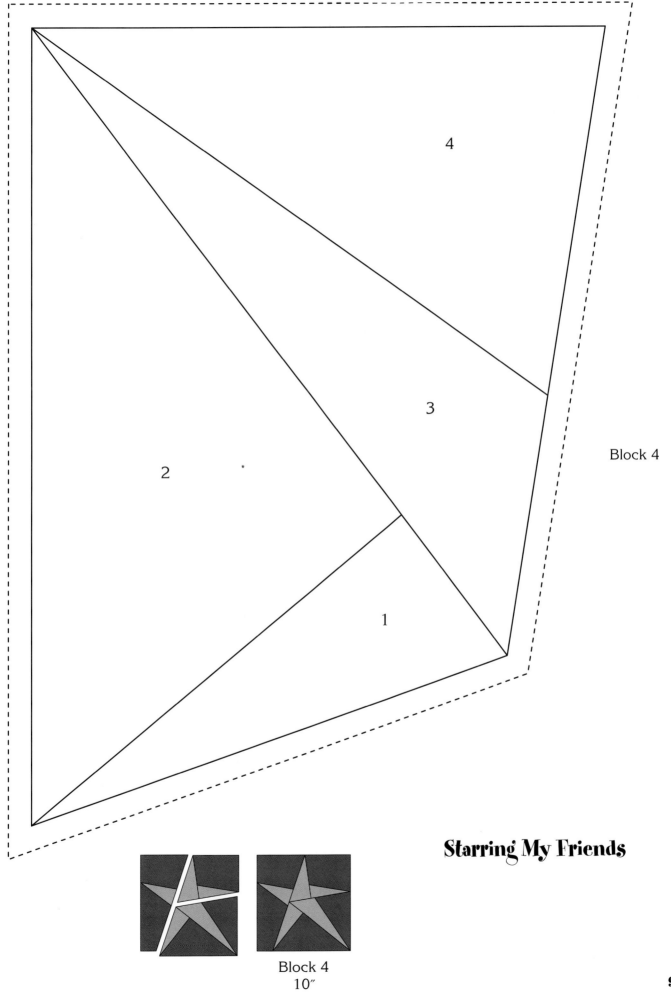

4

3

2

1

Block 4

**Starring My Friends**

Block 4
10″

# Starring My Friends

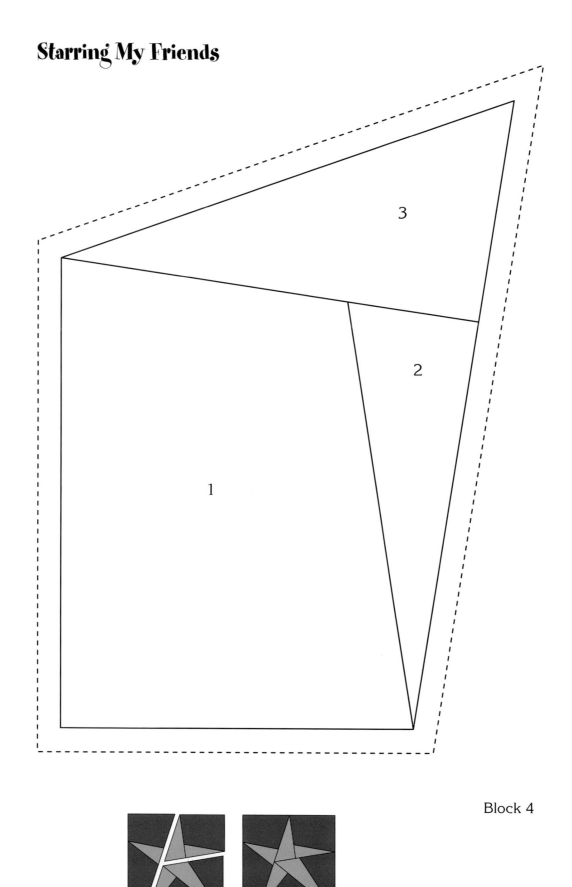

Block 4

Block 4
10″

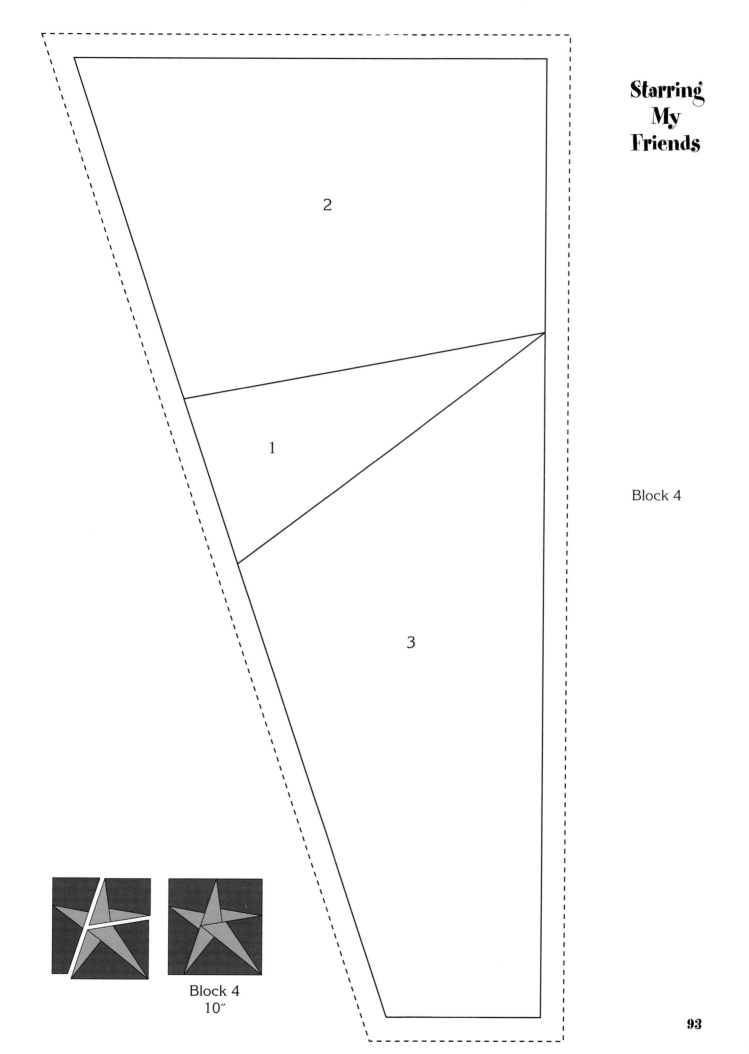

2

1

Block 4

3

Block 4
10″

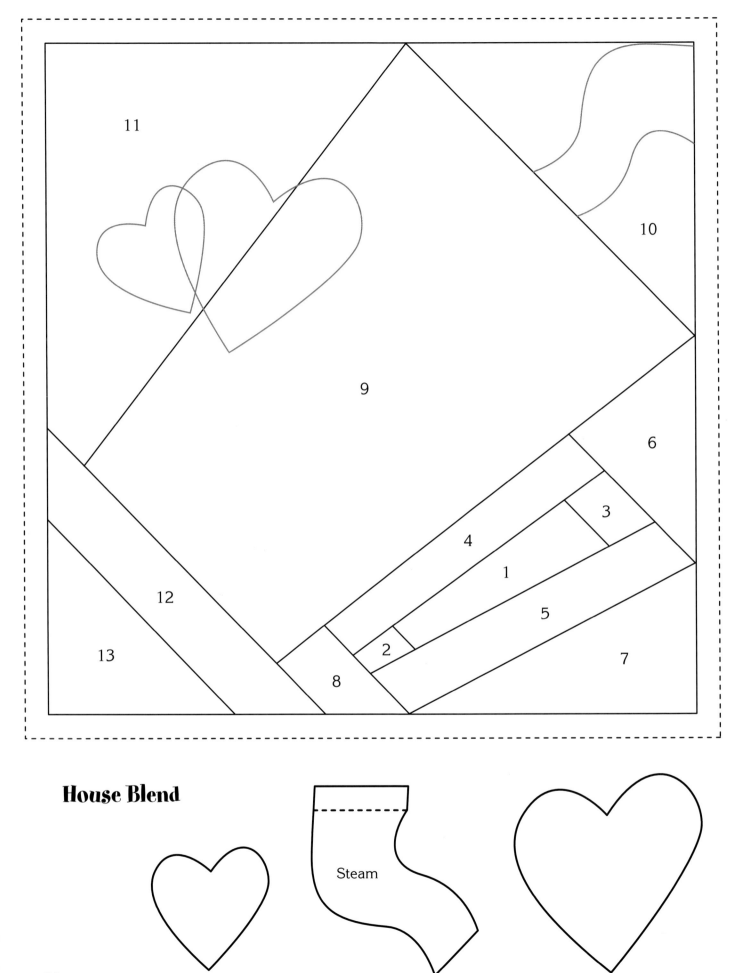

## House Blend

Steam

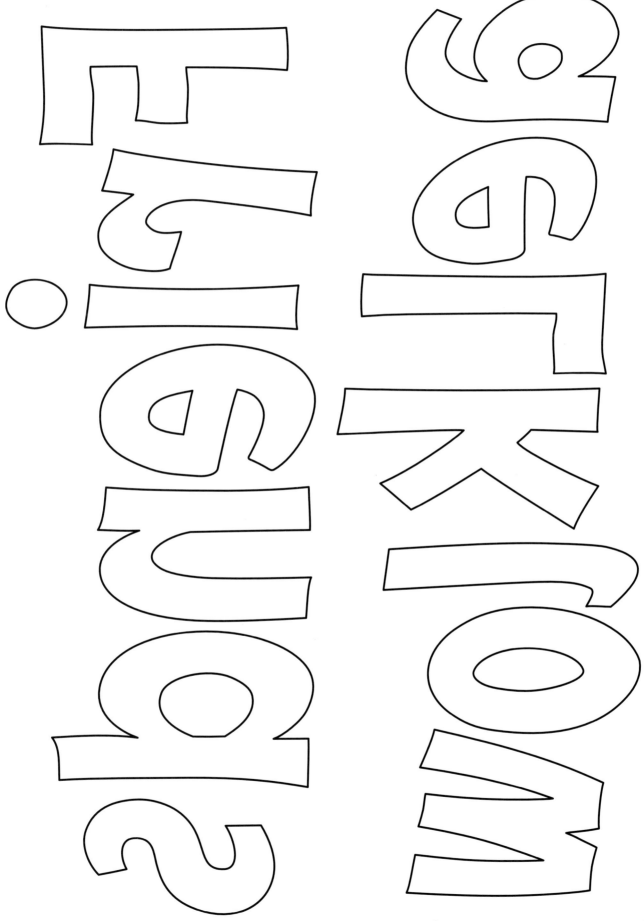

# Friends Are Like Flowers

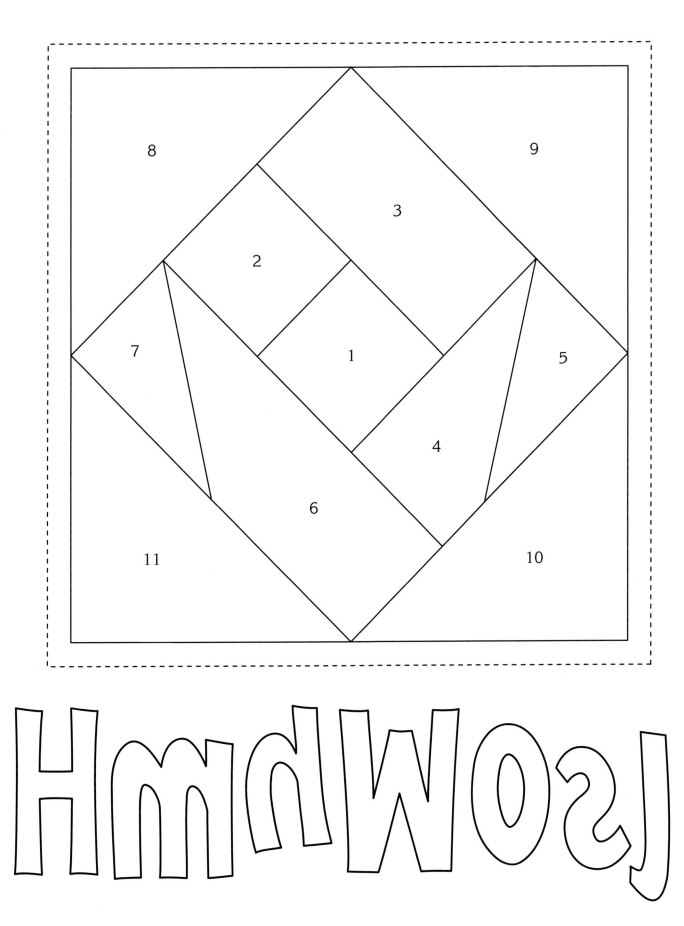

# Friends Are Like Flowers

# Friends Are Like Flowers

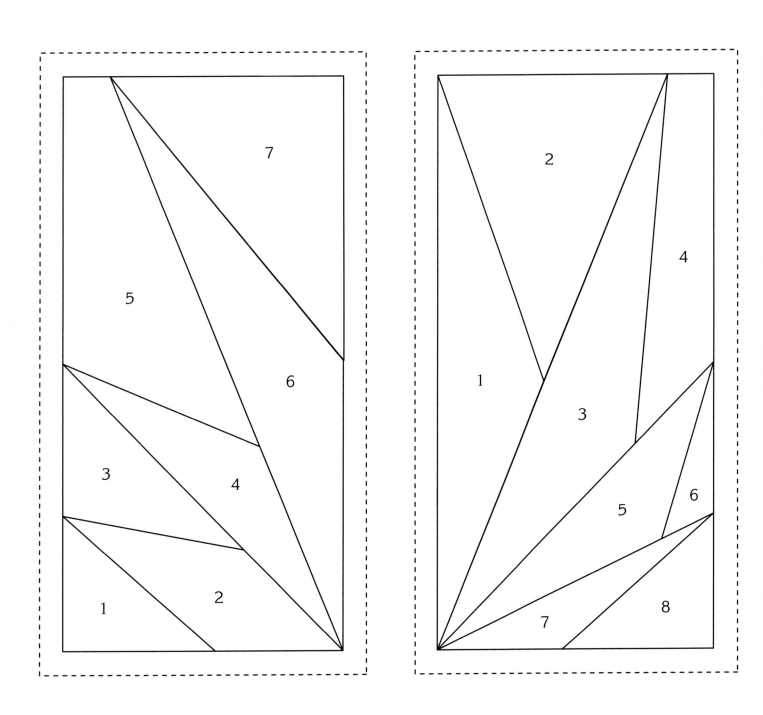

# Friends Are Like Flowers

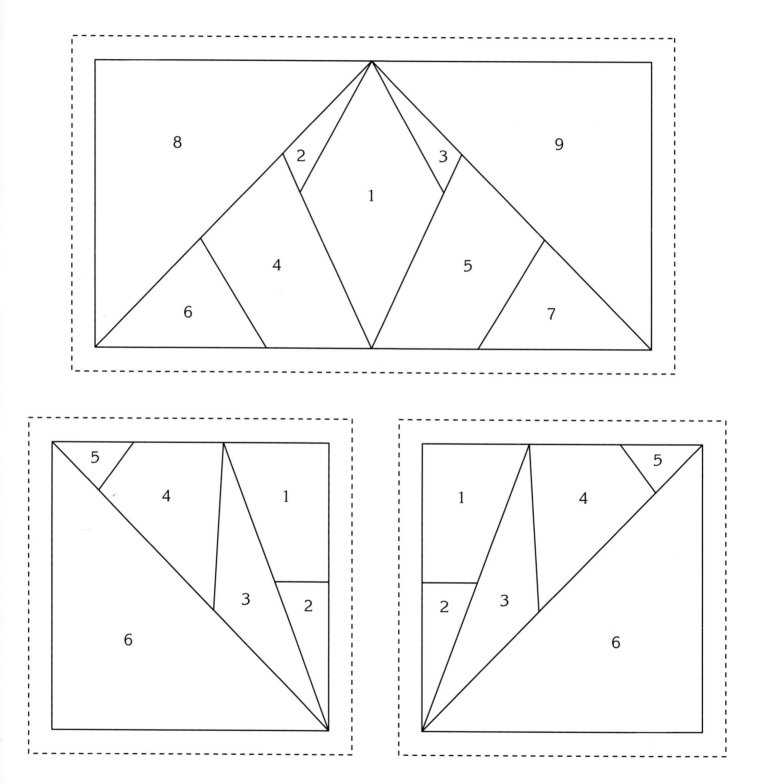

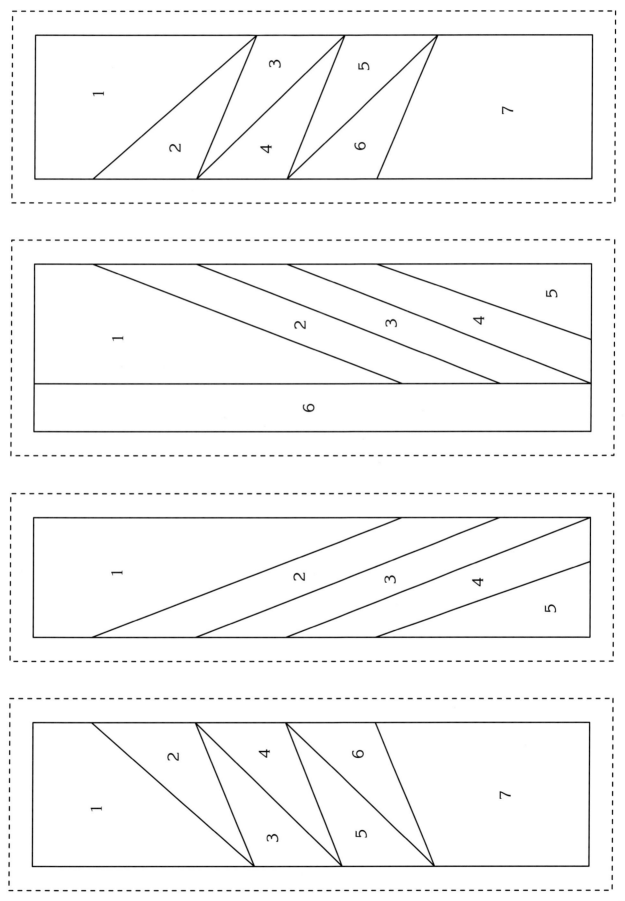

# Friends Are Like Flowers

Make 2 photocopies of this page

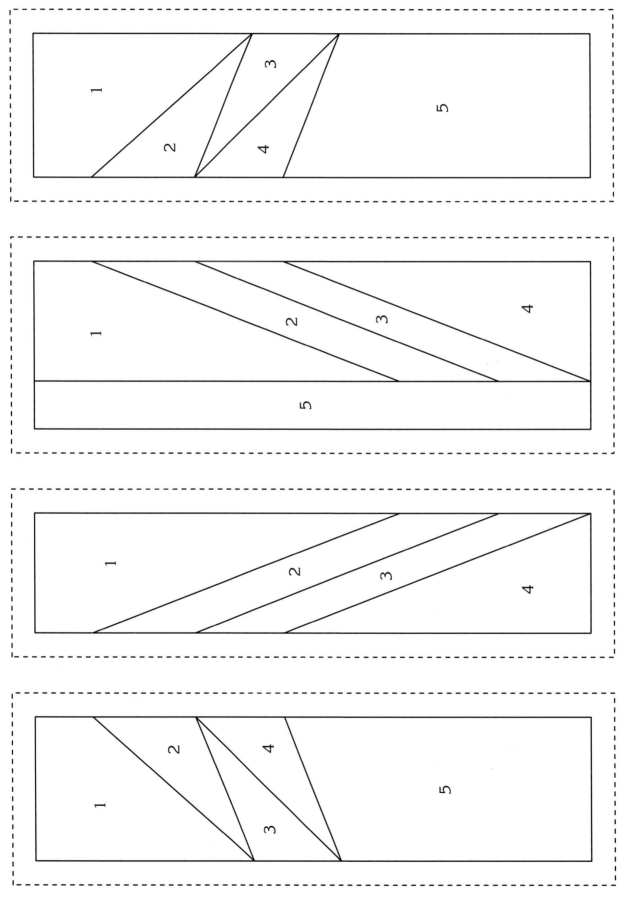

# Friends Are Like Flowers

Make 2 photocopies of this page

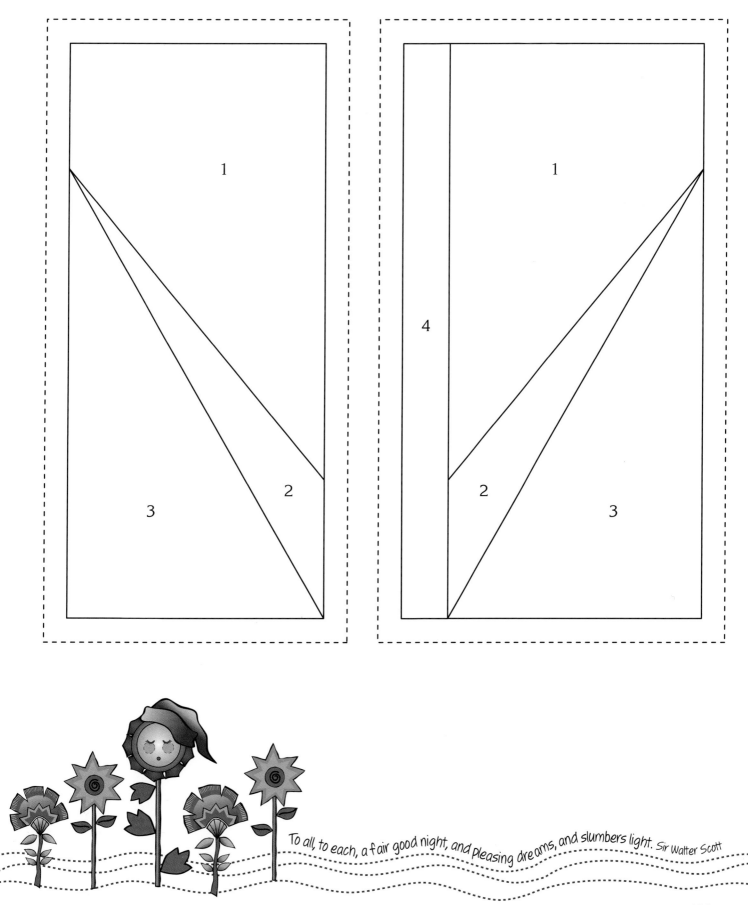

*To all, to each, a fair good night, and pleasing dreams, and slumbers light. Sir Walter Scott*

# Creative Quilting Projects from Possibilities®

**HEARTS APLENTY**

If you need a gift for a loved one, this collection of 19 quilts and small projects is perfect. Has a variety of techniques, styles, and skill levels.

**DIVIDE & CONQUER**

*Divide* a bed-sized quilt into workable sections & *Conquer* the task of machine or hand quilting it. Four methods. 17 original quilts.

**COMFORTS OF LOVE**

Give the gift of love with one of six cozy patch-work and/or applique quilts. Coordinating pillow covers complete the look.

**HOME FOR THE HARVEST**

Celebrate the fall season with 18 quilts and more than 20 small projects. Themes include back-to-school, Halloween, & Thanksgiving.

**BEDWARMERS**

Wrap your comforter in patchwork with one of three styles of comforter covers. Plus coordinated toppers, pillow covers, & pillow cases.

**JOY TO THE WORLD**

Full of holiday quilts for different skill levels. Contains delightful projects such as gift bags, stockings, tree skirts, and place mats.

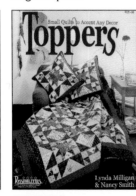

**TOPPERS**

Toppers are beautiful quilts for displaying over bed pillows, on the back of a couch, or over a bedspread or comforter. A variety of styles.

**QUILTS & MORE**

Over 25 projects using photos transferred to fabric. Instructions and full-sized patterns for making special family heirlooms.

**HOUSEWARMERS**

Warm your home with the beauty of homemade quilts. Add personal touches to any room. Nineteen quilts & 25 smaller projects.

**TIME FOR A CHAIN**

Detailed charts for rotary cutting give measurements for single, double, and triple Irish Chains in two or three block sizes each.

**P.S. I LOVE YOU**

One of the top quilting books in America. Includes 17 quilts in cradle, crib, and twin sizes. Nursery accessories included. Exceptional collection!

# POSSIBILITIES®

...Publishers of DreamSpinners® patterns, I'll Teach Myself™ sewing products, and Possibilities® books...

These books are available from your local quilt shop or from Possibilities® at:

8970 East Hampden Avenue
Denver, Colorado 80231

Phone 303-740-6206 • Fax 303-220-7424
Orders only U.S. & Canada 1-800-474-2665
Order online at www.possibilitiesquilt.com

**P.S. I LOVE YOU TWO!**

A national top seller, this book features timeless projects for making cherished gifts for babies and children. A multitude of techniques is included.

# forever e. friends

## Sewing the Seeds of Friendship

Y ou are invited to join Nellie Peach and Missy Plum as they bring out the best in each other through the joy of friendship. Nellie and Missy are best friends who were losing touch because of the demands of work and family. They decided to do something about it, so they created forever e. friends to nurture their friendship, share their love of quilting, and have fun!

forever e.friends
Spring Quilt

Join Nellie and Missy each month on their Internet adventure as they make time to quilt, get together, and lend a hand to others.

## Sign up online at
### www.possibilitiesquilt.com

**OR** sign up by mail below

---

Please mail membership information and payment to: Possibilities®, 8970 E. Hampden Ave., Denver, CO, 80231 or call us at 1-800-474-2665.

For office use only

J F M A M J J A S O N D

_____
Date

_____    _____
Name                                          Phone Number

_____  _____  _____  _____  _____
Street                     City          State   ZIP/Postal Code  Country

☐ Discover/Visa/MC    # _____    **Total $45** *

☐ Check/M.O.  ☐ Cash                               *U.S. funds only. Canadian customers please add $1.
                        _____                International customers add $3 for S&H.
                        Exp. Date

Email Address  ▢▢▢▢▢▢▢▢▢▢▢▢▢▢▢▢▢▢

**Welcome, Friend!**

_____    ▢▢▢▢▢▢▢▢▢▢▢▢▢▢▢▢▢▢
Refer-A-Friend Name                   Email Address

Join Possibilities® on their newest adventure, **forever e.friends**! The team at Possibilities® has created an Internet-based friendship club which entitles members to a wonderful array of quilted projects, monthly sewing tips, recipes, and more!

The world of **forever e.friends** offers members everything they need to create a wonderful block-of-the-month project plus a whole lot more! You'll connect with friends and have a great time! The price of membership entitles you to a wonderful feast of benefits:

- Patterns for 12 original blocks which can be assembled in a variety of ways—quilt, wall hangings, seasonal wall hangings, pillows, and more! Blocks are mostly applique with just the right amount of patchwork.

- At least 5 additional quilt patterns plus more than 10 additional small projects.

- A beautiful and handy binder for organizing membership information, patterns, and recipes.

- A packet of basic sewing information for every skill level plus monthly sewing tips for each project.

- Hints and ideas for organizing your own **forever e.friends** club.

- Tasty recipes for you and your friends to enjoy together.

- A monthly letter from Lynda Milligan and Nancy Smith, authors of Possibilities® books, to help you keep your spirit of friendship alive!

- Automatic entry into the **Friends In Colorado Getaway Weekend**. See details below.

- Free shipping on all of your Internet orders placed at www.possibilitiesquilt.com (U.S. Orders Only).

All of these benefits are available for members only, so sign up today! Simply visit www.possibilitiesquilt.com and follow the links to membership signup, or you may fill out the front of this card and mail it in along with your payment. As always, please call us toll-free at 1-800-474-2665 if you have questions.

We look forward to having you as our new friend! Welcome to **forever e.friends**!

## Friends in Colorado Getaway Weekend

We will choose one of our club members at random to win a weekend getaway for two to Colorado. We will fly you and your friend into Denver, Colorado*, treat you to lunch with Nancy and Lynda, take you to a lecture with a nationally known quilter, enroll you in a class with that teacher, and give you lots of shopping time at Great American Quilt Factory!

*Winner and friend must fly from a continental U.S. departure point. No purchase necessary. Void where prohibited by law. Open only to legal U.S. residents. For complete rules and entry information send an SASE to: Possibilities® Attention: Friends in Colorado Getaway Weekend Rules, 8970 E. Hampden Ave., Denver, CO 80231.

Not only will you be entered when you join **forever e.friends**, you and your friend will receive an additional entry when she joins. Just ask her to list your name and email address as a refer-a-friend! If 10 of your friends join, you could get 10 extra chances to win!

# Management in the
# Active Classroom

**By Ron Berger, Dina Strasser, and Libby Woodfin**

Design by Lauren Parent and Michael Kelly

Copyright © 2015 by EL Education. All rights reserved.

EL Education
247 West 35th St., 8th Floor
New York, NY 10001
212-239-4455

# Acknowledgments

As with all the books we write, *Management in the Active Classroom* has been a truly collaborative effort. Thanks to the entire field staff of EL Education who dug into our first edition of the book and provided deep, thoughtful, and comprehensive feedback that has guided this revision. A few staff members went above and beyond on this revision, and they deserve special thanks: Lily Newman, Jenny Henderson, Rayna Dineen, Dinah Consuegra, and Anne Vilen.

A small group of Mount Holyoke College Master of Arts in Teaching students, led by professors Beverly Bell and Catherine Swift, also engaged with the text and provided valuable feedback from their perspective as pre-service teachers. Thanks especially to Jane Chapin, a graduate of that program, who took time during her first year as a teacher in Boston to Skype with us about her impressions of the first edition.

Thanks also to the staff of Harlem Village Academies, led by Deborah Kenny, who worked with the book for more than a year and offered feedback during professional learning sessions with Ron.

There were many teachers and school leaders who graciously agreed to be interviewed and who contributed their time, expertise, and resources to this effort, and many more whose classrooms have provided the inspiration, examples, and practices that informed this work. The voices of novice and seasoned practitioners combined to help us make this a better book. We couldn't have done it without you!

And lastly, we offer a special thanks to our videographer, David Grant. David has brought these practices to life. He is not just an artist in film but also a visionary educator. We are deeply grateful.

# Videos Available

Almost all of the practices in Part 1 and many in Part 2 of *Management in the Active Classroom* have an accompanying video. Each short video shows the practice in action in classrooms across the country.

Look for this icon and visit: http://ELeducation.org/classroom-management-videos

Check back from time to time; our video library is always growing.

# Part 1:
# Foundational Structures and Practices

# Part 1: Contents

# Group Work

# Deeper Support for Challenging Behaviors

# Part 1: Introduction

*In Deb Ortenzi's middle school science classroom at World of Inquiry School in Rochester, New York, there is not a sound.*

*It seems to be a near magical transformation. Through the open door of the classroom in this urban public school, students first enter chatting animatedly, automatically picking up the entry ticket placed for them at the front entrance. Ortenzi herself is joking outside in the hallway with students, gently pushing them along to their classrooms with her voice—"Keep it moving, folks, bell's about to ring!" In her classroom, as each student settles down in a seat with an entry ticket, their eyes focus, their bodies become quiet and still. The entire class is present and working.*

*What Ortenzi knows, however, is that the transformation is not magic. It is the result of weeks and months of creating trusting relationships, setting strong classroom norms for behavior together, sharing responsibility with her students, and practicing routines and protocols, over and over again.*

*"It was definitely a journey. In the beginning, they didn't want to step up. They wanted us to do tasks for them, or they rebelled when they were asked to do it on their own. It took them a year to get over the fact that they were going to work," she laughs. "But we just kept reminding them of their routines. We still do. With patience and consistency, we get there."*

*Ortenzi comes in and shuts the door shortly after the bell rings—but there is no need for a bell. The learning has already begun.*

There's a certain instantly recognizable energy present in a high-achieving classroom. You can see it in the faces of the students: lighting up as they make new connections between their background knowledge and their reading, or settling into deep concentration on an entry ticket. You can hear it in the respectful but warm conversations that occur between student and teacher, and in the way students take control of their classroom routines and procedures with only the gentlest of reminders. You can touch it: the poster of jointly written classroom norms, the materials organized and ready for students when they enter.

A successful classroom is obvious to all our senses. But the steps to take in order to create that classroom often are not. Ironically, a robust body of research has identified effective classroom practices: we know what works. However, few educational researchers or teacher preparation programs in the United States address effective classroom management (Emmer, Sabornie, Evertson, and Weinstein, 2013).

As a result, teachers can be at a loss, particularly as novice educators, as to what "magic" is needed to keep students engaged, on task, accountable, compassionate, and safe. It can seem to be a kind of "secret sauce," or perhaps something only certain teachers are born with. Teachers who have the magic often have a difficult time explaining what their magic is—and yet they will also tell you that the most brilliant, creative lesson plan in the world will not work without it.

In fact, effective classroom management is not magic, secret, or a lucky gift given to a chosen few. It is this: the teacher, with his or her students, taking full responsibility for developing thoughtful, proactive, foundational management structures that are implemented and reinforced throughout every learning experience. It starts with the belief that students can and will succeed with effective support, and it is one of the most valuable investments of time a teacher can make. The best news of all is that it is something every teacher can learn, practice, and master—and in this resource, we give you clear, straightforward tools for how to do it.

"From the 'Do Now' to how we move from one idea or activity to another, we rehearse that with the kids so that they learn. Now, a lot of it just happens naturally because it's so routine. It's ingrained," says Ortenzi.

Good classroom management practice comes under many names: "the orderly classroom," "the rigorous classroom," or "the focused classroom." We invite you to think of it as **the self-managed classroom**." By using the term "self-managed," we don't mean to imply that classrooms will run themselves or that students don't need the authority and support of their teachers—academically and behaviorally. Rather, self-management is an ethos and a belief system that permeates the classroom and says students have the power, within themselves, to make wise choices that best serve them as learners and people and maintain a respectful classroom culture. Self-discipline is the end goal of all management structures. Students and teachers in the self-managed classroom are people who have self-knowledge, self-compassion, and self-control.

All individual selves are honored and respected.

The classroom is a community in relation to the larger world.

Students and teachers are independent and self-regulated.

**The Self-Managed Classroom:**
Respectful, Active, Collaborative, Growth-Oriented

As a result, students in a self-managed classroom do not constantly need authority figures to compel them to exhibit correct behavior; ultimately, with guidance and practice, they own and enact that behavior themselves. Students reach this point through the consistent implementation of the formative assessment practices of modeling, practice, and reflection.

"My kids know what to expect," says Ortenzi about self-management. "They don't need me if I have to step out for a minute to talk to someone in the hall."

Finally, students in a self-managed classroom also understand that a "self" does not stand alone. A healthy sense of self necessarily includes a strong sense of community. Self-managed classrooms know and nurture their place as a learning community unto themselves and alongside other classrooms with their own identities within a broader school community.

# What Does the Self-Managed Classroom Look Like?

Self-managed classrooms share basic characteristics. These characteristics are rooted strongly in high behavioral and academic expectations, which then in turn positively reinforce and support each other.

## A self-managed classroom is <u>respectful</u>.

Respect is the bottom line for all academic and social interactions in the classroom. The teacher explicitly leads and models for students an unwavering disposition of respect in the way she interacts with the class and with her colleagues. Students are held to impeccable standards of respect toward each other and toward adults. Norms for respectful communication are set, modeled, and enforced without compromise. Cultural differences in the classroom are honored and respected. Students are not simply directed to "be respectful," however. They discuss respect every day; they hold themselves and each other accountable for respectful behavior. They are considered partners in the learning process, deserving the respect and expectations given to adults: engagement, support, and accountability. As a result, students feel safe and trust one another.

## A self-managed classroom is <u>active</u>.

In a self-managed classroom all students contribute to the learning experience and are held accountable for that contribution. Multiple entry points are evident, honoring different learning styles, strengths, comfort levels, and development. Self-managed classrooms help students learn about their own social and academic strengths and contribute to the class in significant and varied ways. Students and teachers shift through multiple configurations of learning (whole-class lessons, group work, independent research, guided work) with grace and speed, with the ultimate goal of student independence in mind. Self-managed classrooms are silent and still at times, when that fits the nature of the work. Students can sit up straight when needed, following the speaker with attention and courtesy. At other times, self-managed classrooms are alive with movement and a productive "buzz" of discussion, problem solving, critique, and creation when the work demands activity and collaboration. Like a real-world workplace, the classroom is often busy with a range of focused and productive independent and group work at the same time.

## A self-managed classroom is <u>collaborative</u>.

A self-managed classroom is committed to collaborative, social construction of knowledge—a community of learners pushing each other's thinking and building each other's understanding—in whole-class, small-group, and paired work. Students are impelled and compelled to share their ideas and understanding with different groups and analyze and critique each other's ideas. Students often take leadership roles in classroom discussions and protocols, particularly at the secondary level. Students work together to maintain a classroom climate that is physically and emotionally safe and positive, keep their classroom space neat and organized, and produce high-quality individual and group work. They have individual and collective responsibility for the quality of the classroom culture and learning. It is not just the teacher's responsibility—it is their shared responsibility.

## A self-managed classroom is <u>growth-oriented</u>.

In a self-managed classroom, making mistakes is part of the territory. In fact, students and teachers understand that mistakes are not only normal but a necessary sign that learning is occurring. To that end, students demonstrate, analyze, and celebrate academic courage—taking risks to speak up in class, ask questions, pose ideas, and try out new concepts and vocabulary. They are not afraid or embarrassed to show they care about learning. They understand and discuss the concept of growth mindset—that practice makes you stronger, that engaging in harder work and more challenging problems "grows your brain." They thrive on embedded cycles of practice, feedback, and documented growth in academics, communication, routines, and procedures.

# Effective Classroom Management Is Built on Relationships

This book on management in the active classroom provides a set of interconnected structures and practices that can help teachers effectively manage classrooms to build more respectful, self-reliant, and responsible students. But these structures and practices—and any set of management practices—can be effective only if they are implemented in a classroom culture built on positive relationships.

Whether the students you work with are a group of 25 second-graders who spend most of the day with you, or 125 ninth- and tenth-graders who see you for 50-minute periods, every student wants to be known and valued—by you as teacher and by peers. The better you know your students, the more effective you can be. It is possible to run a classroom without knowing students particularly well through stern and rigid, or entertaining and clever, teacher-centered lessons. It is even possible to keep students engaged much of the time through ritualized, fast-paced practices that keep eyes on the teacher. But to build a self-managed classroom where students are engaged, self-motivated, and self-disciplined while working actively and collaboratively, fostering good relationships with those students is the foundation of success.

Classroom management often breaks down when a student is struggling academically, socially, or emotionally. If you have built trust with that student, you have a foundation to intervene, subtly or demonstrably, to support and redirect him or her. It is especially important to be able to cite specific positive attributes of students when working with them—especially when their behavior is challenging—so that there can be a genuine basis for your faith in them to succeed. This doesn't guarantee an easy solution, but without this foundation, there is little to build on to help the student grow.

Knowing students well and explicitly teaching skills and protocols needed for self-directed classroom management are commonly understood to be central parts of the job of primary and elementary teachers. By contrast, many secondary teachers feel that they were hired to teach a subject (e.g., math or history) and not to spend time getting to know students personally, explicitly support their social skills and behavior, and establish and practice classroom routines. However, secondary teachers will be much more effective when they become "teachers of students" rather than simply "teachers of content." Long after students may have forgotten the historical names and dates they learned in class (which they will access online), they will flourish in college history classes and in life if their history teacher has imbued them with the life skills to be resilient, incisive thinkers and researchers; to have courage and integrity in expressing and critiquing ideas orally and in writing; and to have the skills to be an effective, collaborative worker.

We believe that great teachers teach from the heart: they have a love of their subject areas, and beyond this, they believe in, and care deeply about, their students. They genuinely feel that their students are capable of more ambitious success than their students themselves imagine. Because the purpose of this book is to support great teaching, the structures and practices described here are designed to be joined with this positive belief in the capacity of students to succeed at high levels—independently and collectively.

## Classroom Management for All

One of the greatest challenges for any teacher is finding strategies that work for all students. Just as academic instruction must be differentiated to meet the needs of diverse learners, often classroom management must be differentiated to meet the needs of the diverse young people in our classrooms. One-size-fits-all approaches may work some of the time, but they rarely work all of the time.

Responding to students' varied needs is an essential ingredient in any approach to classroom management. It starts with relationships—knowing students well, building trust, and listening to and responding to their needs. It also must include *learning* about the individual realities that students bring into the classroom with them. If, for example, you have a new student with an autism spectrum disorder, *learn* about that diagnosis. Read, ask questions, and collaborate with colleagues, specialists, and especially families to identify strategies that will make your classroom just as productive and supportive for that student as it is for other students. Understand the cultural differences among your students (and you) and what that means when building a positive classroom culture. Ask questions, be open to change, and don't assume that your way is the right way. Even though we may suggest making eye contact with students, for example, or occasionally resting a hand on a student's shoulder to subtly get her attention, these actions may not be comfortable or appropriate for all students. Know your students, talk to them about what they need, and adjust accordingly. Most importantly, see this book as a resource for creating the conditions you need to be responsive to *all* students.

## The Relationship between Classroom Management and Student Engagement and Motivation

The best management tool is creating engaged and motivated students. When schoolwork is personally meaningful, appropriately challenging, and invites creative and critical thinking, it brings out the best in student behavior. The same group of students who may be considered "behavior problems" or "unfocused" in one classroom may be "model students" in another classroom where the work is compelling. On the flip side, effective classroom management also creates the conditions that allow all students to engage in their academics. The structures and strategies in this book are not meant to be a magical solution to problems caused by a curriculum that does not respect the capacity and imagination of students. Rather, they are designed to be joined with respectful and challenging work.

"Student engagement is so much higher when they're active and collaborative—role playing, creating, getting up and moving around," Deb Ortenzi says. "The learning goes up tenfold. They enjoy respectfully working together."

Classroom management is most successful when students are not only academically motivated, but also motivated to be their best selves. This is most effective when students are primarily motivated not by compliance to rules (though compliance is necessary) or by external rewards and tracking systems (though for some situations or students, those may be helpful). The most effective management comes when students are primarily motivated by their aspiration to be good and positive members of a classroom community that they respect and value.

The most powerful engagement and motivation is not created by clever structures. It is created by a sense of belonging to a positive academic community. It is useful to think of "engagement" as the fulfillment of three conditions. These conditions are rooted in the psychological research on intrinsic motivation by Edward Deci and Richard Flaste (1996), and cited by such thinkers as Daniel Pink (2011). When these three conditions are satisfied, students are fully engaged:

- A sense of **competence (I can succeed here)**

- A sense of **community (I belong here)**

- A sense of **choice (I am trusted to make wise choices here)**

It is easy to see where this approach to classroom management is different. Traditionally, classroom management conceives of students as agents to be guided and controlled for the smooth, orderly operation of a school. Management is something done "to" students. While we recognize the essential need for adult guidance, the self-managed classroom is also created *with* students, promoting self-discipline and self-guidance, and thrives in classroom and school cultures that promote a sense of competence, community, and choice, where students can become their best selves.

*Learning the skills to be respectful collaborators will serve students well throughout their lives.*

## Self-Managed Classrooms and Academic Standards

The way a teacher chooses to structure and run the classroom sends a powerful message to students about their capacity and responsibility, and helps define the nature of the learning process. When management structures align with the cognitive demand of the Common Core State Standards and other higher-order academic standards—demanding individual responsibility and independence, critical thinking, and collaborative work—then students can thrive in a coherent academic culture that promotes real-world skills. In simple terms: the classroom can promote college, career, and civic readiness through responsible self-management, rather than constrain student growth in a classroom that is exclusively teacher-driven and compliance-based.

When a teacher succeeds in sending messages that support the highest aims of the Common Core, a synergy results that makes the standards not only meaningful and accessible, but also attainable. In this way, both classroom instruction and classroom management can and should be aligned to the Common Core.

Consider these seven descriptors of college- and career-ready students, from the introduction to the Common Core ELA Standards.

- They demonstrate independence

- They build strong content knowledge

- They respond to the varying demands of audience, task, purpose, and discipline

- They comprehend as well as critique

- They value evidence

- They use technology and digital media strategically and capably

- They come to understand other perspectives and cultures

Our experience has taught us that a self-managed classroom—one that is respectful, active, collaborative, and growth-oriented—is one where this vision of a college- and career-ready student not only lives but thrives. Consider also that many of the standards themselves require that students work collaboratively, making management strategies for an active classroom a key ingredient for success. What follows are two examples from the Common Core speaking and listening anchor standards:

- Speaking and Listening Anchor Standard SL.1: Prepare for and participate effectively in a range of conversations and collaborations with diverse partners, building on others' ideas and expressing their own clearly and persuasively.

- Speaking and Listening Anchor Standard SL.3: Evaluate a speaker's point of view, reasoning, and use of evidence and rhetoric.

## About This Book

This book is divided into two parts: Part 1: Foundational Structures and Practices and Part 2: Protocols and Strategies to Build Engagement, Collaboration, and Responsibility.

**Part 1** comprises 23 practices—in six sets—that we have identified as essential to creating and running a self-managed classroom. This is not necessarily a "cover to cover" read. Some practices will be familiar to—or even mastered by—teachers. Other practices may be new or areas in which a teacher feels she needs some further honing of her skills.

**Part 2** contains multiple academic protocols and strategies that provide students with predictable structures for collaboration and discussion and enable them to be leaders of their own learning. Again, this is not a cover-to-cover read—each protocol or strategy can stand on its own or be grouped with others in ways that sharpen the effectiveness of your curriculum and your practice in general.

## Video

The majority of the practices in Part 1 and some in Part 2 are accompanied by videos of the practice in action in schools across the United States. All videos can be accessed at: http://ELeducation.org/classroom-management-videos.

# Teacher Presence

Some teachers just seem to have "it." They command the room. They hold students spellbound, willing, and ready to focus on learning. For teachers who feel that they don't possess this seemingly elusive quality, classroom management can feel like a daily challenge. Sadly, they may end up defeated, feeling that they will never have "it." This does not have to be the case. We believe that much of a teacher's presence in the classroom—the thing that students intuitively respond to—is composed of actions teachers can take that can be taught, practiced, and mastered. From tone of voice, to body language, to the physical space surrounding them, teachers can learn to manage themselves and their environment for the benefit of their students—and serve as models of self-respect and self-discipline in the process.

## Teacher Mindset: I Know Myself, I Know My Students, and My Students Know Me

Underneath a teacher's presence is a foundation: attitude and mindset. How can you think about yourself, your role, and your students in such a way that you create a strong presence in your classroom? Researchers Carol Rodgers and Miriam Raider-Roth (2006) describe presence this way: "[We view] teaching as engaging in an authentic relationship with students where teachers know and respond with intelligence and compassion to students and their learning. We define this engagement as 'presence'—a state of alert awareness, receptivity, and connectedness to the mental, emotional, and physical workings of both the individuals and the group in the context of their learning environment...the quality of these relationships is not a frill or 'feel-good' aspect of schooling. It is an essential feature of learning."

When you have presence as a teacher, you know who you are: your strengths, weaknesses, passions, and values. You act as your authentic self as a teacher, whether with a quiet, soft-spoken strength or boisterous, fun-loving energy. You project confidence and make your students feel safe and accountable. You bring that knowledge to bear upon your work and invite your students to share in that knowledge with you. You are not a different person when you leave the classroom. The student who meets you on the street should see the same person who teaches her every day.

As you know and value yourself as a teacher, you work hard to know and value your students. You understand what makes them tick and what makes their eyes light up. You know their cultures and backgrounds and are sensitive to their needs. You convey your firm belief in their capabilities. When you do this, you are able to connect the learning to your students in a way that engages them wholly. You are also able to create a relational feedback loop: you can see how your teaching impacts your students, and you shape further actions accordingly.

Seeing and knowing students in this way is the foundation of a strong presence in the classroom—students respect your authenticity and feel respected in return. Setting up your classroom in a way that builds on this authenticity and promotes learning is an extension of your presence. It is inviting, personal, organized, and stocked with resources that students learn to use and care for respectfully. It celebrates beautiful work and learning. Confidence and trust grow from there.

## What You'll Find in This Section

- Body Language

- Voice

- Managing Emotions

- Setting Up Your Classroom Environment

# Body Language

**Your physical presence in the classroom conveys powerful messages to students**

_Jill Znaczko is giving directions to her seventh-grade ELA class at Expeditionary Learning Middle School in Syracuse, New York, when she notices a student fiddling with a cup and a pen. Without skipping a beat, she walks over to the student while continuing to give directions to the class. Gently, without speaking a word to him, she puts her hand on his shoulder. He puts the pen and cup down immediately and refocuses. No other student has even noticed the interaction._

_"I think a teacher can communicate a lot through body language during any classroom experience," Znaczko says. "Teachers can express what's important, what students really need to look at. Body language can also communicate to the class when it's time to focus...and if I stand next to a student who may be off task, oftentimes [it] gets them right back on task without me having to address them at all."_

## What It Is

Body language is an important form of nonverbal communication in the classroom. You can use body language—a look, a position, a signal—to communicate simple, positive, and respectful messages to your students without saying a single word. It's the ultimate "economy of language." You can also help students become aware of what their own body language is saying (e.g., slumping in their chairs, putting their heads on their desks). This metacognition is an important step toward independence.

The most powerful communication from you comes before you even say a word—your posture, your look, and the energy you exude send a powerful message. That message can be "I am not sure I can keep things under control and make you feel positive and successful." It can also be the opposite message: "I am confident and in total control of the classroom. You are safe. I believe in your potential to be good and successful." When a substitute teacher enters a room, the students will look at her, she will look at the students, and it is often clear before a word is spoken how the lesson will go. A new teacher—even when not fully confident—can learn to use posture, facial expressions, looks, and pauses to project this assurance. Over time, that confidence becomes real.

## What It Looks Like

The most important feature of body language is to project personal confidence in yourself—your ability to lead the group—and confidence in the potential of the students. This does not look the same for all teachers. Some stand tall with a formal presence—clothing, grooming, and manner all very professional. Others are a bit more rumpled and casual, with a relaxed manner. In both cases, however, they project a strong and reassuring message: I am not worried, frantic, or nervous; I know who I am, and I can handle anything here.

It is critical to remember that your body language can also convey negative messages. Sighing, eye rolling, "looming" threateningly over a student, sharp gestures, or even something seemingly benign like rarely getting up from behind the desk at the front of the room can be just as powerful as a smile or a thumbs-up. It's important to remember that almost no gestures you make are truly neutral, and students pick up on even the subtlest of cues (and can interpret them in a variety of ways, particularly when a variety of cultural backgrounds and life experiences are represented in the classroom).

Teacher Presence

If an adult enters a classroom and moves and stands with confidence, looks at students with direct eye contact, and projects authority, students are ready to listen. The sense of authority projected can be friendly or serious. Either way, students feel safe. All teachers can learn to carry themselves like this—with practice and coaching from mentors and peers.

Teachers often develop a powerful collection of "looks" that convey different things, from "I saw that and I know you are just fooling around. I'm not really angry, but get back to work" to "Don't you dare consider keeping that up or you will be in serious trouble." They need only give "the look" and students are back on task, without a word. They also have a set of looks that convey understanding and compassion, so that even across the room a student can feel heard and cared for.

Proximity is another powerful tool of teacher body language. Simply by standing near a material or a visual and looking at it, you can convey the message "There's something here to which you should be paying close attention." Similarly, by standing near a student who might be off task and/or making meaningful eye contact with that student, you can say, "You need to direct your attention to your behavior" without embarrassing or singling out the student. As with any aspect of classroom management, you must be aware of and sensitive to how culture, background, and personal sensitivities can impact students' interpretations of proximity, and particularly touch.

On the **elementary** level, you will see many teachers using proximity to their advantage by crouching down or kneeling to come to eye level with their young students. This is an essential tactic to make little ones feel welcomed and supported in their learning. Your body language on the elementary level, such as hand gestures, might also appear more dramatic and deliberate, to make it easier for young minds to interpret and follow.

On the **secondary** level, using proximity to send a message is especially important as it allows students the time and space to correct any off-task behavior without embarrassment, particularly if you become adept at folding proximity into your typical movement in the classroom. If students are used to you moving around during instruction, it is possible to gently remind or redirect them using proximity without any of their peers noticing what has happened.

On any level, nonverbal hand signals are another powerful tool, which we will explore in greater depth in Practice #13. They enable you to send messages without a word. They also serve the very useful function of allowing you to communicate two messages at once: one with your hands, and one with your voice. For example, you may be giving a set of directions that is new to the students while also heading inquisitive (and interrupting) voices off at the pass by giving a signal for "please hold your questions for now." Teaching students what this signal means early in the year will support their ability to respond to it.

*Positioning yourself at eye level sends students a message that you are focused on and interested in them.*

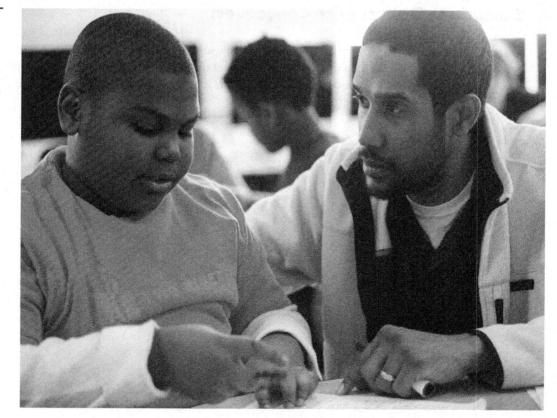

## Why It Matters

Students of all ages—from pre-kindergarten through high school—want to feel safe: physically safe, emotionally safe, and academically safe; safe to try new things, admit confusions, and make mistakes; and safe to learn and grow. Students assess their level of safety first and foremost by observing the body language of their teacher. Do her posture, bearing, and look convey that she is totally in charge of the class? Do her eyes convey that she is going to protect us? Does her look encourage us to engage in learning and try things?

No amount of planning or "teacher moves" can overcome the fundamental message that a teacher's posture, face, and eyes project to students. When a classroom is struggling with focus, behavior, cooperation, or kindness, the first thing to address is this: what is the message you are giving to students, even without words? If you project confidence, self-control, kindness, and excitement in learning, not only will you make students feel safe and ready to learn, but you will also provide a daily model for them of what they aspire to be.

## Planning for Practice

- Reflect on your body language in the classroom by setting up a videotaping session or having a trusted colleague observe you. Do this several times, if you can, to get an honest and objective baseline of your body language in class. From there you can make plans for improvement.

- Create specific and measurable goals for yourself that address something you would like to improve upon. For example: "I will not sit behind my desk more than once during a class period"; "I will position myself in supportive proximity to each of my students once per period"; or "I will use physical proximity as my first non-invasive intervention if I see a student misbehaving."

- Measure your progress. Gather hard data about how often you meet your goals for improvement. Try putting a check next to each period in your planning book to indicate whether you met the goal that period or not. Or create a spreadsheet, table, or graph to chart your progress. This documentation will help you identify patterns and set new goals.

### Scenario to Discuss with Colleagues:

You raise your hand to get students' attention, and initially most of them stop talking. You begin to give instructions related to the lesson, and a minute later several students start to have side conversations. How might your body language impact this situation so that all students have the benefit of hearing your instructions?

# Common Challenges:  Practice #1: Body Language

| Challenges | Possible Solutions |
| --- | --- |
| You don't come across as confident and relaxed because you don't feel that way. You are worried about how things will go. | Practice a confident presence anyway. Be slow, clear, and deliberate in your movements and facial expressions. Practice confident eyes. Make eye contact with students. Take pauses in movement and speech. And finally, be sure that your lesson is well planned and "at your fingertips" so that you can focus your attention on these more affective behaviors. |
| You are unsure of how you come across—how to interpret or monitor your own body language. | It's always difficult to "watch yourself" when teaching. Consider having someone you trust conduct a peer observation specifically to help you interpret and analyze your own body language in class. Or ask a peer to videotape your lesson so you can watch it with an eye on your body language. |
| You are standing or sitting in the front of the classroom for most of the learning time. | This is a habit we strongly encourage teachers to break. Students will feel much more included, engaged, and seen if you make a point of being on your feet and moving around for the majority of the class. Commit to increasing your proximity level in small, manageable increments and build up from there. Intentionally plan for opportunities within the lesson to move around the classroom. |
| The use of technology forces you to stay still at the interactive white board, laptop, etc. | Consider ways in which you can "untether" yourself from your tech. Use a handheld device, for instance, or designate a student or another adult as a "clicker" or an interactive white board operator, freeing you to move about the room. |
| The classroom space makes it difficult for you to move around the room. | Reconfigure the furniture or layout so it is easier to get around. |

Teacher Presence

# Voice

**How you say something to your students may be just as important as what you say**

---

*Julia St. Martin, former high school English teacher at the Springfield Renaissance School in Springfield, Massachusetts, knows what it's like to feel anxious standing in front of a class of students. "But," she says, "the more confident I became, the more confident my voice became. I no longer had 'I need them to like me, I need them to buy in' going through my head as I matured in my own professional identity."*

*St. Martin learned to project confidence—even on the days she wasn't feeling confident—because she saw how crucial it was to her classroom management. Students responded to her more consistently and, most importantly, felt that she was going to keep them safe, physically and emotionally. They knew she was in charge, but also that she respected them. She learned to project a tone that said "I respect you, I believe in you, and I have high expectations of the entire class."*

*St. Martin emphasizes that voice, while it can be controlled and shaped, is always rooted foremost in the teacher's authentic mindset about the students. "Err on the side of a positive attitude," she says. "Kids respect the teacher who respects them."*

## What It Is

A teacher's voice is a complex instrument. The tone conveys so much—encouragement, warmth, excitement, disapproval, sarcasm, anger—and, as a result, it establishes much of the climate in the classroom. Cultivating a confident, warm, unflappable tone and demeanor that lets students know, "I say what I mean and I mean what I say" and "I will show you respect and expect the same from you" is some of the most important foundational work you can do.

Voice is about more than just tone; it's also about the choice of when to use it. For example, if your voice is the only tool you use to quiet your classroom, will you be able to maintain a calm and warm demeanor? Will your students feel that you are yelling over the classroom noise because you don't have control of things? If you choose instead to raise your hand for quiet—a completely silent signal—your students will learn that your voice is used to convey important information in a calm and controlled manner once everyone is quiet. This modeling sets an expectation for how everyone's voice should be used in your classroom: we don't yell, we don't talk over each other, we listen when others are speaking.

## What It Looks Like

Your tone of voice must project confidence in yourself and in your students. Whatever you use, your facial expression and the tone of your voice will communicate the most important message. If your tone is shrill and nagging, students will learn to tune it out. If it is sharp and sarcastic, they will build internal defenses against it. If it is nervous and frantic, they will worry about whether the classroom is a safe place to learn. You will be most effective if you work to achieve a tone of voice that projects authority and calm self-control.

On the **elementary** level, directness, warmth, and calm are key. Nagging or shouting can cause students to feel fearful and troubled, which may make them want to avoid teacher interaction. A measured, quiet voice—once students are paying attention—can be more powerful than a loud one. Some effective teachers intentionally speak softly, and even whisper, to encourage careful listening. Similarly, as little ones are just beginning to learn the rules of respectful communication, they need a great deal of low-stakes modeling to watch and imitate. An elementary teacher can do that very economically through the use of voice.

On the **secondary** level, students need to hear a confident, authoritative tone in your voice to assure them that they are safe. They are very sensitive to criticism and often assume adults are feeling critical of them. Because of this, a tone of respect and understanding is deeply appreciated. Adolescents often decide that classroom talk is the arena in which they will stretch their wings and test your boundaries—either by talking over you or by tuning out. It is rarely malicious, but it should never be ignored. Expect 100% respectful attention from your older students, be clear about your expectations, and don't move forward in the lesson until you have it. But convey respect by letting students know that their voice matters and you want to hear from them at the appropriate time. Adolescents are extremely sensitive to issues of fairness and hypocrisy. If you require that students speak respectfully, for example, it is essential that you model that for them.

At any level, the "self-stop"—stopping at the first sign of interruption or disrespect and waiting for complete quiet and attention—can be a powerful way to convey these expectations. This strategy is helpful for developing a strong and positive teacher voice because it demands full attention and allows you to use a calm voice before a silent classroom, versus resorting to talking over the din of a noisy classroom.

As all teachers know, maintaining a positive and calm voice—especially when we're irritated, angry, or threatened—can be tough. However, putting your attention on how you speak in your classroom, not just on what you speak, is a practice with a lot of advantages for a very small price. If you treat yourself and your teaching with respect through your tone and demeanor, your students will often follow you, before you even begin the conscious process of modeling for them what respect looks and sounds like.

## Why It Matters

Nothing screams lack of control like a screaming teacher. Controlling your voice—both your tone and your choices of when to use it—will bring control to the classroom. Research shows that the human voice is a powerful communicative tool, delivering messages regardless of what is said. We are hard-wired to hear and interpret tone, volume, and nonverbal sounds (Grossman, 2010). Your unflappable tone will exude confidence, and your students will respond. Teacher voice

*Waiting for 100% respectful attention is key to possessing a strong teacher voice.*

is rooted in respect: respect for oneself, respect for your students, respect from your students, and respect between students. Active, engaged classrooms are rooted in respectful behavior.

## Planning for Practice

- With the help of a trusted colleague or audio/visual recordings, take several samples of your use of voice in the classroom. How often do you use a calm, supportive tone? Where do you veer into sarcasm or sharp correction? When do you raise your voice, and why? You may also consider observing other teachers or watching online videos of teachers, focusing on their use of voice and the impact on students.

- Create a very specific and measurable goal for yourself related to your use of your voice in the classroom. Examples include: "I will eliminate the use of sarcasm with my students"; "I will not raise my voice in anger"; or "I will not talk over my students."

- Measure your progress. We rarely think about how we use our voices or the impact on students; therefore, setting goals and gathering data is important. Gather hard data in your plan book or a spreadsheet related to your goal and note the impact on students. Was a tense situation de-escalated when your voice was calm? Did students listen more attentively the more quietly you spoke?

### Scenario to Discuss with Colleagues:

You have just told your students to begin packing up their bags for the next class. A few seconds later you realize that you've forgotten to give them important instructions for the night's homework. You project your voice as loudly as you can to rise above the din in the classroom to give the instructions. Some students pause to listen, but many don't. How could you have handled this differently so that all students could hear you?

Teacher Presence

# Common Challenges: Practice #2: Voice

| Challenges | Possible Solutions |
|---|---|
| You are unsure of how to analyze your own voice. | Have a peer you trust observe you and/or videotape your class. Analyze what you say for tone, candidness, clarity, economy, and respect. |
| Students are talking over you or each other and do not respond quickly enough to "self-stop." | This technique must be tightly and consistently implemented for it to have power. As soon as necessary, implement the "self-stop" (usually with a comment like "Hold on, Elise, not everyone is listening. Let's wait until you've got everyone's attention"). Give students enough wait time so that they learn to settle themselves down without being threatened or yelled at. Consider calmly and quietly thanking individuals who have managed to redirect themselves with a reinforcing message: "Thank you, Shawn. I see you've got your eyes on Elise, and your voice and body are quiet."<br><br>At times you may find yourself allowing the self-stop to drag on too long as you wait for 100% attention. Some students are responding and others aren't. Unfortunately, if you wait too long you risk losing the attention of the students who initially responded to the self-stop (and sometimes you may lose their respect). In these cases, you may need to combine techniques, possibly using your voice to redirect students or, with younger students, singing a transition song or turning down the lights.<br><br>Don't be surprised if you use the self-stop multiple times per day or if you need to practice it throughout the year. It's a powerful tool—if it's maintained well, it can be one of your best. |
| Students feel that the expectation for 100% attention is a punishment. | When students feel they are being bullied or nagged into being attentive, they can feel resentful. If your tone is positive, respectful, and engaging, being attentive isn't so hard. Be transparent about why you need everyone's attention and for how long you need it. For example: "I need 100% attention for the next three minutes so I can explain the process for your guided practice today." Or: "I need 100% attention on Taydrah so we can hear her perspective on the text." |
| Students consistently interrupt one another. | There are many techniques for teaching students to take turns in their conversation (e.g., the good old "hands up"; a passed "talking stick"). The most important one, however, is demonstrating the value you place on it by immediately stopping the interruption and demanding 100% attention on the speaker. You can also prevent interruptions by teaching students the appropriate audience/listening posture. When students turn their body toward the speaker and sit up in an engaged way, it's easier for them to keep their mind focused on the speaker.<br><br>You may also wish to help students understand that interruption is a normal part of discourse and that certain phrases can help keep the conversation flowing without upsetting the speaker (e.g., "I'm sorry, you go ahead" or "I have something to add when you're done"). |

Teacher Presence

# Managing Emotions

**Keeping your cool helps de-escalate challenging behavior**

---

*Deb DePalma is the curriculum coordinator and literacy specialist for Discovery Charter School in Greece, New York, and in her 17 years of work in education she has seen it all—from "perfect angels" to students throwing chairs. Her advice for working with all kids, however, is the same. "Teachers can be so emotionally invested in their kids," she says. "It's wonderful, but the flip side of this can be strong emotional reactions. You can't take them personally, ironically, in the profession that may be the most personal in the world."*

*DePalma is clear that it is the job of the teacher to take control of her emotions, no matter what the provocation is. "You are the adult—she is the child. Don't place blame. If you feel yourself coming from a place of blame, that is an emotional reaction. That's when you have to step away. Any interaction with a child needs to come from a place of compassion." To DePalma, compassion is the lifeblood of the student-teacher relationship. "I will walk away from almost anything students are doing before I speak to them in anger."*

## What It Is

Sometimes a student, or group of students, will push your buttons. They'll get under your skin and make you angry. This happens even to experienced, highly successful teachers at times. It happens to all of us. You'll know the moment when stress, irritation, or anger start to affect your interactions with your students. Your heart may pound. Your voice may rise. Just as in any triggering situation in life, your survival mechanisms will kick in. The rational responses to your students that are the hallmark of a typical day in your classroom may go right out the window.

Sometimes these situations represent a response to a student endangering the physical or emotional safety of another student. Most often, however, they are caused by a challenge to your authority as a teacher, a response by a student that you interpret as disrespectful. You feel you need to demonstrate to yourself and the class that you have that authority. However, that power dynamic may be entwined with personal anger, frustration, and pride, causing you to make poor choices or to "lose it" in your response to the situation. Students also often enter classrooms with trauma histories and social/emotional needs that precipitate behaviors that are difficult for them to control. Keeping your cool in these situations is not always easy, but it has deep rewards. When you can handle challenge or conflict in a manner that displays self-control, you earn the respect of students and act as a model for their growth. For more on working with very challenging behaviors, see the final section of Part 1, Deeper Support for Challenging Behaviors.

## What It Looks Like

Sometimes students just lose it and their unsafe or disrespectful behavior is not a reflection on your relationship with them. Other times, students will have a tangled relationship with you as teacher and act out because of it. They may have positive feelings about you, but they also may hold on to frustration about the role you play in their life or may feel that you have not treated them fairly. Just like children at home who have learned how to provoke their parents, students can learn triggers to "get to" their teachers, to get attention, or to get out bad feelings.

In any case, it is important not to take the student behavior personally. Sometimes it really is personal—the student is lashing out at you or provoking you personally. But primarily students are lashing out at what you represent in your

Teacher Presence

role as teacher. As a parent, it is important to realize that when your two-year-old, or your fourteen-year-old, throws a tantrum and tells you he or she hates you, there is nothing to gain from getting into a battle. Being firm, clear, and unruffled in these times is the goal. It is no different for a teacher.

Managing your emotions in front of your students is often challenging but always worth the work. It is essential that students see you as a figure of confident authority, not one who loses control. What follows are some steps to help manage the stress and de-escalate emotional reactions to crises.

1. Pause before you respond. Do a body check. Is your blood pressure rising? Are your hands shaking or the muscles in your jaw tensing? Are you repressing the urge to shout or speak in anger?

2. If the answer is yes, make sure that the students involved are safe, and then step away from the situation. This does not have to be out of the room. Sometimes all that is necessary is saying something like, "Let's take a break, and then in five minutes I will be back to talk with you about what happened." If it is impossible to remove yourself from the scene, another option is to have the student step out of the classroom, either with a quiet, non-punitive time-out in the hallway, to another teacher's classroom, or somehow escorted out by another adult. You can then give yourself a minute or two, or continue with your teaching, without engaging the student during the moment of crisis.

3. Breathe. Research has shown that breathing exercises can immediately positively affect a person's blood pressure, muscle tension, and stress hormone levels. If you train yourself to consciously breathe whenever you feel triggered, you will have taken an important step in managing your emotions.

4. Give yourself a break. The only way to be truly compassionate with students is to be compassionate with yourself. Before re-engaging with the student in crisis, give yourself a moment to acknowledge the legitimate difficulty of how you feel.

5. When you're ready, re-engage. Don't worry about doing this "too late." While it is important to address student behavior promptly, it is far more important that your interaction with the student is calm and clear. If you need to, go ahead and leave the conversation with the student until some significant time has passed. Just make sure the student knows that you will be following through. Consider if and when to involve the student's family in the follow-through.

*Even when students push your buttons, they deserve to be spoken to with calm and poise.*

6. Soon afterward, reflect. What triggered your negative emotions? Is there a personal issue this raised for you? Is there a problem in your relationship with this student that you can address? How can you avoid that situation in the future? It is often helpful to speak with a colleague rather than stew in your thoughts.

On the **elementary** level, it is important to get your emotions under control as quickly as you can. Strong emotions can frighten children, whether they are feeling those emotions in themselves or seeing them in others. This is especially true for younger students, who may not understand the emotions in themselves or in your response.

On the **secondary** level, staying calm is also important. Knowing that you are reaching a boiling point can be just as unsettling for older students. Take time and space and keep a neutral tone: "This is unacceptable and needs to be addressed when we can give it our calm, focused attention. We will discuss it later."

On any level, consider teaching the previously listed steps to your students as well. That way, you can support one another collaboratively in a shared practice of calm and respect. Chances are, when you need it, they need it, too. See the Deeper Support for Challenging Behaviors section of this book for more strategies.

## Why It Matters

Unfortunately, once you "lose your cool" in front of a class or a student, it can leave a big dent in the mutual trust, safety, and respect that characterize a positive classroom climate—and one that may take a long time to repair. Behavioral research with professional adults working in teams suggests that it takes over six separate positive interactions to counteract the impact of a single negative one. A simple apology—"I'm sorry, I lost my temper"—can make a world of difference.

Strong emotional reactions to triggering events do not represent a personal failing on the part of students or teachers: they are simply how we are wired. Handling these emotions proactively and respectfully is the key. This not only shields students from their impact, but also provides a model for how they can independently self-regulate.

## Planning for Practice

- Take some time to reflect in writing about the situations that trigger your strongest emotions in the classroom, both negative and positive. Make a list of the times in the past week when you've been very angry, overwhelmed, joyful, or calm. See what patterns emerge. It may be helpful to engage a colleague in this work, especially if you need to "deconstruct" a situation when you may have responded negatively.

- Create and memorize a mnemonic or phrase that will help you remember key moves to control your emotions if you've been triggered: "Disengage...breathe...have self-compassion...re-engage...reflect."

- Make a plan for those inevitable situations when either you or a student needs to leave the room. Engaging a student while you are upset will inevitably backfire and cause you to lose more instructional time than if he or she takes a break in another classroom or you ask a colleague to relieve you briefly.

### Scenario to Discuss with Colleagues:

Walter has spoken disrespectfully to you in front of the class. You ask him to step outside the classroom to discuss this with you. He refuses. Other students get excited as they see your face beginning to flush. What's your next step?

Teacher Presence

# Common Challenges: Practice #3: Managing Emotions

| Challenges | Possible Solutions |
|---|---|
| A student's behavior is particularly challenging, and you need to remove yourself from the situation. | This is a challenging situation and may trigger your emotions even more strongly than before. If necessary, get support from a colleague or school leader. Consider creating a set of quick and easy "emergency routines" that you can have in your back pocket for students to work on independently (e.g., vocabulary sheet, independent reading, index cards) to give you the time you need to pull yourself together. |
| Students are engaged in challenging behavior that requires you to be present (stepping away is not an option). | Do what you can to enact the six-step practice described here while you are present. Remember that the practice doesn't have to be a secret; in fact, it may benefit the students to watch you go through some of the steps. |
| You're not sure if you're about to blow up or are simply annoyed. | Generally, the stronger your physical symptoms are, the more likely it is that you need to step away. That being said, reflecting on the behaviors and situations that trigger anger or irritation consistently for you will help you be more aware of what you're feeling. |
| A student is deliberately attempting to make you lose your temper. | A situation like this can be enormously frustrating. Remember that, ultimately, students want and need boundaries and safety—losing control is the worst possible outcome. Consider removing yourself or the student from the situation and having a one-on-one discussion with him or her later. A situation like this may require a long-term approach to the relationship between you and the student—try to get to the bottom of his or her motivation collaboratively and respectfully. |
| "I lost it anyway. Now what?" | We are human. This is going to happen sometimes. Explain, apologize, make amends, and move on. A simple but formal debrief with the students allows them to feel more secure and to see an example of an adult making a positive choice to offer restitution. |
| "I don't feel as if this practice holds the students accountable enough for their behavior." | Remember that your overly strong emotional reactions in the midst of a crisis will not serve to teach the students accountability; it will only make them feel blame or shame. These tactics may work in the short term, but in the end they are unproductive and will likely backfire. Wait until you can calmly address the students and work together for resolution. See Practices #22 and #23 for information about restorative approaches to accountability. |

# Setting Up Your Classroom Environment

**The physical setup of your classroom makes a powerful statement about what's important to you and your students**

*"Our schools are located in a refurbished retail building, so we literally have more space on the walls than any school we know of," laugh Cherisse Campbell and Wanda McClure, who are respectively the middle school director and elementary grades director of Amana Academy in Alpharetta, Georgia. "For a consistent feel throughout our school, we have established some guidelines for how space is used and what goes up on the walls."*

*Campbell and McClure emphasize strongly to their teachers that their learning space is not an afterthought, but rather an integral method of reinforcing the school's climate and academic content. "We have our guiding questions and learning targets posted across all classrooms. Every place you touch as a student throughout the day has them. They will never leave those questions. Commonality like this is important," says McClure.*

*Campbell and McClure also understand that the physicality of a space is, in fact, much more than just what is posted on the walls. It is a reflection of both the academic learning and the cultural norms the teacher wishes to impart to her students. "We're putting real thought behind that—thinking through the 'zones' of learning in a room. Where in the room are you going to teach math, science labs, generalist lessons? If kids are going to have respect for one another and take responsibility for their actions, the space needs to reflect that as well. Students need access to cleaning products, for example. They can't take responsibility for wiping up a mess if they don't have a towel.*

*"You need to be able to point to how your instruction, school culture, and your classroom setup work together," Campbell concludes.*

## What It Is

The physical space of a classroom sends a powerful message to students about how to behave and how to learn. Imagine being a child and visiting the homes of three friends. House One is immaculate—spare, sterile, polished black marble floor, steel and white leather furniture. House Two is a mess—dark, disorganized, dirty carpet, with old dishes and newspapers on the furniture. House Three is artistic—neatly organized, paintings on the walls, wood floors with small carpets, low shelves full of books, art supplies, sports equipment and toys. Consider how differently you would feel about being in each home, and what behavior you think might be expected of you.

You may not have much power over the shape of the building in which you teach, or the shape of the classroom (or classrooms) to which you are assigned. But you often have some power over how you arrange the room and how you care for it. What is the message this room sends to students? What is the first thing they notice when they enter? What will students think about while they are looking at the walls during the day? How does this affirm their culture and identity?

The physical space of the classroom does not exist independently from the instruction and learning that live there. The wall space, seating, "learning zones," and materials in the classroom not only support instruction, but also support strong habits of scholarship, independence, and responsibility. Like other aspects of teacher presence—body language, voice, and managing your emotions—the classroom environment is a backdrop to how a student experiences school.

## What It Looks Like

In the introduction to this book we described the characteristics of self-managed classrooms: respectful, active, collaborative, and growth-oriented. What follows is a description of how the classroom environment supports each:

- A *respectful* space is one where students and teacher feel welcomed, peaceful, and at home. Consider how the lighting, floor, walls, furniture, and decorations contribute to this feeling. Does the space feel personal? Even in a classroom with standard, school-issue furniture, the addition of personal touches—plants, carpets, lamps, framed artwork—can mean a lot. Do the walls feature high-quality student and teacher work, rather than generic images that grow invisible to students quickly and have no connection or pride for them? Is the space organized, labeled, uncluttered, and clean? Are supplies and items from the natural world and, most importantly, living things—classroom plants and animals—all treated with great care? Do the signs, posters, and other materials reflect a diversity of cultures and languages?

- An *active* space allows for students to read, write, and physically interact. Do students have access to the materials they need—stationery, art, and science supplies, math tools and manipulatives, student portfolios? Are supplies organized, labeled, and accessible so that students can take responsibility for getting them, caring for them, and cleaning them up on their own? Is the space uncluttered? Does the room have dedicated spaces for independent work—reading, researching, creating, and building?

*The classroom environment impacts the way students interact with each other and with you.*

- A *collaborative* space has the room and flexibility for multiple configurations for learning: independent work, group work, and whole class lessons. It is arranged so both teacher and students can easily reach one another and the materials they need without tripping over things. It also provides access to materials students need to take care of the space (e.g., paper towels, a broom, a duster, a watering can).

- Finally, a *growth-oriented* space prioritizes effort. Charts of shared values and commitments, academic anchor charts, guiding questions, and classroom norms that support this mindset are posted prominently. The growth of student thinking and quality of work is displayed and updated regularly as new work is created. Documentation panels that show not only finished student work, but growth of student work through multiple drafts highlight this mindset. Showing progress in this way can help students feel accountable, but take care not to imply any kind of ranking of students.

At the **elementary** level, students should be able to find and use materials clearly and easily. Labels should be prominent on shelves, bins, and cabinets—if the classroom has emerging readers, icons and pictures should be paired with words on labels. Shelves should be at a height that students can reach easily, or safe steps should be available. Since most elementary spaces are self-contained, students will need to organize and access their personal belongings as well. Younger students in particular benefit from being introduced explicitly to the setup of the room and materials, and how to keep things organized and uncluttered; this must be practiced until it is second nature for students. Students also benefit from Guided Discovery of a material or a space so that they learn the expectations for its use in the classroom. Guided Discovery will be covered in depth in Practice #11: Student-Led Guidelines for Using Materials and Space.

At the **secondary** level, students spend less time in each classroom, and teachers may need to switch classrooms during the day. Because of this, many secondary teachers feel like they don't have time to "own" their rooms deeply, personalize them, and teach students how to use and take care of the space. Even with the pressure of teaching many groups of students throughout the day, spending the time organizing, decorating with personal touches, and maintaining the classroom space is noticed and appreciated by students and well worth the time and energy. Help students feel ownership of the space by displaying high-quality student work and making self-management tools, such as homework turn-in bins or paper distribution bins, clear and user friendly. And though these students are older, clear organization and labeling of supplies—as we see in elementary classrooms—is very helpful in middle and high school as well. Just as important, time spent teaching students routines of how to care for the room pays off all year long. Many teachers scramble to cleanup organize, and reset the room after students leave for the hallway—all things that students can learn to do.

## Why It Matters

The physical space of a classroom can be an afterthought, particularly after the challenges of planning instruction. We maintain, however, that it is integral to supporting students on their journey to self-management. If the physical classroom itself works against the principles of self-management, much of your time and energy will be spent "fighting" the space rather than teaching and learning. The act of physically interacting with one's environment also powerfully engages students at the most basic level. If students' voices are reflected within the space, and if they have an active say in how the space is used, they become naturally invested in keeping the space hospitable and pleasing for themselves, their peers, and you.

## Planning for Practice

- Take a few minutes to physically walk around your room or learning space. Try to imagine what your students experience when they come into the room, get settled, and move around. Is the space inviting? Is student work proudly displayed? Are students able to access the materials they need? Can everyone move around easily, without tripping over backpacks or desks?

- If there are areas of the classroom in need of improvement, spend some time discussing the problem with students. Often they will have great ideas for making needed improvements to the learning environment.

- Choose an idea or two that is relatively easy to implement and commit to doing so. Success breeds success, so don't be surprised if this small step leads to other ideas for improving your classroom setup.

# Common Challenges:  Practice #4: Setting Up Your Classroom Environment

| Challenges | Possible Solutions |
|---|---|
| "My room is never beautiful and neat. Every year I think about that, but then it gets pushed aside. When would I have time to focus on that when I need to prepare my lessons and materials?" | For the most part, how a room will look all year is set in the summer, before the year begins. If students enter a room at the beginning of the year that is neat, beautiful, and labeled, they can learn to maintain that. Dedicate real time before school opens for this: cleaning, organizing, decorating, labeling, personalizing. Even if you spend weekend or evening time in your classroom grumbling while doing this, you will be happier and more effective all year long. If you are tackling this challenge mid-year, consider focusing on just one area of the room for starters. |
| "I have so much to do during the day. I can't even think about how my classroom looks." | Get students helping, all day long. Create routines and structures in which students organize and clean at the beginning and end of lessons and activities. If there are big jobs that you can't seem to get to—organizing the classroom library, cleaning out the science supplies—put a team of students on the job. |
| Learning space is less than ideal (e.g., in a basement, windowless, cramped, the cafeteria). | It's often the case that teachers have very little control over where they teach. We encourage you to creatively consider all the options of your space, and personalize and beautify it as much as you can. For example, in a windowless room you can create your own windows using tape as an outline and filling the space with photographs or student artwork of beautiful scenery. |
| Materials in learning spaces quickly become messy or disorganized. | Students need explicit instruction on the use of learning spaces and their materials, and need to have clear expectations to maintain them. Particularly with younger students, using a Guided Discovery to introduce learning spaces and the norms for proper use will help them independently take care of the space. Also, for younger students, be sure that learning spaces have simple visual cues (like photographs of students using the space appropriately) to remind students of the norms. |
| You don't have a dedicated learning space (you travel between classrooms or share space). | Consider how you can negotiate with the people who share your room for 1) some dedicated wall space and 2) a seating arrangement that supports collaborative learning. If the teacher you share the room with is unwilling to change the seating arrangement, consider challenging your students to become experts at timed desk moving at the beginning and end of the period. Large poster paper with sticky-note backing can also make posting and reposting anchor charts easier, if necessary. |
| Your seating is not flexible (chairs welded to desks, bolted to the floor, etc.). | In this situation, consider routines and protocols that allow students to move their own bodies to work collaboratively. Students can huddle in small groups with clipboards or form a circle on the outside edge of the room for debriefs. If you have space, consider bringing in an added table that allows students to collaborate. |
| Your school has a limited budget for classroom materials. | Shop at thrift shops, yard sales, or discount stores and buy in bulk when possible. Get support from families. Consider collecting beautiful things from the natural world to create an inspiring classroom space. |

## Scenario to Discuss with Colleagues:

Your school has a problem with items going missing, but you want students to have access to art supplies throughout the day in your room. What are the possible solutions?

# Norms

Rules, constitutions, guidelines, expectations—the behaviors we wish students to exhibit in our classrooms go by many names. We call them *norms*. Schoolwide and classroom norms are the foundation for respectful behavior among students, between students and teachers, and among teachers. Norms provide students with a rationale for why boundaries exist, cutting down on the frequency of the ubiquitous "But why can't I ___?" question. The norms tell them why not, and this appeals to students' sense of fairness and supports their self-discipline. The response doesn't need to come from the teacher: "Because I said so." Instead, students understand that the reason why not is based on a norm that they agreed to live by.

Norms that simply hang on a poster in the classroom or teacher's room, however, will not create a positive school culture; they need to be discussed and used daily to guide interactions and behavior. Students must understand and own the norms, and hold themselves and their peers accountable for the specific behaviors that define those norms. Most teachers know this instinctively. What may be more challenging for teachers is taking the norms seriously enough to use them to guide their own actions and relationships with colleagues and students, and model that for students. It is easy to have a poster on the wall with the word "Respect"; it is not easy to keep oneself accountable, every day, for respectful talk and action. This takes dedicated time, every day.

## Teacher Mindset: You Can Do It, They Can Do It

The journey toward self-management demands a supportive approach to a student's growth as an individual and as part of a learning community. Students need support and compassion as well as clear boundaries and guidance.

Crucial to the success of norms is your belief that you can hold students accountable to norms and that your students can hold themselves accountable. The key difference between arbitrary, punitive boundaries and self-managed boundaries is this: students are partners in developing, owning, and maintaining them. That doesn't always mean that students create all the norms from scratch, every year. But if "Respect Each Other" is a norm that already exists in the school, each class of students can define the behaviors—in their own words—of what that looks like (e.g., "We respect each other. That means we: 1. Talk directly to kids, not behind their backs. 2. Respect teachers, even substitutes. 3. Use respectful words about race, gender, abilities. 4. Honor the different cultures and backgrounds of our classmates and teachers by not making assumptions about what they believe and value").

When teachers compel students to hold true to their own norms—and hold true to the norms themselves—they are giving the students two important messages. The first is that the norms are worthy enough to respect. The second is that the students are worthy enough to abide by them. "Don't say you'll try to abide by the norms," a teacher should advise her students. "Say you'll do it. I have faith in you."

## What You'll Find in This Section

- Creating Class Norms

- Connecting Classroom Norms to Schoolwide Norms

- Problem Solving and Consequences for Poor Choices

# Creating Class Norms

**Tapping into the hopes and dreams of your class provides guidance for the norms you'll live by all year**

**Norms**

*Tricia Davis, a high school history teacher at Tapestry Charter School in Buffalo, New York, doesn't pull any punches. "I'd watched teachers 'co-create' constitutions with their kids before," she says, "and honestly, the whole thing struck me as baloney. It can become an exercise in looking for your own rules, you know? 'Guess the rules in my head.' It's disingenuous. But then I learned to ask students an open-ended question instead: 'What are your hopes and dreams for how this class is going to run? You can tell me things you want to see, things you don't want to see. Just be honest.'" Davis and her students then use this information to create honest, authentic norms.*

*"I ask the 'hopes and dreams' question at the beginning of the school year, and it really sets the stage for trust building. Kids feel relieved and safe. They can say things that they are reluctant to say about classrooms that have not been supportive of them in the past. If you loop with kids, it ends up being a recursive process as well—they can call out stuff you've done, and you learn to be a better teacher.*

*"This doesn't mean I don't have rules, though," Davis adds. "I usually present my kids with a very short list of two or three non-negotiables too." She also includes humorous, kid-friendly norms. "Well, most of them are quite serious. But I also have one or two fun ones. I think it shows kids that you're really listening to them and appreciate their ideas." Davis was surprised to learn that the hopes and dreams approach was originally created and used by an elementary teacher. "Really?" she says. "It works perfectly for secondary kids. Adults, too."*

## What It Is

Through a series of open-ended questions, teachers and students co-create behavioral norms for the classroom. The norms are then posted prominently and serve as the foundation and a reference point for all future conversations about interactions among students and between students and teachers. A set of norms is usually concise (no more than seven), kid-friendly, and applicable to all members of the classroom community. Though norms are usually developed with students at the start of the school year, they can be developed at any time and should be periodically reviewed and revised if necessary. As with all classroom management practices described in this book, students need practice and feedback to reinforce the norms.

## What It Looks Like

In many schools, there are foundational character values, habits of work, or schoolwide norms that define the school culture. If so, those norms can be discussed and analyzed by students as a starting place (for more on this, see Practice #6: Connecting Class Norms to Schoolwide Norms). If shared values do not exist as an active part of the school, classroom norms can be built from scratch. In either case, it is useful to make a set of specific classroom norms that are personal and particular to that group.

There's no one right way to go about co-creating norms with students. The key element is helping students identify and articulate how they want to treat each other and be treated by others. Ruth Charney, author of *Teaching Children to Care* (2002), suggests breaking this process up into several short sessions over one week to help students maintain stamina and focus. The teacher's hopes and dreams, as well as any schoolwide norms, can "stand in" as temporary behavioral guidelines as this process is conducted.

One approach for creating norms is to use Charney's "hopes and dreams" approach, which asks students to reflect on their hopes and dreams for the year. Charney starts by providing a model. She states her own hopes and dreams, being sure to translate them into concrete behaviors children can understand:

- "I hope you will be curious learners. I hope to see you asking questions about everything we learn, every day."

- "I hope you speak to one another respectfully. I hope that you won't use sarcasm or put-downs with each other."

Next, students are asked to generate their own hopes and dreams in writing or in pictures. From this list, students, with the guidance of the teacher, create norms that reflect their hopes and dreams. The teacher may begin with a class brainstorm of norms or rules on chart paper, including those norms the students are familiar with from past years. From there, the ideas are consolidated and simplified into the positive norms the students will use throughout the year.

Norms can go by many different names, such as "classroom constitutions," "classroom commitments," or "classroom promises." No matter the name, the key is to generate a positive, thoughtful discussion and for the teacher to distill the suggestions into a clear and effective list.

On the **elementary** level, norms may be simplified and supported by picture cues or graphics. Young students may need lots of modeling and guidance through this process, such as help in distinguishing in-school activities from out-of-school activities. Drawing an activity they like or dislike in school may be a concrete foundation from which to start. After brainstorming potential rules and norms, ask students to identify one single norm they feel is the most important and consolidate from there.

On the **secondary** level, students can be given sticky notes and asked to write anonymously for any part of this process. Notes can be placed on a larger piece of chart paper and grouped to find the patterns that will establish the consolidated norms. Secondary students may also develop some fatigue with the norm creation process as they move from class to

*Co-creating norms that are meaningful to students ensures that they will come alive in the classroom.*

class at the start of the school year. To the extent possible, teachers should work collaboratively to make this process as coherent as possible for students so that the norms are meaningful to them.

At any level, the language of the norms is critical. Norms should be framed positively (e.g., speak respectfully to each other) rather than negatively (e.g., no put-downs). Students also need to be able to understand the norms and see how they can act upon them. For example, students may decide that the norm "be kind to each other" isn't specific enough or that it's so common as to be meaningless. Instead they may choose language like "when you see that someone is down, emotionally or physically, help them up." This may not be the language you would choose, but that's less important than the resonance it has for students. Working with students to develop a "looks like" and "sounds like" list for the norms will help make them more actionable. In the end, the most important thing is not exactly what the norms say, but how they are used. They must be discussed, referenced, and upheld every day to be a living part of the classroom.

## Why It Matters

Co-creating norms embodies the essence of self-management. Students know and appreciate immediately that they are not being asked to regurgitate your thoughts, but are genuinely included in the process of governing themselves and their classroom. Seeing you as part of the community that agrees to uphold the norms also helps students understand that they are collaborative partners with you in this process.

Norms, when followed seriously, create the safe, bounded space that allows students to express themselves authentically, support one another, and feel safe enough to take risks and make mistakes. When implemented at the beginning of the year, norms creation also serves the powerful role of being the first message the students hear about how their classroom is going to run: "I care about what you say. I care about what you think. We're in this together."

## Planning for Practice

- If your school has some kind of code of character, be sure to start your norms conversation with it. Ask students to think about what it will look like and sound like in their classroom when they are living by that code.

- Decide ahead of time how you will hear from all students and how you will then condense their hopes and dreams into a manageable and meaningful list of norms that everyone can agree to live by. Will you have an open discussion? Will students privately journal? Will they write on sticky notes?

- Consider the non-negotiables you have for your classroom and plan for how you will steer the conversation toward their inclusion in the norms, while still allowing students to have ownership of them.

## Scenario to Discuss with Colleagues:

Normally not a loner, Jacqueline has been opting out of group work. You've noticed her usual group of friends occasionally looking at her and whispering. How might your classroom norms help you handle this situation?

# Common Challenges: Practice #5: Creating Class Norms

| Challenges | Possible Solutions |
|---|---|
| Younger students have trouble understanding the abstract language of "norms" or even of "hopes and dreams." | Provide lots of models before asking students to identify their own hopes and dreams. Try to have the hopes and dreams connected to experiences rather than "stuff" (e.g.,"I hope other kids will include me in games"). You may also consider using a picture book, such as *Thank You, Mr. Falker*, by Patricia Polacco, in which the main character has a dream to learn how to read, to help younger students grasp this concept. |
| Older children resist or reject the exercise. | Sometimes older students have developed negative attitudes toward school and may tell you that they have no ideas or make sarcastic suggestions. Be empathetic and supportive in your response. Remind students that these norms are also about how they themselves will be treated; even disaffected students typically have strong feelings about how they wish to be treated. Revisiting the process from time to time as the school year goes on may also help students have a more personal/emotional connection to the norms. Letting older students voice what doesn't work well for them can also support their motivation to engage in the process. |
| Norms are being phrased negatively. | It's all right for discussion of a suggested norm to begin in this way, but you will need to help students reframe it positively. If the students say, "No running," you can ask, "If we don't run, what do we do instead?" to elicit the positive form of this norm: "We walk safely in the school." |
| Your school year's already begun. | It's never too late to co-create classroom norms. You can start the process with students reflecting on what's been working or not working for them in terms of the culture of the classroom. Students could share those thoughts as a jumping-off place for developing the norms. |
| You and your students established classroom norms at the beginning of the year, and students followed them consistently for a while, but now they are slipping. | Build in time for students to reflect on and assess as a group the norms they are doing well with and the norms they need to work on. Students could set class or individual goals related to what they need to work on. Norms should be assessed regularly, even daily if necessary. |
| You meet with five different sections of students each day. How can you possibly display each class's norms in a manageable way? | Consider generating one common list of norms based on conversations in each class. You can combine the various charts into a final draft and have students in each class approve it or suggest amendments. Aligning the list of norms to pre-existing schoolwide character traits may also suggest how to create one list for all classes. A final solution may be to hang the anchor charts in your classroom in layers and assign a student the job of flipping the anchor charts each time he or she comes into the classroom. |

Norms

# Connecting Class Norms to Schoolwide Norms

**Build community by helping students seamlessly connect the norms of your classroom with those of the school**

---

*Crossroads Middle School in Baltimore has consistently been at the top of the city in student achievement. The school has attracted many visitors to see the beautiful student project work and joy in learning that is evident there. Educators are intrigued by their success: the school's results and positive culture are atypical in the city.*

*When students are asked about this success, their responses often point to The Five Promises—the school's code of character—which are a part of every classroom, every meeting, and every lesson, and serve as a guide for all students and all staff. The Five Promises:*

- *Commitment to Quality*

- *Perseverance*

- *No Excuses*

- *Contribution*

- *Honor and Integrity*

*One student remarked, "If you do your best to produce high-quality work, persevere through obstacles, admit when you are wrong, contribute to the community, and show honor and integrity, you are bound to succeed." The promises form the basis for all classroom commitments, celebrations of student success, and means for addressing problems.*

## What It Is

While the bulk of this classroom management book is about classroom-centered practices, this practice asks teachers to connect their work with the students in their classroom to commitments shared by the wider school community. Every school has some form of code of conduct, often embedded in a school handbook. These school codes range from a list of disciplinary guidelines, to norms, to positive character traits, to "words to live by." In most schools, they live primarily in a handbook or poster, and are not a living part of the school culture and daily discussion. To make them come alive, they need to be discussed and reinforced in every classroom.

# What It Looks Like

We suggest three strategies to make a Code of Character a force for improving quality of life and learning in the school:

1. All members of a school community commit to a Code of Character (what it is actually called does not matter) that lists positive dispositions of character (e.g., courage, compassion, respect) rather than behavioral rules (e.g., no improper uniforms, no running in hallways).

2. Individual classrooms analyze those character values or norms and name specific behaviors and evidence of what that actually looks like (e.g., We are Courageous. This means we: Stand up for our classmates when they are being treated badly; take the risk to ask questions and make mistakes in class).

3. These commitments and the embedded behaviors are discussed every day—in classroom meetings, advisories, and lessons—and students are publicly affirmed and celebrated for displaying positive habits, and held accountable for breaking them.

It is important that school faculties also embrace these same values and model them for students. This requires that teachers work together to name what those values would look like for the faculty—what behaviors with each other and with students would demonstrate respect, compassion, courage, etc. (e.g., I respect my colleagues. This means: I arrive on time to shared duties; I speak directly to my peers when I have a problem). This is not easy work for a faculty, but when teachers feel proud to model positive values as a professional community, students feel the difference and learn from that model.

School commitments should include both relational character (treating others well; being a good person) and performance character (being dependable, hardworking, responsible). That way, following commitments directly relates to school and life success.

School commitments, as with classroom norms, should be consistently seen and heard by students and modeled by teachers. References to them should be woven into instruction and any conversations teachers have with students about behavior, habits of scholarship, and values. They should undergird the disciplinary code in the school and in classrooms. Students who break school or classroom rules are also breaking their shared commitments, and the disciplinary process is strongest when it focuses on analysis and reparation connected to those commitments. As one Crossroads Middle

*Norms must reflect and acknowledge that the classroom lives in relation to the school community.*

School student commented: "A rule is something you have to do. A promise is something you're committed to."

On the **elementary** level, as with many of these practices, keeping connections to school norms as simple and concrete as possible assists young learners in internalizing what they mean. Especially with primary students, translating words like "persistence" to phrases like, "I keep trying and don't give up" will help them better understand how every student from the oldest to the youngest in the school can work together toward common goals.

On the **secondary** level, it can be an empowering process to do a "close read," as a class, of pertinent sections of a school's code of conduct or schoolwide norms. You may decide to help students develop new classroom norms based on this schoolwide document. Or you may choose instead to leave the schoolwide document as is and instead work with your students on translation and interpretation. If a schoolwide norm is a simple word like "respect," for example, engaging students in a discussion of what that will look like and sound like in their classroom can be an effective way to bring the norm to life. Rather than every teacher working independently to develop classroom norms, this practice supports students' smooth transition from one class to another, helping them experience coherence in expectations from room to room and connecting them to their wider community.

## Why It Matters

Individual classrooms don't exist in a vacuum. Connecting the norms in one setting to those in larger settings supports the whole child, helping all students be their best selves in the classroom, the school, and the larger community. When behavioral norms are substantially different across classrooms, common spaces in the school such as hallways, lunchrooms, and playing fields can become places that are not consistently respectful and positive, places where teachers need to continually reprimand behaviors. When norms vary widely, students will learn to adjust their behavior in different environments: they may be courteous and focused in one classroom, for example, and discourteous in another. Coherent and consistent expectations support students on their journey to self-management. They also support staff members who enter multiple classrooms (e.g., special educators, specialists, support staff, school leaders)—common norms provide a common language of respect. Perhaps most important, the quality of student culture is in relationship to the faculty culture. When teachers model common commitments of mutual respect, students will follow.

## Planning for Practice

- Take the time to do a thorough "close read" of your school's code of conduct or schoolwide norms. Take notes, discuss with and ask questions of colleagues, and generally get comfortable with the document. Consider the connections and overlaps with the classroom environment you want to foster.

- Help your students examine the school's code of conduct or schoolwide norms and make connections to the way they want their classroom to be. Strive to help students make abstract norms concrete and actionable. Help them answer questions like: "What would it look like if we were to live the schoolwide norm for respect in our classroom?"

- Make the norms visible in your classroom and get in the habit of referencing them. If they lose their punch with students, revisit them and support students to recast them in words that will hold more meaning and influence for them.

Norms

## Common Challenges:
## Practice #6: Connecting Class Norms to Schoolwide Norms

| Challenges | Possible Solutions |
|---|---|
| My school does not have a well-defined code of character. | You can work to engage your faculty in creating one or revising a dormant one; or, if you have little support for this, you can pull out the dormant code for the school and bring it to life in your own classroom, by redefining it in positive, concrete terms with your students. |
| My older students roll their eyes when I use the character language of the school. They're sick of it. | This can be one of the side effects, ironically, of a strong and repeating emphasis on norms. It can also be a sign that your students do not feel connected to the school's norms. Work on translating "worn-out" norms into meaningful, concrete language that students can relate to. Also, be conscious that the school's norms are not continually used for admonishing students for poor behavior. When they are tied to daily affirmations of positive behavior, particularly student-to-student affirmations, they are not something to dread. Showing students data about the link between commitment to the norms (e.g., completing homework, being on time) and academic success can also serve to build engagement with the norms. |
| The norms my students created with me don't connect to the norms of the school. | You may have to dig for connections if your school's code of conduct is particularly dense with legal language or if your school uses an existing program that doesn't feel like a great match. If you have secondary students, use the existing text as an opportunity to do a close reading and create with students a student-friendly version that reflects the aspiration of those norms. |
| Our norms have lost meaning for my students. | Students may need to recommit to a vision of what the norms look like in action and why they matter. Consider having small groups present on each norm and offering ideas for what each looks like and sounds like. |

## Scenario to Discuss with Colleagues:

Your schoolwide norms are these five statements:
- Be responsible
- Be respectful
- Be trustworthy
- Be caring
- Be ready to learn

Last year you had ongoing problems with students being distracted by their cell phones during class, and you want to ensure that you prevent that behavior this year. Even though the school rules require that cell phones be put away during class, students would often sneak them out. How would you connect this issue to one or more of the five schoolwide norms to support students to agree to a classroom norm about cell phone use? How would you help students own that classroom norm?

# Problem Solving and Consequences for Poor Choices

**Consequences in your classroom should help students learn and grow**

---

*"The whole idea," says Rayna Dineen, veteran teacher and educator for over 30 years, "is that you should do your best to talk to kids and work with them in the same way you would speak to an adult friend who needed help and guidance. You would never speak to a friend the way I have sometimes heard adults speak to children.*

*"Consequences aren't punishment," she says. "They are a form of specific, kind, and helpful feedback. That way, they are something a kid can grab onto; it doesn't feel out of left field. For example, I was working with a little guy who was so enthusiastic about being near his friends that he was literally sitting on top of them when they circled up for whole group instruction. This repeatedly happened day after day. I saw the teacher react to this behavior by yelling at the child and angrily moving him, and sometimes giving him a punishment, such as taking away recess. But where is the logic in that? There is no connection for the child between the act and the consequence. Even just moving him didn't help him understand what he needed to do differently.*

*"So I recommended that the teacher get a little squishy seat for him to sit on, so he could see where his physical boundaries were. You could use a carpet square, or even just a box taped on the rug—anything to help him clearly see where his seating area was. This could feel like a punishment, of course, if you're not careful. If you make a face and throw down the cushion and growl, 'That's it! You're sitting here from now on!' that will feel like a punishment to the student. Instead, you go down to eye level and you whisper. You say, 'Hey—you know how your sitting on top of other kids kind of bugs them? I have an idea to help.' You can show the child the seat or carpet square you have found for him. Of course, it's ideal if every child has a similar seat or area as well, so this one child doesn't feel singled out."*

## What It Is

When teachers are concerned about classroom management problems, often the first thing that comes to mind is students breaking rules. Often we focus on extreme cases—students who really "lose it"—and how well the school administration follows a "discipline ladder" of consequences when these meltdowns happen. Teachers rightly have fear of those extreme situations and sometimes feel that their own classroom management is compromised because the school leaders don't support them with consistency.

We suggest separating this kind of "crisis management"—those very difficult situations when school leadership intervention may be needed—from daily classroom management. Crisis management should not be the vision that guides the work of your daily classroom management. Though it is important to have clear schoolwide systems for crises and school leadership that supports them, classroom management should always strive for positive reinforcement and behavioral correction that helps students learn and grow. It is important to acknowledge that there may be a few students who have deep challenges behaviorally, and special systems, protocols, and consequences must be designed for them. Some students may have Individual Education Plans (IEPs) that require very specific responses from you. That does not mean that the management system for the whole class should be designed primarily to address those particular students when they are in crisis.

Here we focus on problem solving and consequences that encourage the growth of students' self-management and self-discipline. For more on very challenging behaviors, see the Deeper Support for Challenging Behaviors section of this book (Practice #19–Practice #23).

## What It Looks Like

In applying reminders, redirections, and consequences, your choice of words is critical. Students should hear "you made a poor choice," not "you are a bad kid." The language we use often confuses or combines these messages. All of us in life make poor choices and acquire bad habits at times—students are no different. We need to use the language of choice to let students know that they are not doomed to be a bad kid—they made a poor choice, they can make better choices, and we are going to support them in that and also hold them accountable for their choices. For more on the language of choice, see Practice #14.

Often, a reminder or quick redirection of student behavior—without a major intervention or consequence—is sufficient to change a poor choice by a student. You may be able to simply walk behind a student who is disrupting a small group work session with silliness, tap the student gently on the shoulder and whisper, "Make a better choice of where to sit until you are ready to work," and walk away. If your relationship with that student and the classroom culture is strong, that student may simply move and get to work with no disruption in the flow of the class.

If a consequence for a poor choice is warranted, however, consider the guidelines of *relevant, respectful,* and *realistic* consequences. A *relevant* consequence is one that relates directly to a student's action. For example, a student who is doodling on a desk might be given cleaning supplies and asked to clean the surface of his desk, or even other desks in the room.

*Relevant, respectful, realistic consequences for poor choices help students learn and grow.*

A *respectful* consequence is one that is delivered, as Rayna Dineen states, "as a friend." "Consequence," in this instance, is not a code word for "punishment" and is not held out over the student as a threat: "If you roll your eyes at Jack one more time, Lanna, there will be consequences." It might, in fact, be more useful to abandon the loaded term "consequence" altogether in your mind and think of your reaction to misbehavior as feedback, from which your students can learn and grow. You might say to Lanna, "Lanna, rolling your eyes is disrespectful. It makes Jack feel as if you do not care about him enough to treat him well. How can you respond to what Jack is saying in a more respectful way? That's what I expect to see you do next time."

A *realistic* consequence is one that is within the power of the student to do—and within your power to enforce. Having that student wipe down the desks in your room is within the student's power, is not overly harsh, and can be supervised by you. Threatening to have the student wipe down every desk in the school may terrify him, but it is not realistic. An unrealistic consequence, by its nature, is one that cannot be put into action. This is the worst kind of consequence. It teaches the student that you do not mean what you say.

On the **elementary** level, consequences need to be delivered firmly, but very gently. Small children often wear their hearts on their sleeves and can take consequences extremely personally. Be as warm and reassuring as you can while still standing firm on your decision to address the behavior.

On the **secondary** level, saying what you mean and meaning what you say is of the utmost importance. Older students can take advantage of your lack of follow-through in a flash and may attempt to snare you in a challenging cycle of negotiations. In cases like these, it is important to remember that relevant, respectful, and realistic consequences can also be firm and uncompromising. In some cases, especially in a classroom with widely respected norms and a healthy sense of community, older students may also be given more autonomy in determining their own consequences. Once they see that you are negotiating this feedback with them in good faith, they will usually come up with truthful and appropriate options for you to collaboratively decide upon. Their understanding of how to determine their own relevant, respectful, and realistic consequences supports their self-management.

At any level, poor behavior often stems from conflict between or among students. In this case, just applying consequences for disrespectful behavior doesn't solve things. Teaching students skills and protocols for conflict resolution can help. Asking students to write and share positive things about each other can go a long way toward healing hurt feelings. Young students can use sentence frames such as "I'm sorry for_____" and "I know this caused you to feel_____" to guide their mediation.

## Why It Matters

Perhaps nothing you do carries more weight with students than how you manage misbehavior. It's where the rubber meets the road for them: all your norms, circles, advice, and advisory periods mean nothing if you don't deliver on what you say, when it really counts. Fair and logical consequences make students feel safe and supported and strengthen the classroom community.

## Planning for Practice

- Collect some data on the consequences for poor choices you have used with your students over the course of a week or two. Ask yourself of each one: was it a relevant, respectful, and realistic consequence for that student's behavior? If not, consider what you could have done differently.

- Intentionally practice more relevant, respectful, and realistic consequences for poor choices. Collect data on the impact on student behavior you notice as a result.

- Plan instruction proactively. The best approach to discipline is to plan your lessons tightly so that students are engaged. Choose an upcoming lesson to examine for "weak spots"—places where students might get distracted, confused, or off-task. Think about what you can do to remedy those problem areas.

# Common Challenges: Practice #7:
# Problem Solving and Consequences for Poor Choices

| Challenges | Possible Solutions |
|---|---|
| You find yourself being inconsistent in the kinds of consequences you are implementing. | Have someone you trust videotape or take notes of you teaching. Write down exactly what you say, word for word, and study it. What triggered the consequence? Why did you deliver one consequence one way, and another in a different way? What is the next step you can take to equalize your treatment of students? |
| You fear that you're being too harsh when delivering consequences. | Reconsider the language you are using when addressing problems. Adopt the language of choice—wise and poor choices—to separate judging the action from judging the student as a person. Consider your own emotional state—are you frustrated and upset with yourself for letting this get out of hand? Make a wise choice yourself in the tone you use with students. |
| Your students don't respond to these kind of consequences. They don't take it seriously. Only punishment seems to have an impact. | It's going to take some time for students who are used to "punishment" to see the logic in your approach. That's okay. Persevere. If they up the ante by increasing their misbehavior, continue to administer relevant, realistic, and respectful consequences. Have conversations with students, both individually and whole class, to discuss the issues and understand the causes. |
| Your school's discipline ladder is not relevant, realistic, or respectful. What can you do? | Do everything you can to address the behavior appropriately in your classroom. If it comes to the point where outside intervention is required, work collaboratively with your administrators to create consequences that make sense for each situation. See the Deeper Support for Challenging Behaviors section at the end of Part 1 of this book for more. |

Norms

## Scenario to Discuss with Colleagues:

You've redirected Marta, but she's still taking her working group off task. Even moving her seat to a different group has not worked. What should you try next?

# Routines

Our approach to classroom management is based on the premise that the end goal is for students to independently make good choices and hold themselves accountable for their behavior. Though this is the goal, there really is no finish line. Self-management is always a process in need of refinement. Establishing routines is an essential part of this process. Routines give students a roadmap for important moments during their day and allow them to internalize and take ownership of their choices and move quickly into new learning experiences. This internalization, engagement, and ownership is achieved through the mindful scaffolding of routines.

"Scaffolding" is a very important concept here: very rarely, if ever, are students ready to handle routines independently from the get-go. It takes weeks, if not months, for students to learn to be independently productive and efficient in their movements, especially if they have regularly experienced more teacher-centered management models in the past. This is true across all grade levels. Once they get there, however, teachers (and students) describe the experience as effective, engaging, and empowering. Remember that you are not alone in this work. Sharing and implementing the same routines with a buddy teacher across classrooms, subject areas, grade levels, or schoolwide amplifies the power of the practice.

## Teacher Mindset: Build Students' Capacity for Independence

Entering a classroom, or transitioning within a classroom, students should know exactly what is expected of them and why. It should happen smoothly whether a teacher, a substitute teacher, or even no teacher at all is in the room. It should be automatic. This is achieved by establishing concrete routines and rituals that students come to know and expect, and by practicing those routines and rituals until they are second nature. Just as in other settings in students' lives, such as church or sports practice, they can find it reassuring to know that things are predictable, clear, and sequenced. Particularly for English language learners or students with special needs, routines support their ability to gain independence.

In Ruth Charney's *Teaching Children to Care* (2002), she discusses the three "stages" of scaffolding students on their way to independence. She begins by teaching students the basics of the classroom and the schedule, teaching them how to use routines to make things run smoothly and to make interactions positive and respectful. In step two, she allows students to carry out routines without guidance, often in small groups, but steps in where needed to reinforce, remind, redirect, and critique the process with them. Step three is when students are trusted to run things themselves, although the teacher always provides affirmation and constructive feedback to keep things running well.

## What You'll Find in This Section

- Transitions

- First Five Minutes/Last Five Minutes

- Paper Management

- Student-Led Guidelines for Using Materials and Space

- Classroom Responsibilities

## Practice #8

# Transitions

**Efficient transitions save valuable time (and effort) and prepare students for learning**

*Tasha Rimany, a first-grade teacher at Alice B. Beal Elementary School, in Springfield, Massachusetts, was assigned an interesting group of students one year. Her class included a student who was blind, one who was Deaf, one who needed metal canes to walk, and a few students with attentional and behavioral challenges. Students entered the classroom each morning at staggered times, some walking to school, some on the buses, some in special vans.*

*When students entered the room, they immediately and independently put their backpacks away, made choices of activities in the room, and for five to ten minutes worked silently with blocks, Legos, art supplies, or books. Each morning at the same time, music would begin—"Zip-a-Dee-Doo-Dah"—and the students would instantly begin cleaning up supplies and putting everything back in its place. They were not frantic, but focused, knowing that in two minutes the music would stop and they needed to be all cleaned up and sitting in their spot on the rug ready to learn. Students put things away with great efficiency. The Deaf student was cued by the instant change in behavior that the music had begun; the blind student was supported by another student to put things away and get to the carpet; the student with canes made his own way to the carpet with expert care. By the time the music stopped, every student was at his or her place on the carpet, ready to begin their morning meeting.*

*When Rimany was asked how things could possibly run this smoothly with this challenging group of kids, she laughed. "Practice," she said. "You should have seen us during the first week of school."*

## What It Is

Transitions are any point in instruction when students must switch focus from one activity to another, within a lesson or between lessons. Planning for and practicing transitions is important—the more independent students can be with transitions of all types, the more efficiently your class will run. All transitions can be improved with attention, guidance, and practice. Common transition times include:

- Students coming in from the hall → Beginning formal instruction in class

- Whole-class instruction → Group work

- Handing in homework → Formal instruction

- One section of a lesson → Next section of the lesson with a different format

- Planned instruction → Spontaneous "teachable moment" instruction

## What It Looks Like

All good transitions have the same characteristics. They are *efficient*, *practiced*, and *purposeful*. Some transition routines can also be fun for students, especially if combined with things like artful silent movement, music, dance, gestures, chants, or percussion.

*Efficient* can mean a literal timing, as in "You have six seconds to put your papers away in the front pocket of your binders and put your eyes on me." In fact, counting down a time can elicit excited engagement from students and support them to make the transition independently. Using a timer that all students can see also allows for a sense of collaborative effort as students help each other keep track of the time they have for the transition. Overall, a timed transition means that orderly speed is of the essence. Decide how much time you have to reasonably spend on a transition, let the students know your expectation for that time, and hold them accountable. If a literal timing of the transition is not the best choice, students can still learn to be efficient and brisk when they know what the expectations are and are held accountable.

How do you hold students accountable for a successful transition? You *practice* it. You practice it in the beginning of the year, after long vacations, when something disrupts the transition, or the day of the formal dance when the class is too excited to get its act together. Practice is not punishment. It is the way in which you empower your students to know exactly what you (and they) need to do to have a self-managed classroom.

To practice a transition, use the following steps:

- Model the transition.

- Ask the students what they noticed about the transition (e.g., "When you raised your hand, other students did too").

- Summarize the transition and have the students repeat the steps.

- Call on a student to demonstrate.

- Repeat the noticing.

- Have everyone practice until the transition is 100% correct for all students. (Don't settle for less.)

- If desired, add a step of paradoxical modeling (modeling a poor transition). Students often have high engagement during paradoxical modeling, since it puts them automatically into the position of experts.

When engaging in practice, remember to consider aspects of teacher presence, such as Body Language (Practice #1) and Voice (Practice #2), to convey the message that you know the students can succeed, especially if you're engaging in a

*Periodically practicing the procedure and expectations for a transition will help it run smoothly.*

bout of practice after a poor transition: "I think we need to practice this transition a bit again, since we just came back from winter break. I know you know this cold, so let's see if we only need to run it once. I know you can do it." Consider also asking the students to create or review transitions in collaboration with you. As the subjects of transitions, students often have insights into the best ways to handle transitions that you may not.

Lastly, a transition is *purposeful*. It involves concrete, manageable steps toward a specific end. As a result, a successful transition involves much more than saying, for example, "Get into your groups," and hoping for the best. Instead, good transitions have been thought through, planned, and scaffolded for students, one step at a time. Similarly, transitions require your full attention. They are difficult to carry off successfully if you are trying to do too many things at once. Especially when a transition occurs within a lesson, it will be most effective when you plan out the exact language and steps of the transition ahead of time. The transition will be most engaging for students if there's an explicit connection to a warm-up activity, "Do Now," a previous lesson, or a detail from their lives (e.g., "You were just working on ecosystems in science. In our literature work today we're going to talk about family systems, which is similar").

At the **elementary** level, particularly with primary students, it is common to have some students who are genuinely overwhelmed by transitions. They may have challenges with organization, memory, or change in general. These students may require personalized support or strategies to help them handle the transitions, especially at first. See Appendix A for transition routines and activities for primary students.

At the **secondary** level, transition problems often occur because students want more social time. Be understanding but firm about keeping social time out of transitions. When possible, building social time into transition routines can help keep adolescents more focused and efficient (e.g., "You have two minutes to put away your stuff and find your group and one minute to chat with your group"; "You can walk and talk with one partner during this transition"). Consider a plan that will gradually increase student independence during transitions (with regular opportunities for feedback).

## Why It Matters

Respectful, active, collaborative, growth-minded learners do not waste time on transitions. Not only are poorly executed transitions disrespectful of learning by sapping instructional time, but active, engaged students know that mucking around in a transition is boring. Instead, they own and have mastered the transition through their repeated bouts of feedback and execution, especially if they have collaborated with you to develop the transition. Finally, students on their journey to self-management require a growth mindset; they understand that transitions are a skill to practice and improve upon.

## Planning for Practice

- Think through an upcoming lesson from beginning to end; concretely identify when the transitions will occur and what activities students are transitioning from and to. Choose one transition that you'd like to tighten up and write your plan for the transition right into your lesson plan.

- Practice the transition yourself so that you can identify a few simple, concrete steps to guide students.

- Be intentional about the introduction of a new or improved transition. Set aside five or ten minutes for as many days as necessary to practice a new transition until students have internalized it. Students, as always, can often contribute valuable insights for how a transition can improve.

### Scenario to Discuss with Colleagues:

You've noticed that students are handing in their daily homework very slowly and in a disorganized fashion. By the time you've collected all their work, over five minutes have passed. How would you "reset" the homework routine to ensure that students are following the procedure efficiently?

Routines

# Common Challenges: Practice #8: Transitions

| Challenges | Possible Solutions |
|---|---|
| Students wish to move forward without 100% accuracy (e.g., some students were off task; the transition was well-executed but too slow). | Practice, practice, practice. Hold the students to the highest standard: 100% accuracy. Don't give in to negative feedback from the students about practicing—if you hold them accountable now, they will know you mean what you say for the rest of the year. Strongly celebrate growth and meeting the target. Consider turning the transition into a group challenge by having students track data on how long it takes them to complete the transition 100% successfully. |
| Students indicate that they're confused about certain steps of the transition. | Review the transition steps with the students to make sure they are concrete and manageable. Have students practice with any changes or clarifications. Use an anchor chart as a means of capturing and posting the steps and any changes. |
| You've given too many directions for the transition at one time, and students are not able to follow all of them successfully. | Consider reducing the number of steps. Especially with younger students, if that is not possible, create a visual of the steps and lead students through a couple at a time (e.g., "We are first going to complete steps 1 and 2: Find a sharpened pencil and a partner. When you have formed a partnership, make a bridge with your arms and we will move to steps 3 and 4"). |
| Students treat transition practice as a punishment (or, if older students, as a "babyish" activity). | Remind students of the reasons for the practice and the need for transitions, and express confidence that students can master this skill. With older students, connect transition protocols and routines with the way they are used in real life: in the military, in professional sports, with public safety drills by professionals. |
| Students rush the transition and become disorderly (materials flying around, etc.). | Remind students that a transition is not a race. There are two goals: speed *and* order (or safety in primary grades). Practice again, looking specifically for orderliness or safety. |
| Secondary students use the transition as a time to talk with friends. | Secondary teachers need to be particularly tight with transitions to make sure students don't get sidetracked. Transitions may have to be silent if students can't be efficient, but be cautious about giving whole-class consequences for individual problem behaviors. Another option is to use music in the background. A song can make the transition more fun and give students a focus other than socializing. |
| Young students struggle with transitioning as a large group. | Transition students in small groups and make transitions engaging. For example: "If you have two syllables in your name, you may walk to your table" or "Triangle group, please waddle like a duck to your table." |

Routines

# First Five Minutes/ Last Five Minutes

**The beginning and end of every instructional period are critical instructional opportunities**

---

*"All right...come on in...handout at the door. Ladies and gentlemen, your eyes are up on the board and you see that there is no homework for tonight," says Lisa Zeller, seventh-grade teacher at World of Inquiry School in Rochester, New York. "Your 'Do Now' is independent and silent, please," she reminds them. "There's always a screen on the board when they walk in," Zeller explains. "It's the same every day. It will tell them where they need to sit, if they need to take anything out on their desk, and it will also tell them what they need to complete for their 'Do Now.'"*

*Deb Ortenzi, another middle school science teacher at World of Inquiry, also carefully structures the first five minutes of her instructional periods. "We have the same ritual every day: They come in, they grab that 'Do Now,' which is a half piece of paper, and they go to their assigned seat. They know they have the first five minutes to get their homework out, make sure they have a sharpened pencil or some writing utensil, and that their 'Do Now' is getting done.*

*"At the end of class it's always the same thing [as well]: They flip [the 'Do Now' slip] over and do the ticket to leave on the back, which is usually a recap of the day, a self-assessment on the learning targets, and sometimes a question to get them thinking about the next day's lesson.*

*"That ritual has gotten rid of the time waster of asking kids to sit in their seats, stop talking, get ready...It just happens naturally now, because it's so routine," says Ortenzi.*

## What It Is

There are multiple ways of structuring the first and last five minutes of a class period to have both academic and practical value. No matter how it is done, however, it should be taught, practiced, and reinforced as a routine.

Sometimes the first and last five minutes of a class can slip by us. We're already rushed, trying to take attendance, get the papers collected (or distributed), the materials ready (or put away), address the student who was off task during the last period, or greet or say goodbye to the rest of the students in a way that is present and thoughtful. The list can be endless (and frustrating), particularly if your school schedule deliberately uses exceptionally brief passing times as a means of crowd control.

Yet consider this: in a typical 180-day school year we lose the massive academic potential of these transitions—potentially 1,800 minutes a year. There is important learning that can be done in those precious minutes! Additionally, the closing synthesis of a lesson can be a crucial step in checking student understanding and enabling them to apply their learning to new situations.

The first five minutes and the last five minutes of a class, as a result, need to be planned just as carefully as the rest of the period. They should be not only crisp, predictable, and academically effective, but structured so that you can simultaneously accomplish details such as attendance and homework collection in a consistent manner without

Routines

sacrificing instruction. Additionally, when done well, they set the tone for a high-functioning, self-directed learning community.

## What It Looks Like

As we saw in the vignette from Lisa Zeller's and Deb Ortenzi's classrooms, one effective practice is ensuring that students have a quick, independent, meaningful academic assignment to do directly upon their entry into the class. Such activities have myriad names: "bellwork," "bell ringers," "entry tickets," "Do Nows."

Admit or exit tickets that ask students to reflect upon their learning are not only an effective way to manage the first and last five minutes of class, but also an important formative assessment opportunity for teachers. Students answer questions or do activities that allow teachers to check for understanding. For more on admit and exit tickets, see Part 2 of this book.

Student responsibilities (e.g., turning in work, storing gear, rearranging furniture, getting or returning supplies, straightening and cleaning) can also be built into opening and closing times. At the secondary level, this must be super quick and efficient, as periods are short and lesson time limited; at the elementary level, these responsibilities may take more time. See Practice #12: Classroom Responsibilities for more on this topic.

The first or last five minutes of a class may also be used fruitfully to connect students personally to their learning. Brief surveys, or a prompt that asks students to describe in writing a personal experience that illustrates the learning target, all serve to personalize the work and honor the students' individual selves.

Students may also benefit from a very brief, guided physical "reset" before starting or completing their learning with you. Three deep breaths, a quick stretch, or a mini-meditation can make a rushed transition to a completely different subject or classroom a little easier for students—and for you—and allow everyone to be more receptive to a new set of information or directions.

At the **elementary** level, teachers can also benefit from a simple, clear routine at the beginning and end of the school day. As students enter over the course of 30 minutes, for example, clear expectations can be set for activities that are appropriate to engage in after young students put their things away, let the teacher know their lunch plans, and so on. An

*Grabbing a "Do Now" on the way into class helps students settle quickly into learning.*

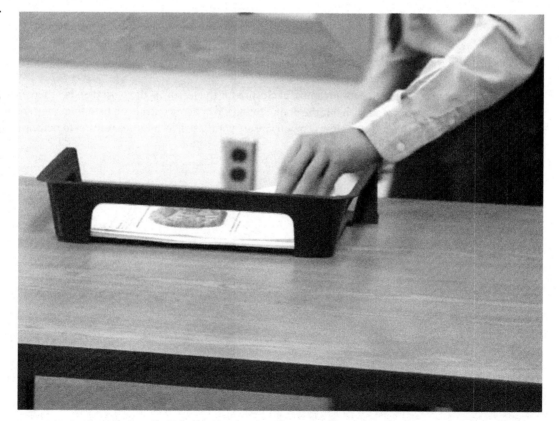

elementary teacher may want to plan for the first 30 minutes and the last 30 minutes of the day as well as the five at the beginning and end of lessons.

At the **secondary** level, the first and last five minutes are critical transition times. Routines will not only help maximize time on task, but also support students to take ownership of the transition rather than relying on direction from the teacher. Post the routines and consider having rotating student "teaching assistants" manage and monitor them to build leadership and support internalization of the process.

## Why It Matters

The importance of planning for the first five and last five minutes of a lesson is about much more than simply not losing minutes to disorganization. The first five minutes set a tone of organization and focus for the whole lesson, and the last five minutes are a vital chance to check for understanding, anchor learning firmly, and make the next steps and homework clear for students. Student-managed routines, such as "Do Nows" and exit tickets, can be highly effective structures.

## Planning for Practice

- Make a list of the "housework" activities you want and need to have completed daily in your classroom: attendance, lunch arrangements, summative checks for understanding, pre-assessments, homework retrieval and recording, notebook checks, and so on. Make this master list as comprehensive as possible.

- From your list, select those that will reasonably fit into a first five minutes or last five minutes routine. You may have too many activities to fit into this time. Choose those that will give you the most "bang for your buck" in terms of the activities you must prioritize and those that students can take ownership of completing somewhat independently.

- Set aside five or ten minutes for as many days as necessary for the repeated practice of the new routine until students have internalized it. You'll know you've been successful when students enter your classroom and get right to work without reminders and when they leave the room without a flurry of paper shuffling and rushed questions.

### Scenario to Discuss with Colleagues:

There does not seem to be time for meaningful closure for the lesson as the period ends—there is a rush to pack up, announce homework, and rush out the door. Students can't concentrate on listening; they are anticipating social connections in the hallway. How can you "reset" your last-five-minutes routine to make the time more instructionally purposeful?

# Common Challenges: Practice #9: First Five Minutes/Last Five Minutes

| Challenges | Possible Solutions |
|---|---|
| Students take a very long time to get settled in the beginning of class, despite a well-structured routine. | Examine the routine to analyze what's taking so much time (e.g., waiting in line to pick up the Do Now, digging through backpacks for pencils). Once you know what the issue is, determine how that specific part of the routine can be streamlined. Have the students practice, perhaps using timed drills to increase engagement and meaningful feedback. |
| Secondary students rush out of class when the bell rings. | When introducing expectations for your last-five-minutes routine, ensure that students understand and practice what it means to complete the routine. Sometimes that will mean that they don't leave the room without turning in their completed exit ticket, even if the bell has already rung. Other times, when a written exit ticket is not required, it may simply mean waiting for word from you that class is officially over (e.g., a simple "see you tomorrow"). Classroom norms for respectful interactions can also serve as a foundational understanding for students who may be tempted to rush out even if you're in the middle of a sentence. A well-timed reminder of the norms can be a powerful tool to change the behavior. Old habits take time to change. If students have been rushing out of class at the sound of the bell for many years, they may need to practice a new way of doing things. |
| Students don't remember what they are supposed to do in the first- and last-five-minutes routines. | Consider creating an anchor chart that contains the steps of the routine and posting it prominently in the room. In younger grades consider adding photographs of students engaging in the routine as visual cues. Refer to the chart until the students can manage the routines on their own, and then take it down. |
| Managing "housework" (e.g., attendance) while also conducting a first/last five minutes academic task is too overwhelming. | Build student capacity so that they can assist you (e.g., collecting and handing out papers, cleaning up materials). These types of student responsibilities can be official, rotating jobs. |
| Students straggle into class late or are lagging in their work at the end and don't have time to complete the established routine. | Ensure that the work that was missed in the first or last five minutes is completed. If the entry ticket is more critical than a portion of group discussion, for example, pull the student out of his or her group to complete the entry ticket. Similarly, if an exit ticket is missed, require that it is completed after school or for homework. Consider also if this is an opportunity for a whole class discussion of the norms pertaining to habits of work. Students may need to refresh or reframe these norms to make them more meaningful in order to stop an unproductive pattern. |

# Paper Management

**Good systems help track and keep student work organized in your classroom**

---

*Todd Stiewing of the Santa Fe School for the Arts and Sciences has developed key practices to keep his third- and fourth-graders organized. "First," he says, "I have a set of four bins that organize the paper they use for assignments: recyclable paper, graph paper (I've made my own with one-centimeter squares), clean photocopy paper, and clean wide-ruled paper. I also have a bucket of half-sheets of paper for quick-writes and the like.*

*"Since I've incorporated that system, we use and discard far less paper. The system helps kids understand that there is certain paper that is appropriate for certain tasks, like drafting drawings. The 'good paper,' the clean photocopy paper, is reserved only for final copies. The kids have started talking about them with real reverence. 'Can I use a clean piece of paper?' they say with amazement. It's like a nugget of gold. It's a real, cherished piece of paper for a special final product.*

*"We also purge. This is important," he says. "We do this every time we start a new unit or a new project. We'll go through their subject folder and take out anything from the previous unit and transfer it to their working portfolios, so they don't overload those little pockets, and the students don't get overwhelmed. I also never let them recycle anything unless they run it by me first. You never know what will work to show mastery in an end-of-year portfolio, for example. One student put a piece of paper in her portfolio that for most kids would have been scrap, but she said, 'This is when I finally got how to work out a long-division problem.'*

*"But you know, what paper management comes down to ultimately is conversations about quality work," Stiewing summarizes. "We talk about quality. We talk about drafts. Kids say to new kids, 'Oh, boy...you don't know about drafts yet! We don't work on things once...we work on things for a long, long time.' Kids are good about taking their peers under their wings and explaining the whole point of staying organized. 'This might be something you want to show to your parents at the end of the year,' they say."*

## What It Is

Even in an increasingly digital age, students still do a great deal of work that involves paper. Helping them keep multiple papers straight is a challenge for any teacher at any grade level. It's frustrating for all involved when students lose things or they care for things so poorly that they can't do their best work. Papers are not simply scrap (or scrapped), but living records of a student's thinking and effort over the course of time. They are essential reflection tools and records of growth.

Part of building independence and self-management in students is supporting the growth of their organizational skills in keeping on top of the assignments given to them, the work they are turning in, and the work they are getting back. "Put this in your binder" is not enough: good paper management requires simple, effective, student-owned and strictly defined routines. Classroom management and student growth are both much stronger when clear, practiced systems are established for students to be in charge of all of this themselves.

## What It Looks Like

The classroom is most effective when systems are in place for students to manage papers for all kinds of purposes:

- Storing paper and cardstock of multiple types that students can access

- Handing out paper assignments

- Collecting student work, forms, permissions

- Returning student work

- Storing assignments in student binders

- Storing student work in a categorized system in binders and portfolios

- Tuning up student binders and portfolios

There is not one system and set of routines that will be optimal for all teachers or all grade levels. The key is that you have a clear system and set of routines that works for you and your students.

Paper routines have the following characteristics: they are fast, simple, and easy. In particular, they need to eliminate the time-suck that handing out and handing back papers can be. Ideally, that work will be done almost entirely by students themselves, individually or in teams.

Some specific suggestions include:

- Create a crate system, organized by class, with folders labeled by student names. In these folders, collect and return homework and other materials, and also "pass out" materials for the upcoming class. This is an excellent way to make sure that specific students receive the differentiated materials they need. Make checking the folders a part of your first-five-minutes/last-five-minutes routine (see Practice #9).

*Using "seat sacks" or folders to distribute papers is an effective way for teachers to ensure that students receive differentiated materials when they need them.*

Routines

- Make handing in papers a timed, crisp routine. If you use rows, have students hand papers over to the student at the end of the row, where you can pick them up efficiently. If you have centers or round tables, designate one person to be "the collector" and pick up the papers from them. As always, time and practice these routines until they are a matter of habit for the students.

- Color-code your handouts so that each type of paper is a different color: notes in blue, homework in green, and so on. This can also be dovetailed with binder use so that each section uses a different color. If colored papers are too expensive or difficult to copy quickly, colored stickers or marker dots can be put on papers. As always, student helpers may save you time by doing this work. You may also try simply numbering the papers you hand out so that they create a cumulative page system for student binders. (An alternative might be to label each handout with the name of the binder section in which it belongs.) It might be a good idea to have students keep a "table of contents" in which they write the page number of their work and the topic as a regular routine.

- If you choose to use portfolios in your classroom, develop consistent routines for organizing student work. Time should be dedicated at regular intervals for "portfolio tune-ups," where students clean up and organize their portfolios. Portfolios are a powerful means of students owning, assessing, and reflecting upon their own work in the classroom.

- Digital documents will require their own set of handling, storage, and backup routines. Ideally, systems for organizing, naming, and formatting documents, and organizing desktops and file hierarchies on a school server, or on individual laptops or tablets, will be established as common protocols across the school. If not, teachers must create systems for this in their own classrooms. Just like paper routines, digital document standards and routines must be taught and practiced, and "tune-ups" of digital desktops and files must be scheduled routinely.

On the **elementary** level, consider keeping paper routines as simple as possible. Labeling and organizing tabs in a three-ring binder, for example, might be beyond the developmental or physical capabilities of younger students, whereas a simple system of color-coded pocket folders would work well.

On the **secondary** level, consider which items should live in the classroom: once those items leave, it is very difficult to ensure their safety. For example, have students use a "home" folder to bring papers they need home, instead of transferring their binders or class folders from school to home every day. This approach also makes long walks with multiple materials easier for students physically transferring from class to class. Creating a school- or team-wide system for organizing homework and/or papers going home might also be helpful.

## Why It Matters

When students hold both themselves and each other accountable through clear routines for keeping their papers neat and organized, they embody the collaborative and active characteristics of the self-managed classroom. Paper routines put the responsibility for paper management on students, not the teacher. They also teach the students that papers are not "one and done" items: they are treated respectfully, and necessarily used multiple times as students grow in their learning.

## Planning for Practice

- Jot down the various papers you deal with on a daily basis: spelling journals, reading logs, daily homework, or long-term writing assignments. Identify a single simple paper challenge you want to address. Perhaps your students habitually turn in papers without their names on them, or homework distribution and collection takes far too long.

- Brainstorm simple ways to address the challenge. Again, it is always a good idea to ask the students to participate in this process. Not only do they know their own challenges with paper, but they have experience in many other classrooms where different paper systems are in place.

- With your students, choose an idea to implement and identify the criteria for success. After a week or so, assess progress and revise the procedure if necessary until students can be successful.

# Common Challenges: Practice #10: Paper Management

| Challenges | Possible Solutions |
|---|---|
| Students turn in wrinkled, mangled papers. | The main reason this happens is that a classroom has low standards for what can be turned in. If papers are never accepted when they are wrinkled, students will learn to rise to this standard. You can support students who have challenges with this standard by suggesting or providing strategies for transporting or storing papers (e.g., transparent paper protectors that fit inside the binder or folder). In the end, it is about holding students to a high standard. |
| Work is handed in as a "lump"—homework, drafts, permission slips, etc., all together. | Use labeled trays (letters and permission slips, math, science, etc.) for students to sort their papers as they turn them in. Incorporate this routine into the first five minutes of class with other entry tasks. Put students in charge of organizing and maintaining this system. |
| Class binders or folders are overloaded with items students review only periodically. | Storage files labeled by student name, sometimes called "working portfolios," can be kept in the classroom to hold completed summative assessments, writing pieces, reflection trackers, or logs. These files are separate from the main binder or folder students use in class. |
| Students recycle materials they need at a later date. | Set up a routine where folders and binders are "purged" regularly. Make sure students know that no paper is thrown out without your approval first. Consider distributing a checklist of things to save and have students work with partners to identify and save those documents. Pairing students is a great way for them to learn organizational strategies from each other. |

## Scenario to Discuss with Colleagues:

For the third day in a row, several students are missing an important graphic organizer that they need for class. They have been taking the paper home to fill in while they are reading. What strategies might you try to ensure that students have the materials they need during class?

Routines

**Practice #11**

# Student-Led Guidelines for Using Materials and Space

**Letting students explore and plan how to use materials and space effectively invests them in treating resources well**

*For primary and elementary students, the Responsive Classroom model uses a particular approach to introducing materials and space called Guided Discovery, which is described in detail in the following pages. "We have an electric stapler in our room now because of Guided Discovery," says Keri Gonzalez, first-grade teacher at Genesee Community Charter School. "We tried a bunch of stuff. Little handheld staplers, big manual staplers...but what the kids discovered from their exploration of this particular tool is that you have to pinch it together really hard to get the staple to go through the paper, and their little hands have trouble with that. Plus, when they're pushing hard to get the stapler to work, it jams. So now, we carefully use the electric stapler." By following the steps of a Guided Discovery, Gonzalez and her students were able to develop norms for the use of the new electric stapler.*

*A process like this "doesn't solve all the problems, but it allows them to be so much more independent. The kids are more responsive and invested," she says. "It's so important to hear what kids have to say about their own materials," Gonzalez adds. "One time I had some blocks that weren't going away properly in their bin. I asked the kids, 'What do you think the problem is?' and they told me that the blocks were so big, they couldn't fit into only one bin with the time they had to clean up. We got a second bin, and we solved the problem totally. Imagine if I had just lost my temper with them instead and said, 'Oh, you kids! You never put your blocks away!'"*

## What It Is

When students have access to quality tools and resources—office supplies, books, computers, tablets, science equipment, math tools, art supplies, construction materials—they are empowered to learn, create, and do great things. Unfortunately, even in classrooms that can afford to have such resources, students often do not have access to them except within highly restricted times and conditions. Teachers may be concerned that students will misuse, break, or lose supplies or that students will hurt themselves. They may feel that supplies are precious and limited and therefore must be carefully protected. These reasons are sensible, but it is certainly possible, through thoughtful planning, to give students access to these resources and also keep the materials and the students safe.

What makes the difference? In classrooms where resources are readily available and students use them effectively and prudently, substantial time has been spent creating guidelines for the use of these resources. Those guidelines are most powerful and most closely followed when students themselves have contributed to their creation. This does not mean that the school, or you as teacher, can't establish some non-negotiable guidelines regarding safety or propriety to start the process. After this, however, students are capable of working with you to create (and perhaps later revise and improve) rules that allow for the fair distribution of resources and keep areas in the classroom useful and safe. This is important work in developing students' self-management skills.

To cite an example, many schools have microscopes that are protected and unused, sitting dusty in cabinets and closets. The Alice B. Beal Elementary School in Springfield, Massachusetts, was able to purchase new classroom microscopes with a grant and immediately had its fourth-grade students learn to use them expertly. Those students then created a student-friendly user's guide to the scopes—a written booklet with diagrams and instructions—and trained all the younger students in the school to use the scopes. Classes then created their own rules for how to use them carefully, and the microscopes became a tool used frequently in all grades.

## What It Looks Like

At the primary and elementary level, the Responsive Classroom approach to Guided Discovery provides an excellent example of how this can be achieved. Ruth Charney, in her book *Teaching Children to Care* (2002), highlights five steps to Guided Discovery:

- Introduce the material. This may mean sitting in a circle on the rug with younger students, with an electric stapler in the middle. With older students it may mean a "field trip" down the hall to the computer lab. In any case, bring their focus to what material or space you want them to "discover."

- Spend some time brainstorming with students what they notice about the material or the space (e.g., it looks sharp, it's out of sight of the teacher's desk, it might spill).

- Allow students to explore the material or area. This may mean passing it around from student to student or letting them mill about a particular area of the room.

- Once they have explored the material or area, ask them to share any further noticing they did. Help them generate ideas about possible ways to use the material, including unintended uses or possible safety concerns. Have students model proper use and, if appropriate and safe, improper use.

- Ask students to suggest and come to agreement on the "rules" they want to set up for using that material or area. Young students especially may benefit from signs around the room that remind them of proper use. To further support their sense of ownership of the classroom, you may consider assigning different materials or areas of

*Co-creating the guidelines for classroom materials with students will help them use the materials safely and effectively.*

Routines

the room to individual students or small groups. They can create signage and help you monitor how things are going throughout the year and determine if the class needs a refresher discussion about using that material or space.

At the **elementary** level, whether or not one uses the Guided Discovery steps, students will typically need lots of support to learn to use materials and areas in the classroom. Teachers may spend several weeks slowly introducing students to scissors, cubbies, reading nooks, and the like. As each new material or space is "opened up" to students, they become fully invested in their classroom environment. As with any classroom expectation, students may need frequent reminders or refreshers if they slip in their ability to independently hold themselves accountable for proper use. You may decide halfway through the year to close off the reading nook, for example, until you can lead students through another Guided Discovery to reinforce how they take care of the space.

At the **secondary** level, students are much more physically and cognitively capable of understanding the issues around using materials well, but are not necessarily more prudent or thoughtful. They have the potential to be excellent stewards of their classroom and the school, if that becomes their self-expectation and that of a classroom community to which they are emotionally committed. Despite this, middle school students are often the least trusted of all students, often being given fewer choices and access to resources than kindergartners. This is understandable: adolescents often have poor impulse control and make unwise choices, and part of their maturation includes testing authority and rules. However, when adolescents feel they are "treated like babies" by adults, they often respond by acting immaturely. Conversely, when they feel they are respected with real responsibilities and held accountable for those responsibilities by others whom they respect, they often step up in responsibility. The same student who is irresponsible in class may be an excellent baby-sitter that evening. Because teenagers are so deeply cued to peer respect and social connection, guidelines created and enforced by their classmates for use of supplies and technology can bring out the best in them. When guidelines are co-created with peers and students hold each other accountable, they are less apt to try to get around the rules.

## Why It Matters

When students help to establish guidelines for the use of materials and space, they "own" those guidelines. If guidelines are exclusively rules imposed by adults, they will be followed by students who conform, and challenged and possibly subverted by students who resent their imposition. If students themselves help create and enforce guidelines, they no longer seem arbitrary and unfair. If they break those guidelines, they have deep knowledge of why they were created in the first place. In an active classroom, access to powerful learning resources and spaces opens up all kinds of new doors to learning. When students learn to self-manage the physical classroom and school in responsible ways, those doors don't need to be locked.

## Planning for Practice

- Identify the materials or areas in your classroom that could benefit from carefully delineated routines, either because of the special materials there (e.g., computers, art supplies) or because of problems that tend to arise in that area (e.g., students fighting over beanbags in the reading nook). Choose one material or area to focus on immediately and create a schedule for when you plan to tackle the others.

- Commit to implementing a Guided Discovery session or a whole class discussion on how to improve use of the material or space. Work with students to create creative signage or other reminders about special instructions or rules they've agreed to.

- Consider inviting a colleague you trust to your room to help you reimagine some solutions to chronic problem areas.

## Common Challenges:
## Practice #11: Student-Led Guidelines for Using Materials and Space

| Challenges | Possible Solutions |
|---|---|
| You have too many new materials and spaces to introduce to students at the beginning of the year. | Create a plan for introducing students to materials gradually at the start of the year, and be mindful of the amount of new information that students can process and apply at a given time. Provide ample time for students to become familiar with a couple of materials, and create guidelines for using them, before introducing new ones. It will likely be most effective to introduce students to the new material just before they will put it to use in the course of a lesson or activity. |
| Students offer off-task suggestions for use of the material or area during planning discussions. | If they don't understand the constraints and issues, explain them patiently. If they are just trying to be funny, don't get angry, but let them know that you are interested in real ideas. Give your time and energy to useful comments and build a good set of guidelines to pilot with the class. |
| Certain students don't always follow class guidelines. | Problem-solve this with the class, without assigning blame to particular students. You can incorporate this into the lesson debrief so that students can reflect on what worked and what didn't. If necessary, follow up with individual students to get to the root of what is not working. |

## Scenario to Discuss with Colleagues:

You have bought beautiful new sets of colored pencils for your middle school students to use. They are high quality and very expensive. You have not introduced them to your students yet. How will you do it?

**Routines**

# Classroom Responsibilities

**Giving students classroom jobs invests them in taking care of their space**

---

*"I stole the idea for my job chart from another teacher," laughs Deb Ortenzi, middle school science teacher at World of Inquiry School in Rochester, New York. "It's really simple. There is only one job: the facilitator. The facilitator gets to do everything I don't have time or hands to do: answer the phone, answer the door, pick up and distribute papers, and generally assist me during class. There's one facilitator per day. At the end of the week, another five kids rotate in. So everyone has an opportunity to be the facilitator within the month.*

*"The kids are really invested in it. I don't even have to tell them to rotate the names—they do it themselves at the end of each week. Plus, it's a really cheap time investment—maybe 45 minutes at the beginning of the year [to prep the materials (3x5 index cards with Velcro on the back) and walk students through the responsibilities of the job]. Learning what to say when answering the phone or door is also teaching them how to do that stuff in real life. I attached little scripts above the phone and door, so they knew what to say, and then we rehearsed it together."*

## What It Is

By creating classroom jobs for students to handle regularly, teachers invite their students into the running and maintenance of the classroom. Not only does this help the teacher delegate tasks that can be easily completed by students, but it also creates one more dimension of real-world learning for the students on their journey to self-management. It helps every student learn responsibility and take pride in their classroom, and can be much more effective and efficient than a single teacher trying to keep on top of things. For some students who try hard but struggle academically, the real-world responsibilities of classroom jobs are a place where they can shine and contribute with distinction.

In elementary classrooms, where students are in the same room all day, a job chart can assign every student individually or as part of a small team to be in charge of almost all the setup, cleanup, and logistical routines of the day. In secondary classrooms, like Deb Ortenzi's example above, it is not typically feasible to have jobs for every student every day (beyond responsibilities that every student takes on, such as moving tables and chairs and cleaning up after themselves). In those cases, a set of jobs that a small group of students rotates into daily or weekly can be useful. Some jobs, such as classroom or school ambassador (welcoming visitors to the classroom and school; leading school tours for visitors; meeting with school guests on student panels) may be jobs that are earned through particularly responsible behavior.

## What It Looks Like

At the **elementary** level, a job chart with student name cards in pockets, or a job wheel that rotates, is particularly useful. Job assignments change, typically weekly, so that each student gets the chance to do each job and the responsibilities are shared equitably. At the beginning of the year, the teacher needs to explain exactly what each job entails and discuss that

Routines

with students. The directions for each job can be entirely teacher-created but are even more powerful if students can give input into the guidelines for completing each job well. Some job charts have those directions written right on the chart itself or on cards that a student can refer to if he or she forgets.

The nature of the jobs on a job chart depends on the needs and routines of the classroom. Sometimes the jobs need adjusting partway through the year when the teacher or class realizes that some important jobs have been left out, or that certain jobs need more students assigned to them. Some jobs that one might see on a job chart include:

- Areas: floor, chairs, tables, desktops, counters, play area, cubbies, coatroom, lockers, windows

- Supplies: art, science and math, paper shelf

- Classroom library

- Classroom plants and animals

- Paper passer

- Lunch count and lunch money

- Portfolios and student files

- Bulletin boards

Some classrooms have used real-life professions to name their jobs (e.g., mailperson, treasurer, custodian, mover, librarian). Many classrooms have shelves and buckets of cleaning supplies, stored at student level, so that students can access tools such as brooms, dustpans, floor sweepers, vacuum cleaners, cleaning sprays, and rags.

In addition to teaching and discussing the importance of each job, and what each entails, at the beginning of the year, there is an ongoing need to keep quality control over how well jobs are being done. This should be discussed regularly in classroom meetings; it does not necessarily need much detail if things are going well, but success should always be reinforced with positive feedback and problems addressed as they arise. If there is a high level of trust and respectful communication in the classroom, it can be useful to have a "Job Inspector" role for a pair of students, who spend their

*Classroom jobs help students invest in the upkeep of their materials and space.*

cleanup time walking around the room with a job list on a clipboard, checking off things as they are completed correctly. While this can create debate at times, and job inspectors can be accused of being unfair or bossy, those issues can be discussed and resolved, and there is a big upside: it cuts down dramatically on teacher oversight and nagging.

At the **secondary** level, like the facilitator role in Deb Ortenzi's classroom, jobs may apply only to a single student or small group and have special responsibilities. An absence buddy, for example, volunteers to keep notes, handouts, and assignments for another student who is absent that day. This can be vital help for a teacher, so that he or she does not need to create a packet of materials to send home and ask other students for notes. Secondary student mentors and tutors may volunteer to work with students in that class or help out in other classes. In general, secondary teachers will often opt for a smaller number of classroom jobs than elementary teachers, given the rotation of students in and out of their classrooms every day.

## Why It Matters

There is perhaps no simpler way to enact the central tenets of a self-managed classroom than to have jobs available for students. Jobs open the door for active, collaborative contribution by the students to the health and well-being of the classroom community. Students demonstrate their respect for the learning process and for others by completing their jobs to the best of their abilities and growing through the effort; teachers demonstrate respect by trusting their students with the tasks.

## Planning for Practice

- Make a master list of potential jobs that will genuinely contribute to the well-being and efficiency of your classroom and make your life as a teacher a little easier.

- Plan a sustainable job rotation. You may choose to assign 20+ jobs equitably to all of your students or you may opt for a more manageable handful of jobs that can be rotated every quarter. You may also opt for a singular helper or pair of "classroom assistants" that rotate daily or weekly. Be sure to choose a system that won't overwhelm your own abilities to stay organized and that will contribute to your students' sense of ownership of the classroom.

- Think about accountability. For a job to be taken seriously by students, it needs to be taken seriously by teachers as well. How can you quickly and easily monitor whether a job is being done well? A check mark system, a student job supervisor, or a regular job evaluation period might all work for you. If you teach with an assessment system that weights character traits, effort, or habits of scholarship, consider how you might fold in students' responsibility and independence with their jobs into this system.

### Scenario to Discuss with Colleagues:

Most students are doing a good job with getting their classroom responsibilities and jobs completed, but a few students are consistently irresponsible. How might you address this problem?

# Common Challenges: Practice #12: Classroom Responsibilities

| Challenges | Possible Solutions |
|---|---|
| Students are fighting over the "best" jobs. | A fair system of rotation is the answer, along with reminders to students to be team players. |
| The jobs you need done accurately, like attendance, aren't getting completed the way you need them to be. | Provide more training, group discussion, and critique. Whole-class discussions on the topic of doing things well are worth the time. Also, consider whether your rotations are too frequent. Sometimes students may need several weeks to learn how to complete a job successfully. |
| There is debate about the overlap of jobs (e.g., are supplies on the floor part of the "supplies" job or the "floor" job?). | Discuss these problems with the class and let them decide. Post descriptions of each job and add the disputed task to the appropriate job description. |
| Students are doing their jobs instead of their classwork, or students aren't doing their jobs at all. | Make doing jobs part of your entry or exit routine if needed, and/or tie them directly to your classroom schedule in some way. Either way, be sure that students are aware of when they should be doing their jobs just as clearly as what the jobs are. Regularly build in opportunities to reflect on the classroom jobs. Invite students to discuss any jobs that need refining or that need to be added to the classroom jobs list. Use job inspectors. |
| Some jobs take longer than others to complete, and it's challenging to schedule the time so all jobs are completed in a timely manner and with quality. | Adjust the number of students assigned to each job. |

Routines

# Communication

The way teachers convey information and the way they see and hear what students convey through their words and actions sets the tone for everything else in the classroom. A teacher's tone of voice and body language, highlighted in the Teacher Presence section of this book, are a key part of this communication. This section will focus more particularly on the words and nonverbal messages that teachers use and how they choose to use them.

Underlying all of the practices in this section is our assumption that teachers will use their voices calmly and respectfully, that they won't resort to yelling or shrill talking over, and that their body language will project warmth, interest, and confidence. Maintaining this tone and employing consistent patterns of communication that allow students to feel seen and heard will support them to be strong communicators themselves.

## Teacher Mindset: Responding to What You See

Much of what we focus on in this set of communication practices is less about what teachers say and more about how they "listen to" and respond to what they see. To encourage independence and self-management in students, your guidance to students settling in at the beginning of class can shift from the teacher-directed "You should be seated, quiet, and writing now. I don't want any talking. See me if you have questions" to "I notice Marcel, Quentin, and Marielle got right to work. I see Trevor helping Crystal find a pen—thanks for helping her out, Trevor. Kayla, where can you look or whom can you ask if you're not sure what you should be working on right now?" Your noticing and reinforcement of the positive behaviors you want to see gives other students a chance to take responsibility for doing what they need to do.

"Seeing" in this way is a consistent, constant reflection of students' actions through your oral commentary in the classroom. Like a play-by-play announcer in sports, you are telling students what is happening; unlike a sports announcer, you are also using your commentary to compliment, remind, and direct the action. It is a communicative patter that provides feedback at all times, allowing students to build the skills they need and feel safe enough to make good decisions about their behavior and learning. Keep in mind, however, that a key part of effective communication is knowing your students well. Learn what works best for them; some may respond better to private, rather than public, praise.

Teachers can build habits of orally noting and acknowledging what they see in students—to make sure students feel seen, heard and understood—and then move on to guide, redirect, or even reprimand those students gracefully (e.g., "I notice you are looking frustrated in this work. That makes sense; it's hard. No need to be bothering Tanisha; move over to this table and I can help you with this." "You guys were doing a great job being on task until just a few minutes ago. Make a good choice here to be focused, and I can keep you together"). The most effective language for redirecting students is always about noting poor choices, not implying that they are bad kids.

## What You'll Find in This Section

- Nonverbal Signals

- Choice and Options for Students

- Critique and Feedback

## Practice #13

# Nonverbal Signals

**Enhance communication in the classroom without saying a word**

---

*Most teachers use nonverbal signals to some degree: "hands up to be called on," for example. Anne Perrone, who teaches bilingual third grade at Manzanita SEED Elementary School in Oakland, California, a dual-language school, has widened these horizons. She and her colleagues Dale Rogers-Eilers, Priscilla Parchia, Elizabeth Cato, and Marijke Conklin have developed a series of content-driven, academic hand signals to use with their students.*

*"We developed signs for 'I agree,' 'I disagree,' 'I have something to add,' 'I have a question,' and 'I have some evidence,'" she says. "There are also signs we use for analyzing stories: 'This is setting,' 'This is a character trait,' and so on."*

*Students at all levels pick up simple signals with ease, increasing their attention, engagement, confidence, and production. Perrone states, "It buys the kids their own time to think, so there's less interrupting and less restating. It also is student-driven. Critical thinking is not completely tied to teacher questioning anymore." She finds that hand signals have also significantly increased the confidence and production of her English language learners.*

*Perrone feels that hand signals allow her a much more accurate read of the classroom. "I can tell who's listening and who's not by how many academic hand signals they use," she says. "And I can reassure my students through them as well. If a kid throws up the hand signal that means 'I have a question,' I will always call on him or her."*

## What It Is

Nonverbal signals serve many purposes in the classroom—they communicate directions, for example, or the need for permission, a question, or a connection or common understanding. Because they are visual instead of (or in addition to) auditory, nonverbal signals help students understand what is being conveyed through multiple senses. They empower students and teachers to communicate efficiently without disrupting the flow of the lesson. They also enable easy communication for students who may struggle with typical means of talking in class, such as students with attention issues or English language learners.

Nonverbal signals can be very helpful in maintaining the power of quiet during a silent work time. When students are engrossed in silent work, there can be requests to the teacher for help, for getting supplies, or for the restroom that go unnoticed by the class and do not break the spell of concentration. When students are listening to a guest speaker or attending an event, a simple hand gesture from the teacher, or even a fellow student, can redirect or remind students of polite behavior with no interruption of the speaker. A sign that means "excuse me" or "I'm sorry" can communicate remorse and respect without interrupting a lesson or the directions being given.

## What It Looks Like

There are some signals that are understood in all classrooms, such as raising hands to ask or answer questions or dimming the lights for quiet. There are others that may informally take hold within a school community, such as the silent American Sign Language (ASL) sign for applause, or snapping to indicate applause instead of clapping. Others

Communication

need to be agreed upon, taught, practiced, and reinforced in the classroom. If possible, a faculty should work together to reach agreement on some common signs that will be used across the school; professional development time may be fruitfully spent learning and practicing the signs. Though this coordination will not be feasible in every school setting, it makes life much easier for both students and teachers. When there are a set of common signs across the school, specialist teachers, substitute teachers, and school leaders can use them in any room they enter; on a secondary level, students know that they can use the same nonverbal signals any period of the day.

Schools and classrooms can invent their own signs, but should consider the great resource of ASL. There are already signs for anything students and teachers would like to communicate, represented in picture dictionaries of ASL. Not only does this save time in inventing signs, but it also honors a powerful language that many students are excited to learn and use. Classrooms in which the students and teacher use ASL frequently can have focused, silent work times where useful communication between student and teacher and among students still thrives.

Some of the most useful schoolwide signs include the following:

- A sign for "freeze and listen," such as a bell, gong, or raised hand

- A sign to indicate a need, such as "I need to use the restroom" or "I need to sharpen my pencil"

- A sign to indicate a level of comprehension, such as, "I don't understand"

- A sign to indicate agreement or support

- A sign that means "eyes on me" (or him/her)

- A sign that means "cut that out"

- Signs for directions, such as "take a seat," "line up," "clean up," "wait a moment," or "finish"

- Sign for silent courtesies, such as "please," "thank you," "excuse me," and "I'm sorry"

- Signs to check for understanding (e.g., thumbs-up/middle/down)

*Hands up for quiet is one of the most useful nonverbal signals at any grade level.*

Communication

At the **elementary** level, nonverbal signals are a wonderful way to help students develop impulse control. Rather than blurting out what they need or waving their hand wildly in the air, even the youngest students can learn simple signals for when they need things (e.g., tissues, the pencil sharpener). Signals that indicate understanding or connections with other students are also especially supportive of young students' developing ability to empathize with others and really listen to what they have to say. The ASL sign for "I agree with you" is particularly useful in empowering students to silently add a "me too"; many students can do this simultaneously without causing an interruption.

At the **secondary** level, nonverbal signals are important tools for redirecting students or getting their attention without singling them out and potentially embarrassing them. They can give students a sense of independence and maturity (e.g., not having to ask verbally to go to the restroom). Students can also ask for help discreetly, can politely interrupt you when you are busy (using an "excuse me" sign), and can apologize directly and discreetly to you or other students for making poor choices with the "I'm sorry" sign.

## Why It Matters

Nonverbal signals empower students to communicate with you actively and respectfully during class, and promote eye contact and attention. They promote a quieter, more efficient, and focused classroom; they allow for more discretion and dignity in meeting the needs of students; and they allow you to redirect individual students or the class without interrupting the flow of work. They empower students to express themselves more effectively and appropriately.

## Planning for Practice

- Make a list of some of the situations that could be streamlined in your classroom using nonverbal signals. What signals could you teach students to use in these situations? Consider consulting an ASL dictionary or an ASL teacher in your vicinity to choose signals that make sense for your classroom.

- Think beyond behavior. Challenge yourself and your students to use academic nonverbal signals to indicate things like "I agree with you" or "I have a question for you when you're done." These kinds of signals can make instructional time more productive for you and your students.

- Introduce signals slowly. Consider introducing nonverbal signals in "chunks," particularly if you're already well into your school year. Choose one or two you'd like to focus on at a time and emphasize them strongly with lots of practice until students are habitually using them.

### Scenario to Discuss with Colleagues:

Passing time between classes is extremely short. As a result, when your students come into your classroom, despite your established routine of silent reading for the first ten minutes, they often inundate you with personal needs requests such as for a drink or a bathroom visit. How could you use nonverbal signals to address this issue and make silent reading time more productive (and more silent)?

# Common Challenges: Practice #13: Nonverbal Signals

| Challenges | Possible Solutions |
|---|---|
| Students have trouble remembering the signals. | Create an anchor chart of the signals to post in the classroom. Especially for younger students, consider including photographs or drawings of the signals. You may need to periodically review the signals with students. |
| Students don't always use or respond to signals. | Practice. This is especially effective "at the time of need": if a signal doesn't work the first time, have the students "reset" by respectfully reminding them of the signal and trying it again. |
| Older students use the signals in a distracting manner (deliberately or accidentally). | To clarify whether or not the mistake is accidental, speak with the student privately after class. Provide the student with the information he or she needs to use the signal correctly and give him or her positive reinforcement for correct usage thereafter. |

Communication

**Practice #14**

# Choice and Options for Students

**Using the language of choice and giving students options builds maturity and ownership**

*At King Middle School in Portland, Maine, almost all projects offer students "controlled choice." Every student is working in the same format, practicing craftsmanship, learning the same skills, and building common knowledge. Within this common structure, however, students are given choices that allow their individual or small-team work to be personal and distinctive.*

*When Karen McDonald and Caitlin LeClair's sixth-grade students studied the civil rights movement, they each contributed to a published book that honored the courageous stories of local civil rights heroes. Students needed to consider important choices: whom would they interview and how would they tell their hero's story with power and integrity? When Scott Comstock's seventh-grade students created a field guide to local wildlife, the format and skills again were common, but the choice of species to research in school and out in the field was a powerful one. When Peter Hill and Gus Goodwin's eighth-grade classes all designed and constructed model wind turbines that generated electricity, the final products were distinct and creative.*

*It is not feasible or optimal to give students open choices about all they will learn and do in school, but when controlled choices are built into assignments and projects, students take ownership and pride in creating something of value that is personal and unique. The same is true when talking with students about behavior. When behavior is framed as a controlled choice, students take more ownership over their actions.*

## What It Is

The concept of choice, whether behavioral or academic, is central to management in the active classroom for three reasons:

- First, the language of choice is a particularly effective way to describe and understand the decisions, good and bad, that students make. School (and life) is not about naturally being a "good student" or "good person," but about making good choices and taking responsibility for the choices we make. Everyone can make a poor choice, and everyone can make a wise choice. William Glasser's books (e.g., *Choice Theory* and *The Quality School: Managing Students Without Coercion*) are excellent resources for this framework.

- Second, students (and adults) assume more ownership of their actions and work when they are engaged in making choices. Even limited choice can mean a lot (e.g., all students are required to create a portfolio of their work with required sections and components; however, students can personally design the cover, and there is a student-designed section for personal interests).

- Third, students can learn how to make good choices only if they have the chance to practice. If students are always told what to do, they can't build self-management skills. This is painfully clear on college campuses, where so many freshmen flounder academically and emotionally—and perhaps drop out—because they have not learned to manage their time and make smart choices academically and socially.

Giving students options is an important part of their development as independent, critical thinkers. From the low stakes—a choice between paper colors or seating arrangements—to the high stakes—a choice of final projects or a consequence for misbehavior—engaging students in the act of choosing among options is an important part of every teacher's job. Choices need to be strategic and, often, constrained. It's not about choosing any option; it's about presenting options that meet students' developmental and academic needs and giving them your respectful trust to make the best choice.

The feeling that we have the power to make choices in our daily lives is integral to our psychological health. When teachers use the language of choice in their classrooms as a foundation for their classroom management, it makes students autonomous, valued partners who own their learning. It says to them, "I trust you enough to make your own decisions."

## What It Looks Like

What follows are some examples of how the language of choice can support positive behavior.

For describing student decisions:

- "Davian, I see you chose to work by yourself on this. Good choice! You look focused here."

- "I see that Tiana is seated and has gotten right to work—thanks for making that choice, Tiana."

- "This group had trouble together yesterday. Make wise choices today, if you want to stay together."

For offering options to redirect students:

- "Jonathan, I see that you are having a hard time settling down to the bell work this morning. I can give you a choice: take a quick stretch and try again, or get a drink of water and try again."

- "I can see that you two are upset with each other. You can either sit with me now to talk it through or you can take a five-minute break—one of you in Mrs. Jackson's room and one in Mr. Washington's room—before we sit down together to talk it through. What's your preference?"

*Offering students constrained choices supports their self-management.*

With students dealing with behavior challenges, it is often the best course to offer a small range of options for action—two or three maximum. The wide-open "What do you choose?" can be too overwhelming. Limiting choices also gives the teacher control, while simultaneously helping students manage their choices successfully. In designing lessons, assignments, and projects, it is always helpful to consider where controlled choice can be embedded. Is there a part of the assignment or project that can be more engaging and personal with student choice? In building the schedule for a lesson (or in elementary school, for the full day), are there good times and structures for building in choice?

At the **elementary** level, "choice times" are often times when students can use fun classroom resources—games, blocks, puzzles, art supplies, technology. It is possible to expand this to "academic choice times," where centers or stations are open and resources are available (e.g., all students are working on mathematical understanding of fractions, but are making choices about how to learn).

Behavioral choice can be framed very deliberately for younger students so that "choice" becomes part of the shared language of the classroom. Praising students for "good choices," asking them to reflect on "different choices," and encouraging them to use the word "choice" when describing their actions not only simplifies the verbal coding of choice in a way little ones can understand, but also consistently reinforces classroom norms that support the growth and independence of students through thoughtful choice.

At the **secondary** level, where "choice times" can be more difficult to implement, academic choice can be implemented through the thoughtful and targeted differentiation of lessons. Differentiation can occur through multiple means: offering different academic activities for levels of readiness, allowing students a choice of activity that aligns to their interests, or providing options for different approaches to group work. Secondary students are eager to assert their independence and feel in control; as a result, controlled, thoughtful choice is one of the most powerful means to meet secondary students "where they are" developmentally and naturally open up their hearts and minds to learning.

Older students are superlatively sensitive to any language that sounds "babyish" to them. Asking "Was that a good choice?" may strike them as condescending. If the tone is laced with judgment, a more neutral "Not a good choice, Tiffany" can be more effective. Develop a bank of phrases that are adult in their tone. Ask yourself how you would reflect on a choice with an adult friend: "How did that work out for you?" or "What would you have done differently if you had the chance to do it again?" Reinforce choice while acknowledging the autonomy of the older student.

## Why It Matters

Choice opens the door for students to participate actively in their learning, by taking full responsibility for their actions and learning to plan their time and effort. When teachers give students options, they model respect for the students' autonomy. They also reinforce that learning is collaborative: students and teachers are partners in the learning community. The language of choice also brings home to students that they have responsibility for the choices they make. They can blame their friends, their parents, or the school for a poor decision on their part, but in the end, this was a choice they made.

## Planning for Practice

- Reflect on some of the common poor choices students make in your classroom (e.g., talking over you during instruction, gossiping).

- Write mini-scripts for how you can redirect the students during these situations, using the language of choice. Choose one or two to start with and practice them until they are automatic.

- Distinguish between academic choices and behavioral choices. While "choice" is a powerful tool in both academics and behavior, they are not the same animal. Increased student autonomy in one does not translate into increased student autonomy in the other. Be sure to balance the kinds of choices you are offering students and consider carefully why you are offering them.

Communication

# Common Challenges: Practice #14: Choice and Options for Students

| Challenges | Possible Solutions |
|---|---|
| A student makes a poor choice of behavior. | Ask the student to reflect on his or her choice briefly with you: "Was that a good choice?" (or a respectful "Did that work out for you?" to older students). "Why not?" "What was a different choice you could have made?" |
| A student says, "I don't like any of those choices." | Make sure the choice is phrased as "you can choose…" versus "Which would you like?" Sometimes a student may not "like" any choice you give him or her, but this is not actually the goal. Rather, you are offering the student autonomy within the limits you set. |
| A student says, "I don't know what to choose." | Say something like, "That's okay. I will give you a couple of minutes to make a decision. When I come back to you, I'd like to hear what you've decided." Make sure you are offering a small range of choices, two or three at most, for the student to consider. |
| A student refuses to make a choice, either passively or actively. | Say something like, "I'd really like for you to make this choice yourself, but a choice needs to be made. If you don't make a choice for yourself, I'll need to make one for you so we can move forward." |
| For academic work, it is too hard to manage the classroom and get quality work if students can all choose different things. | Use a common assignment or project with common skills and timing. Within that, allow students genuine choices in the specific topic of research or individual extension. |

## Scenario to Discuss with Colleagues:

A student loses her temper in class. When you speak with her later about her poor choices, she responds that she doesn't feel that it is a "choice" for her. This is who she is. How would you handle this comment and refocus her on the choices she is making at school?

Communication

# Critique and Feedback

**Learning the language of kind, specific, and helpful feedback supports student growth**

---

*An eighth-grader at Expeditionary Learning Middle School in Syracuse, New York, is sitting next to his critique partner and leans in with advice: "For your praise, I put, 'I like how you used various pieces of evidence, and you did good on elaborating and putting the meanings of the word in the parentheses. A suggestion is that you could elaborate more on these last three pieces of evidence," he adds.*

*These students are using a protocol called Praise, Question, Suggestion to offer each other critique on a piece of writing. "Praise, Question, Suggestion is a protocol that helps students provide meaningful feedback to each other," says teacher Rich Richardson. "We demonstrate how to give feedback based on Praise, Question, Suggestion in front of the whole class first."*

*Through this modeling, practice, and feedback, students learn how to make their critique kind, specific, and helpful. "Over time, students learn the ability to articulate thinking to a peer in an effective way," says Richardson. This model then can serve as a foundation for student to student, teacher to student, or even student to teacher feedback.*

## What It Is

Praise, Question, Suggestion is just one of many protocols for providing critique and descriptive feedback. (For more detail on the steps of Praise, Question, Suggestion, see the general protocols section in Part 2 of this book.) More broadly, critique and feedback is a strategy for productive communication in the classroom, whether between students or between teachers and students. Various forms of critique and feedback can help students reflect on and improve their academic work—as we see in Rich Richardson's class in the opening vignette—as well as their behavior. In either case, critique and feedback must emphasize reflection, effort, and high standards. The process should help students better understand what they have already achieved as well as how they can stretch and grow in the future. Critique and feedback work best when regularly modeled through a formal process with teacher facilitation. The real power of a positive, critique-centered classroom, however, takes root when students begin to value the power of critique themselves and use it informally, respectfully, and effectively with each other throughout the day.

## What It Looks Like

Critique and feedback, whether formal or informal, should be grounded in three norms:

- Be Kind: Always treat others with dignity and respect. This means we never use words that are hurtful, including sarcasm.

- Be Specific: Focus on particular strengths and weaknesses, rather than making general comments like "It's good" or "I like it." Provide insight into why it is good or what, specifically, you like about it.

- Be Helpful: The goal is to positively contribute to the individual or the group, not to simply be heard. Echoing the thoughts of others or cleverly pointing out details that are irrelevant wastes time.

Particularly when we ask students to give peer feedback to each other, we must create the conditions for this to be successful. First, the classroom must be a safe place, with closely enforced norms for kindness and respect. This kind of safety can be hard to monitor, especially when building culture with a new group, but it is imperative that teachers stop a critique when norms have been violated (e.g., work is complimented with a sarcastic expression or tone.) Second, the feedback can't be general feedback—it should focus on one particular skill or behavior that the class has learned together. If we ask students to sit with a writing critique partner and give feedback with no clear focus, comments will almost always be vague and unhelpful. If we want students to critique how they behaved on a particular day, they will need something concrete to reflect on. If students have a focus they understand well (e.g., the use of metaphors in their essay; the efficiency of their transitions), then they can give you and each other productive feedback.

There are myriad ways for teachers to set up processes for critique and feedback. Usually they involve a student presenting his or her work or a teacher highlighting something that needs improvement, either in an individual's behavior or that of the entire class, and another student, a group of students, and/or the teacher engaging in a round of feedback. One "piece" of praise, a question, and a suggestion is one option. Another is framed around "warm" (positive) feedback and "cool" (room to grow) feedback. Still another is framed with "I notice" and "I wonder." All of these frames for giving feedback can be structured to include many rounds, each focusing on something new (e.g., one round on how quickly the class lined up to come in from recess, a second on how thoroughly they completed their classroom jobs).

Using a structured method for critique and feedback is an important and helpful starting place for students to learn the norms, language, and impact of the practice. As the practice takes hold, the language of critique and feedback often starts to "inch in" to informal conversations in the classroom. As they come to value how an honest assessment of their work and/or behavior helps them learn and grow, they begin to more naturally give and get kind, specific, and helpful feedback. "I have a question about…" or "I wonder if…" will likely pop up when students share their work or when they are working with partners or in groups.

Once a classroom builds a positive culture of critique, that culture and the critique process can and should be put in service of critiquing student behavior and class culture on a regular basis. When students are doing an excellent job of upholding class norms or schoolwide character values, that should be affirmed and celebrated during critique; when

*Peer-to-peer feedback can be highly effective with practice and good structures.*

Communication

students have drifted from norms and character values, that should be addressed with kind, specific, and helpful critique as a group.

At the **elementary** level, critique and feedback should generally be given in small, clear chunks that a young learner will be able to follow and implement without difficulty. A graphic organizer with space for students to write down their praise, question, and suggestion or their warm and cool feedback will help keep them on track. For peer-to-peer critique, young students can sometimes be unintentionally hurtful to others by blurting out candid criticisms. They will benefit from modeling and practice in a group, and can be offered sentence starters (e.g., "I like the way you..."; "Maybe you could think about adding...").

**Secondary**-level students will also need modeling and practice with language before they can engage in peer feedback. Adolescents can be particularly sensitive to criticism and often live in a social world where sarcasm and teasing are the norm. It is worth spending the time discussing, modeling, and practicing feedback in whole-class and small-group settings until there is a safe and comfortable environment for it. Though it may seem silly, offering (not requiring) sentence starters can be helpful for these students as well. It is useful to check in via private notecards (e.g., exit tickets that you collect) with students about how critique sessions went.

## Why It Matters

Structures for critique and feedback, including the norms that the entire class agrees to abide by when commenting on work or behavior, supports respectful, collaborative communication in the classroom. Learning to provide kind, specific, and helpful feedback is also a skill that will benefit students throughout their lives, whether on a soccer field, around the dinner table, in a college classroom, or in a professional boardroom. Thoughtful feedback can help others feel seen, heard, and respected. Psychologist Claude Steele (2010) has also identified specific, effort-based praise as one way to build trust among diverse members of a learning community.

## Planning for Practice

- In what ways, patterns, or formats do you currently give feedback to your students (or do they give feedback to each other)? Make a twin list: "academic feedback" and "behavioral feedback." Run down your list and determine a logical place to incorporate a structured protocol.

- Commit to trying a protocol like Praise, Question, Suggestion at the next formal opportunity students have to give feedback, whether academic or behavioral. Teach students that all feedback, whether part of this particular protocol or another structure, should be kind, specific, and helpful. Students may need mini-lessons to help them give helpful feedback and ask the kinds of questions that will help their peers improve their work.

Communication

# Common Challenges: Practice #15: Critique and Feedback

| Challenges | Possible Solutions |
|---|---|
| A student insists that he cannot complete the suggestion(s) you or his classmate has made because he doesn't have the ability. | Assess (or reassess) the suggestion to ensure it is realistic and consider whether the student would benefit from seeing a model. Assist the student in naming concrete steps to address the suggestion and then say something like, "I believe you can do this. Give it a try. I'll come back in a few minutes to see how you're doing." Then leave the student. |
| A student does not seem to believe your praise or that of a classmate. | First, ensure that the praise is truthful and sincere: students have strong radar when it comes to false praise. Second, make sure the praise is concrete and specific; a student who is struggling with writing cannot hear "you are a good writer" but may accept "your opening sentence is gripping." |
| A student is confused about the feedback. | Check feedback to make sure it is specific, clear, and helpful. Review and/or rephrase with the student, and ask the student to put it into his or her own words. |
| Students are giving harsh critique or unspecific feedback to their peers. | Remind students that the feedback must be kind, specific, and helpful. You might consider doing a mini-lesson on how to give quality feedback—use examples of their feedback from previous lessons and help them evaluate it for effective and ineffective comments. Remind students that unspecific praise (e.g., "I really like it") may feel good but does not help them grow as learners and people. If necessary, model respectful critique language (words and tone) for students. Offer sentence starters: "I like how... I wonder if... You may consider... Have you thought about...." |
| Critique of student behavior and class culture doesn't seem honest. | If you feel that students are being too easy on themselves in assessing their behavior, or too hard on themselves, make your own feelings clear in the critique session. Just be sure to be kind and specific: a general comment that behavior is poor is difficult to address; a specific issue or habit can be a focus for improvement. |

## Scenario to Discuss with Colleagues:

The feedback your students give each other is either very general (e.g., "great work") or focused on proofreading for conventions (e.g., spelling, punctuation). How can you help them give each other kind, specific, and helpful feedback? Think about each step you would take to make this practice come alive in your classroom.

Communication

# Group Work

In classrooms committed to building student self-management, group work is key. Collaborating with peers around meaningful academic work supports students' healthy development, academically and socially, in ways that a teacher alone cannot. Collaborative work skills are also heavily emphasized in the Common Core State Standards because of their importance for college and career readiness. The ability to collaborate is cited as one of the top priorities of business leaders; it is an essential skill for workplace success.

## Teacher Mindset: Nothing Is Random

Every group is made up of individuals with their own needs, which lends special importance to the teacher's role in students' group work. Grouping students should be just as carefully planned as any other part of the lesson. It can't be an afterthought. And, once students are in groups, the expectations for the ways in which they work together must be taught, practiced, and assessed—and often retaught—just like any other routine. To do this, using group structures and protocols is vital. Students may have differentiated roles (e.g., facilitator, recorder) or common responsibilities within a discussion or work protocol.

Group work can be orchestrated for a wide variety of purposes and needs—from lab partners to desk groups. Groups can vary in size for different activities—from pairs, triads and quads; to table groups of 5-8 students; to a half-class split. It is important to consider these purposes and needs proactively, as different types of grouping strategies serve different needs. Some examples follow:

- **Homogenous Grouping** allows groups of students with similar abilities, aptitudes, first language, or interests to work together. We do not suggest that these groups be yearlong "ability groups," but ad hoc groups convened for a certain need.

- **Heterogeneous Grouping** allows students who possess certain academic strengths to assist and model for those who may have different academic strengths (and vice versa). Strategies for mentoring and support must be taught.

- **Social/Relational Grouping** takes advantage of students' social relationships to strengthen social bonds, honor already established friendships, or encourage new friendships. Strategic group assignments can be used intentionally to help support students who are new, shy, or fragile or to push cliques of friends to branch out.

- **Random Grouping** allows students to step out of their comfort zone and work with peers with whom they may have little contact.

- **Free Grouping** honors the individual preferences of the students.

No matter the purpose, the success of group work requires that teachers put thought into how students' interactions with each other will impact their learning. Saying "get into groups of four" may not produce the desired result.

## What You'll Find in This Section

- Giving Clear Directions
- Volume and Movement in the Classroom
- Group Work and Group Discussion

**Practice #16**

# Giving Clear Directions

**Delivering clear directions allows students to follow with accuracy and focus**

*Fifth-grade teacher Erin Daly at P.S. 36 in Bronx, New York, knows what it is like to have to manage a diverse group of students: in her classroom, she has regular education students, special education students, and English language learners all learning together. As a result, she knows her directions need to be crisp, clear, and accessible to all students.*

*She begins by reviewing the learning targets for her lesson and then moves into what she wants students to do. "We are going to get into our [preassigned] triads, and we're going to choose one character that we're interested in going a little bit deeper with." She releases the students to get into groups of three: "Go."*

*Daly waits patiently until all students are seated in triads and ready before going on to explain the academic task. She asks them to choose one character to focus on from the novel they are reading and gives wait time for this. "Now that you have decided who you are going to be, we're going to be doing a jigsaw activity...."*

*The entire class is structured in this fashion: Daly gives one clear direction; the students accomplish the direction; she gives the next direction. There is no backtracking, revising directions on the fly, or multiple directions at once. Students know exactly what to do—and, importantly, why.*

## What It Is

Effective directions are crisp and clear—including nothing beyond what they absolutely must—so that students can follow them with accuracy and focus. Although it may seem obvious, group work cannot function successfully without clear, well-planned directions. Since several cognitive demands of students are made while working in groups—moving to the right place, having the right materials, following an instructional sequence, and working collaboratively with peers—it is essential that you think through your delivery of directions beforehand.

## What It Looks Like

Giving **oral directions** effectively is closely tied to teacher presence, specifically Body Language (Practice #1) and Voice (Practice #2). Confidence and clarity go a long way. Additionally, giving directions of any kind will meet with greater success if these steps are followed:

1.  Ensure that students are still and silent before you begin, and that they remain so until you've finished giving the directions.

2.  Describe the action you want students to take, succinctly and clearly. Especially with younger students, don't give too many steps at once.

3. Head off potential challenges if needed (e.g., "Sit down with empty hands").

4. Check for understanding: "Can someone restate what I just said?"

5. Release the students. "Okay—go!"

Providing written directions that are equally clear and efficient will give students multiple points of access. Consider how the directions look on the page. Are they organized and readable? Are they large enough and in a clear font that stands out on the page?

Often there are two kinds of directions that impact group work: the "academic" directions (the instructional sequence students will work through) and the "grouping" directions (the peers students will work with to complete the academic task). If grouping is simple (e.g., "find a partner"), give that direction as well as the first one or two steps of the academic directions (no more), check for their understanding, and release them to get to work. If grouping is more complicated than just finding a partner (e.g., "form triads with students you haven't worked with yet this week"), wait to give academic directions until the groups are organized and ready to work.

At the **elementary** level, students do best with very simple directions. Giving them one or two directions for getting into groups and then refocusing them before giving academic directions is usually a good course of action. Anchor charts, visuals, and consistent routines will also support them to know exactly what to do. You may, for example, set partners for the week using a rotating chart on which you move around pictures of the students to indicate who the partners are. When asked to find their partner, students know to look at the chart and find their partner. Similarly, a consistent routine for what they do once they've found their partner (e.g., sit cross-legged on the floor; make a bridge with your arms) will clearly indicate when everyone is ready for the next direction. Very young children may also benefit from a simple song to sing when certain directions are given (e.g., "everybody clean up, clean up, clean up").

**Secondary**-level students also do best with very simple and concrete directions; social distractions are the challenge, so silent transitions between steps may be needed. Keeping the number of steps announced at once to a minimum and asking for students to repeat or paraphrase the directions supports their understanding and ability to follow through.

At any level, particularly for group work on academic tasks, consider creating "table tents" or instruction sheets that list the steps for the task at hand. This proactive approach supports students to work together to figure out what to do next versus always relying on you to tell them. Also, before giving any directions at all, always wait for 100% attention.

*Asking students to restate your directions will aid their understanding.*

## Why It Matters

Clear directions lay the foundation for respectful, active, collaborative, and growth-oriented learners. When students don't understand what they should be doing, their attention lags, their confidence suffers, and their potential to derail their group increases. Within the "safety net" of clear directions, students feel confident and secure in both their own academic efforts and the expectations for working with their peers.

## Planning for Practice

- Reflect on the process by which you give directions for working in groups. Do the students ever get confused about what they are supposed to do? Do they start moving into groups before you finish the directions? Does it take them a long time to settle down? Identify the problem areas.

- Plan proactively. Shape your next lesson with an eye toward clarifying and tightening your directions. Where will the steps for giving clear directions, described previously, help you?

- Practice by creating a script to guide you in delivering complex directions. Say the directions out loud. Listen to yourself. If you were a student, would you be able to follow the directions without confusion? Consider test-driving the directions on colleagues or a set of willing students before using the directions in a whole class setting.

## Scenario to Discuss with Colleagues:

Your students have gotten pretty good at following grouping directions, but inevitably once they get down to engaging in the academic task with their group, hands go up all over the room and many of them seem confused about what to do next. How might you handle their questions and confusion in the moment? How can you adjust your approach to giving directions in the future?

# Common Challenges: Practice #16: Giving Clear Directions

| Challenges | Possible Solutions |
|---|---|
| Students rush to move before you are finished with the directions. | Give the signal for attention again (e.g., hands up; dim the lights). Wait until you have 100% attention and finish the directions before moving on. Comment positively on student eagerness, but be clear that you won't finish until everyone is still and silent. Also, check your language to make sure you haven't accidentally cued your students to start moving. You might even preface your instructions with "when I say 'go'" so that students know they will be cued when it's time to transition. |
| Students don't follow the directions accurately. | Use your signal for attention again and wait for 100% attention from students. Reiterate the directions or ask for a student volunteer to do so, and then have the students regroup and/or restart the academic work. As students work, comment on or reinforce students who are following the directions (e.g., "I see Jace has gotten out his independent reading book. Thank you, Jace"). You may also consider posting more complicated multistep directions on chart paper so that students can independently refer to them if they are confused. |
| You tend to give and change your directions "on the fly." | Try writing out the directions beforehand as a script for yourself. You may consider using slide technology such as PowerPoint, so that students can follow along with you, or instruction sheets that students can refer to in their groups. You can save these directions for future lessons, and students can become more accustomed to them and take more ownership. |
| You need to change your directions to address an immediate classroom need. | Use your signal for attention. Announce clearly that you have to change the directions and, if appropriate, give a very simple explanation as to why. Be sure that you have 100% attention and then give the new directions. |

Practice #17

# Volume and Movement in the Classroom

**Productive buzz and movement are essential parts of learning but require structure and monitoring**

*"My classroom isn't a very quiet one," laughs Kristin Bacheldor, first-grade teacher at Tollgate Elementary School in Aurora, Colorado. "I feel as if students need to hear each other think, talk, and read aloud most of the time."*

*Bacheldor uses a strategy that allows students to share ideas with each other or to read aloud to each other without bothering others around them. "What I have done," she says, "is explicitly teach them what a whisper is. We'll have a conversation as a class about what a whisper sounds like and feels like. I tell them that 'if I am across the room and I can hear you, that's not a whisper.'*

*"By teaching them this, I empower them to take care of their own noise problems. It does take a lot of work to get there. But with a lot of repetition, modeling, and role play, we achieve our goal."*

## What It Is

Noise and movement can make a teacher nervous. It's hard to shake the iconic image of a principal peeking into a classroom, expecting to see students working silently at desks—the traditional sign that the teacher is in charge and learning is taking place. Some teachers, particularly new teachers, have an almost binary view of volume and movement: either students are sitting totally still—at desks or on the carpet—or it's going to be chaos. There is no vision of a productive in-between state.

In fact, the most important learning in an active classroom often takes place when students are discussing, debating, analyzing, and creating together. There may even be times when the classroom is downright loud—hammers banging, duct tape being stretched out, many groups of students talking together simultaneously. There are certainly times when being silent makes the most sense, and other times when the noise of learning should be evident everywhere. This requires classroom management systems that allow for productive discussion and movement, even exclamations of joy in learning.

We suggest that every classroom have a range of noise levels and movement levels that are understood, practiced, and used effectively. These can be codified in a classroom chart and can be standardized as an agreed-upon schoolwide structure and posted in every classroom. Or this concept can be informally taught and practiced so that students build routines that are naturally respectful of the concentration and work of others. Either way, it is helpful to have names for the different points on this scale (e.g., this is a silent time; whisper time; conferring time; studio time) that will instantly cue students to the expectation.

## What It Looks Like

Perhaps the simplest noise scale is one that is numbered—1 is silent, 2 is whisper, 3 is quiet talk, 4 is regular indoor voice, 5 is outdoor, recess voice, etc. (The points on the scale and names for the points can obviously vary from school to school.) With this system, a teacher can simply say "Level 2," write a "2" on the board, or point to the chart, and students are clear about what is expected.

Of course, for this to work, students need to role-play and practice what those levels sound like, and levels need to be monitored to set a standard. When beginning to use a scale, it is vital that a high standard is established for keeping to a set level, as volume naturally rises. If students can't keep at a Level 3, even with a reminder, the class may need to switch to Level 2 or 1 (silence) for five minutes or for the rest of the work session. When students realize the levels will be enforced, they will learn to self-monitor so that they don't have to be silent.

A similar scale can be used for movement (e.g., red is still, at desk or table; orange is conferring, moving briefly to ask something of a teacher or peer; yellow is collaborating, moving around the room as needed to work with others or materials; green is active work, building or experimenting; blue is outdoor movement, running or jumping). Classrooms with multiple scales in operation can distinguish them from one another by using letters for one scale, colors for another, and so on.

Some schools and classrooms may not want the formality of an official scale and chart. They do, however, want students to understand how to adjust their volume and movement appropriately to the task. During reading times, for example, it's silent and still; during science work, there is indoor talk and collaborative and respectful movement.

Either model is fine, as long as it promotes well-monitored, positive levels of noise and movement that don't require continual nagging and reminders. If you are continually reprimanding, raising your hand, ringing your bell, or shouting over students, the system is not working.

At the **elementary** level, names for levels, or numbers or colors, can be particularly helpful for younger students, as they are very concrete. Whether on a poster or not, if every student knows what "whisper time" is (as in Kristin Bacheldor's class), or what "Green" or "Level 2" means for sound or movement, the classroom can remain productive. These can be fun to practice at first in games or trials until they are clear. The natural energy of young students may cause these guidelines to be forgotten as they get excited in work or play, but if the routines are practiced, students can return to calm when needed.

**Secondary**-level volume and movement control may be able to be handled with less formality. Students can be treated like adults: adult workplaces have no noise scales or movement rules, and adults typically get their work done

*Productive group work relies on a system for volume and movement control that students can follow independently.*

respectfully in common spaces. Some classes of students can rise to this standard and operate genuinely like a group of productive adults most of the time. However, if this is not easy or possible at first for a group, especially at the middle school level, there is nothing wrong with having informal or formal noise and movement scales to build independent monitoring.

## Why It Matters

When there is not a good system and learned routine in place to monitor optimal volume or movement, learning can be greatly constrained. Either students will be forced to stay still and silent at desks, even when collaboration and active work would be helpful, or things may be uncomfortably loud and crazy, with the teacher regularly shouting and reminding students to quiet down. When noise and movement match the task at hand, however, students and teachers feel comfortable and productive.

## Planning for Practice

- Annotate an upcoming lesson, noting the noise and movement levels you think would be optimal for each part of the lesson.

- For this upcoming lesson, consider how you will indicate what you want to your students. How can you make the expectations clear to them? What feedback system do you have in place or will you use? When will you remind students of the feedback system?

- Consider assigning a "noise monitor" student to each working group, or a single noise monitor student for the class as a whole. If you don't have a noise or movement feedback system in place, consider if it would be useful to co-develop one with your students. For older students who may not need or want a formal system, have them help you design a poster, anchor chart, or video describing what optimal levels of noise and movement look like during certain activities in the classroom.

## Scenario to Discuss with Colleagues:

During a "whisper time" work period, one group of students has gotten louder and louder and some other students have complained. How can you reinforce and help students "self-enforce" the expectations for noise and movement so that they all experience the productive buzz of learning, not excessive noise or chaos?

# Common Challenges:  Practice #17:
# Volume and Movement in the Classroom

| Challenges | Possible Solutions |
|---|---|
| Noise in your classroom constantly rises, despite a feedback system | Remember that rising noise levels during group work are natural. Students must learn to self-monitor and to monitor peers. If there is no consequence for always getting louder (e.g., period of silence), students will not learn to respect the guideline. Also, consider asking the students to help problem-solve the challenge of increased volume. You might ask whether there is something that would make it easier for them to maintain a more quiet volume. For example, students might decide their desks are too far apart or that they need one person in their group to be in charge of monitoring the noise and reminding others when it's getting too loud. |
| The students don't seem to know what a whisper or inside voice actually is | When implementing noise-level management, you may need to actually teach students the difference between each noise level and frequently practice what each level sounds like. |
| There are students who do not function well with much, if any, noise in the classroom | Make sure other students understand this. Be sure there are plenty of "whisper" or silent times in the day. If necessary, provide noise-blocking headphones or a "quiet zone" in the classroom for students with particular processing needs. As much as possible, structure your agenda to meet various processing styles of your students. Ensure that you have silent think time built in for students who need that *and* discussion time to meet the needs of your oral processors. Be transparent about this agenda structure with your students. It's often easier for students to maintain four minutes of silence if they know that it will be followed by four minutes of discussion. |

**Practice #18**

# Group Work and Group Discussion

**Structures, protocols, modeling, and guidance build students' collaboration and discussion skills**

---

*Erin Daly, fifth-grade teacher at P.S. 36 in Bronx, New York, is aware that productive group discussion doesn't spontaneously occur in the classroom. "I use conversation starters all throughout the year," she says. "I keep an anchor chart in my room at eye level and often refer to it. I praise students who use these sentence starters and make sure to say something like, 'That would be a great way to start a discussion with your triad.' That way, my English language learners, for example, have a chance to hear the words being said and learn how to use them the standard way. I think these conversation starters work really well for the kids, and they use them often, even general education students."*

*Daly views these supports not as a top-down model of how to speak, but as a means of helping her students share and articulate their great ideas. "All kids have awesome ideas swirling around in their heads, and they sometimes struggle with organizing their ideas to verbalize them in an effective way. These sentence starters give kids the words they need to focus their thinking and allow them to enter into a rich group discussion."*

## What It Is

Most students do not intuitively know how to collaborate in academic work or how to have productive academic discussions. While many four- and five-year-olds have no trouble collaborating to create a giant block city or a poster map of their town, older students do not typically feel uninhibited and free enough to create together. Asked to investigate or analyze a topic or begin a project, some students will hold back and be silent, afraid to share ideas; others may be bossy and take over the work with strong ideas. Without protocols and practice, it is not easy for students to share voices and ideas, consider each other's ideas thoughtfully, critique their own and each other's thinking, and create a plan to work effectively together.

Students will benefit from a set of scaffolding structures and tools to build the skills to work in groups. That set includes:

- **Explicit norms for group work** that compel students to treat each other respectfully, share air time, take the courage to speak up, and build on each other's ideas. These norms are most powerful when co-constructed with students, discussed, practiced, and assessed after group work times.

- **Protocols for group work and group discussion** that define roles, timing, and steps that shape the conversation. Protocols do not need to be used for every discussion, but when they are used a great deal, students will naturally learn how to structure free discussions more equitably and productively.

- **Instruction and practice in academic language** and the phrases that adults use to facilitate discussion. This comprises both vocabulary instruction and practice and also modeling and skills in the phrases that are used to respectfully communicate agreement, disagreement, transitions, and new perspectives.

# What It Looks Like

For the process of creating and using norms to guide group work, refer to Practice #5 on creating classroom norms. The norms for group work are very similar to general classroom norms, but they are specifically focused on creating a climate for safe, equitable, productive discussion and collaborative work. Just as with any norms, they must be continually discussed and assessed throughout the year to keep them alive and effective.

For more on protocols to guide discussions, Part 2 of this book, Protocols and Strategies to Build Engagement, Collaboration, and Responsibility, is a resource for exactly this purpose. It contains many examples of discussion protocols that can be used for all kinds of different purposes in classrooms.

For building the academic vocabulary and discussion fluency of students, there are many strategies that are effective. Many of the protocols in Part 2 will contribute significantly to this goal—the more students use those protocols, the more they will become comfortable in academic discussion. Academic language should be built throughout the day, through explicit discussion and posting of vocabulary during close reading, during academic work in all subjects, and during discussions. Sentence starters can be very helpful as well:

- I want to build on what _____ said.

- I respectfully disagree. I think that _____.

- My evidence is _____.

- Can I add something? I think that _____.

- The text says _____.

**Elementary**-level supports for group work begin with a focus first on how to be kind, how to share, and how to cooperate. Learning, modeling, and practicing words and actions that promote cooperation should be part of daily life in the classroom. Sentence starters can be very helpful for teaching students how to enter and add to discussion, rather than simply sharing their own ideas and opinions. In some schools, students as young as first grade learn phrases like "I agree, and I would like to add that…" and "I respectfully disagree, because…."

*Norms and protocols support productive group work.*

**Secondary**-level students benefit from very clear norms for respect and equity that are discussed and assessed regularly. Since adolescence can be a very self-conscious period in life for many students, a safe environment to collaborate and norms and protocols that demand respect and equity of voice are essential. Students can also work collaboratively in their groups to establish "mini-norms" for their conversations before they begin any work. Additionally, secondary students can practice with more complex sentence frames, such as "I feel this evidence supports my conclusion because...." After using protocols and sentence frames based on adult academic discussion, the goal is for students to internalize language to the point that open discussion in groups is at a higher level much of the time.

## Why It Matters

Effective collaboration and discussion skills will be essential for all students to succeed in college, career, and citizenship. Teachers shouldn't assume that students have the skills they need to have conversations or accomplish tasks together. Building their skills to do this important collaborative work is something that should be a focus at every grade level and in every content area.

## Planning for Practice

- Rate yourself using the following statements: I use group work at least once a class/once a week/once a month/less than once a month. Consider what the reasons for your rating might be. What specific supports or challenges do you experience in planning for group work?

- Spend some time reviewing the group work protocols in Part 2 of this book or another trusted source. Choose one that will help students achieve an objective for an upcoming lesson. Commit to working the protocol into the lesson or building an entire lesson around it. Once the lesson is complete, reflect on the level of engagement and collaboration among students. What did you notice? What do you wonder?

### Scenario to Discuss with Colleagues:

Even with norms and protocols, certain confident and talkative students end up dominating group discussions much of the time. How can you support the group to share airtime and work productively?

# Common Challenges: Practice #18: Group Work and Group Discussion

| Challenges | Possible Solutions |
|---|---|
| Students are not talking in their groups. | Use protocols that compel students to share ideas in turns. You may also consider giving students time to think (and possibly write) before they move into group discussion. This ensures that everyone has a chance to generate some ideas before they are expected to share with the group. |
| Students are being unkind to one another in their groups (interruptions, put-downs, etc.). | Gather the class as a whole group and refocus them on the class norms for respectful discussion. You may wish to stop their group work from time to time throughout the lesson to point out what you notice about their interactions and how they are following the norms. Be sure to notice and reinforce the positive, not the negative. Create a post-conversation reflection tool for students to self-assess how well they followed the norms during the conversation. Students may then use these self-assessments to set goals for future conversations. |
| Students have great ideas, but struggle with articulating them. | Consider giving students a brief period of time to compose their thoughts on paper, using the sentence starters if they wish, before the conversation begins. Make sure students can easily access the conversation starters during the discussion. Create small, laminated copies that students can refer to during their discussions. |
| Students are having trouble taking turns in conversation (often in younger grades). | Consider giving students a physical prop (soft ball, magic wand, stuffed animal) they can hold during the conversation and pass to group members to take turns speaking. The student holding the prop is the only one allowed to speak. Consider modeling with a Fishbowl protocol or conducting a whole-class conversation using the prop first. |
| Students are so concerned with what they are saying that they are not listening to other students. | Create an opportunity for post-discussion reflection where students share one new piece of information they heard from someone else during the conversation. This could be structured as a whole-class conversation or individual written reflection. |
| Students in groups are talking about an unrelated topic. | Sometimes it's enough to simply remind students to stay on topic. At other times you may need to evaluate the quality of the discussion prompt. Is it compelling and relevant enough for students to get deep into conversation and stay on task? |

# Deeper Support for Challenging Behaviors

No matter how diligently we have worked to nurture a positive classroom culture—building norms with students, setting up routines for communication and group work, and attending to our presence in the room—there will still be times when things get messy or particularly difficult. Students and teachers alike bring their experiences, stressors, and quirks into the classroom with them every day, and interact in dynamic and unpredictable ways. It can feel like a pressure cooker, and sometimes things explode.

There is no magic bullet for these situations, though beginning with the foundational practices described in this book so far can make the landing a little softer and the rebuilding a little easier. This is especially true when considering that we don't only need to attend to a student who may be in crisis (or at the very least pushing our buttons), but because we also have to attend to the needs of all students—they can stand on the solid foundation you have all built together until the storm blows over.

## Teacher Mindset: Self-Management Is What Students Want and Need

Despite outward appearances at times, all students *want* to behave. They want the support, connection, and community that all human beings want. What they *need* is transparent and consistent boundaries, calm and respectful communication, and the skills to understand how their behavior affects others. When it comes to working with students who exhibit challenging behaviors, three underlying considerations shape all of our advice: know your students, know your strategies, and know your supports. The synthesis of these three components allows you to choose targeted and impactful approaches that set you and your students up for success.

## What You'll Find in This Section

- Preventing Challenging Behavior

- Challenging Behavior, Part 1: Undermining Authority and Respect

- Challenging Behavior, Part 2: Explosive Students, Explosive Situations

- Restorative Practices, Part 1: Questions

- Restorative Practices, Part 2: Circles

# Preventing Challenging Behavior

**The best classroom management stops challenging behavior before it starts**

*"Adam had a genetic syndrome which involves developmental delays and an intellectual disability,"* remembers Jillian, a 17-year veteran of the classroom. *"He would have intense outbursts that were very disturbing to other students—throwing things, yelling obscenities, and destroying his belongings in a rage."*

*When Adam transitioned from ninth to tenth grade, Jillian, Adam's case manager, and his other new teachers met together during the summer to create a plan that would ease the transition and proactively address some of his more challenging behaviors. They generated ideas for setting up their classrooms and differentiating lessons based on his needs. Also, "given his IEP," Jillian recalls, "he could not receive a typical consequence for yelling out in class inappropriately, but he could spend time with the counselor or dean of students to collect himself and get back on track." So Jillian and her colleagues made a plan for him that involved in-class steps to help him de-escalate, like taking the pass to the bathroom (if he was safe) to take a quick break or heading over to the "reflection spot" in the classroom to flip through a magazine or vent in his journal. If those strategies didn't work, Adam would often go spend time with the counselor or dean.*

*When Adam's behavior was escalated, other students also had permission to stand just outside the classroom door until help came for Adam so that they would feel safe. Jillian and her colleagues worked with all students in Adam's classes—with his parents' permission—to understand his condition and his triggers so that they could be partners in supporting him and could keep themselves safe in case of a severe outburst.*

*"I think it's affirming for teachers to know this is a lifetime struggle for kids like Adam, because we often cannot solve these challenges only in our classrooms," says Jillian. "However, we can support our students to take steps towards growth that they can continue to use throughout their learning journeys. Adam continued to need a lot of support and careful preventative planning. He showed gradual and incremental improvements (like reduced numbers of outbursts and improved work completion). Celebrations of his successes (privately) definitely gave him energy and helped him try. We saw real improvement with our prevention strategies, along with regular, proactive behavioral reminders and frequent check-ins with him on how he felt the plan was going, and adapting based on his feedback."*

## What It Is

Unfortunately, students with challenging behaviors can develop a persistent negative dynamic with their teachers that becomes their source for attention and feedback. Turning that dynamic around requires knowing students well—their motivations, strengths, and struggles—setting high expectations, and expressing your belief in them that they can learn and grow. It also requires planning and intention so that you can prevent challenging behaviors as much as possible and, when and if they happen, you're ready with a productive response. Take a consistent and persistent approach in order to gain students' trust. And, most importantly, be the teacher who never gave up on them. They'll notice and respond.

## What It Looks Like

Prevention is ongoing. If we're lucky and we know about a student with challenging behavior coming into our class next year or next semester, we can make plans in advance. We can arrange our rooms, have meetings, and do everything we can to learn about that student and make the classroom learning environment supportive of his or her ongoing growth. Often, however, challenging behaviors emerge and become obvious as time goes on. The behaviors may only take a week to surface, or they may take months. This is the reality that makes prevention an ongoing process. Whether you know well ahead of time or you've just recognized that a student is exhibiting challenging behaviors, what follows are some steps you can take to support that student:

- **First, consider the other practices in this book as a foundation.** Learning, for example, to manage your emotions when you're upset or your confidence is shaken, speaking in a calm voice, setting up your classroom environment, creating norms that emphasize empathy, acceptance, and growth, narrating the positive, using nonverbal signals and the language of choice, and carefully orchestrating group work are all practices that can help prevent challenging behaviors. We have emphasized these practices throughout this book for their power in creating a positive learning environment, based on respect, collaboration, and mutual trust. That foundation won't prevent all challenging behaviors, but it will help.

- **Connect with the student's "team."** This may include former teachers, counselors, family members, administrators, coaches, special educators, and the student herself. Learn all you can about the student, including her own perceptions of herself as a learner, and gather strategies that work. Commit to ongoing communication and strive for consistent and transparent approaches to behavioral challenges.

*Preventing challenging behaviors requires thoughtful planning and, often, communication with the entire class.*

- **Change the physical layout of your classroom if necessary.** Consider where in the room the student sits. Is he or she in a group? If so, should you think more carefully about who is in that group? Are there places in the classroom where the student can sit quietly if necessary? A reading nook? A beanbag chair? Would it help if he or she could look out the window? Work with the student to figure out what will provide comfort and a feeling of safety in the room.

- **Consider how you design your lessons.** This is a great opportunity to think about how your lessons may or may not be a prevention tool. For example, if you have a student who gets irrationally upset if she feels she's not being listened to, a discussion protocol with very clear rules for when and how each student speaks may help her regulate those emotions. Similarly, planning lessons that involve opportunities for movement and discussion may help those who can't seem to sit still (and often act out because of it). Low skills in a particular academic area can also be a trigger for some students—proactive lesson planning that may involve well-timed movement breaks or strategic pairings of students can go a long way.

- **Identify a predictable and consistent protocol for responding to challenging behavior.** Some teachers give three reminders of the class rules, some give one. Some use a "buddy classroom," some send students to the office. We are not advocating any one particular "discipline ladder," but we are advocating that you create one that is clear to all students, that is firm and respectful, and that you can commit to following through with. Doing this work ahead of time will prevent you from having inconsistent responses in the heat of the moment. It is critical to your relationship with the class and your commitment to student learning that you make every effort to keep students with you in the classroom for as long as possible—sending them out only isolates them further and takes them away from learning opportunities.

- **Create scripts for yourself so that you can remain calm in response to challenging behavior.** A script can save you the trouble of thinking on your feet, which can be very difficult when you're juggling an entire class full of students and you may be triggered by a student's behavior. Once scripts become ingrained, students know what to expect and the predictability will help them on their way to self-management. When creating scripts, incorporate the language of choice whenever possible:

  - "You're making a poor choice right now. Think about a better choice and try again."

  - "You can either stand up and move back to your seat or you can go spend time with Mrs. Cantor. It's your choice."

On the **elementary** level, consider teaching American Sign Language phrases, such as "please stop," to your students or playacting various ways they can respond to situations that may trigger them to act out. This is especially helpful for students who may have a hard time getting their words out when they are being hurt or bothered. In addition, teach students compassionate communication: how to talk about their feelings (e.g., "I" statements), how to listen to each other (e.g., not interrupting), and how to take the perspective of someone else. Many students need instruction to help them express their feelings, especially children with developmental delays, autism, or emotional issues. Practicing emotional communication the same way we might practice our multiplication tables is worth the time it saves you in the end.

On the **secondary** level, it is essential to recognize the growing independence of students at this age. Your proactive plans for prevention should take into account responses that minimize public embarrassment and offer opportunities to correct behavior and "save face." Use structures like advisory to get to know your students so that you can draw on their strengths and interests to build trust. And don't forget that older students also need practice with compassionate communication. Don't assume they know how to express their feelings or listen empathetically to you or their peers. You should also plan realistically for how to respond to unsafe situations with students who may be physically larger than you. Include in your plan a way to call for help should physical intervention be necessary.

## Why It Matters

Prevention allows us to create and maintain a healthy classroom without the distractions of trying to meet challenging behavior in the moment without a plan or foundation, and also trying to teach at the same time. It gives us the space to think things through, martial our resources, and give our full attention to all the needs of our students.

# Common Challenges: Practice #19: Preventing Challenging Behavior

Deeper Support

| Challenges | Possible Solutions |
|---|---|
| I can't predict when students are going to fall apart or crises will happen. | Nobody can. Proactively creating protocols and scripts will minimize your need to think on your feet in the heat of the moment. When things are calm, talk with your students about how they can help during difficult moments. These structures and proactive conversations will allow for greater consistency in your responses and, over time, act as a form of prevention. |
| My school administration doesn't always act in a way that's supportive or consistent. I'm afraid that all of my planning will be wasted energy because administrators are just going to respond to issues haphazardly anyway. | Do everything you can to keep students with you in the classroom. Identify other allies in the building—nurses, counselors, etc.—who can step in to work with a student if you need additional support. Work with the student's team of other teachers and specialists to approach challenging behaviors consistently and fairly across the school building so that the student interacts with the administration as little as possible. Individual classrooms can and do make a difference for students, even when schoolwide systems are imperfect. |
| My school is small and there's no one I can identify to take a student off my hands when they need to leave the classroom. | Identify a "buddy classroom" with an identified spot for your student to sit when he or she needs a time-out. Ideally this buddy classroom will be at a different grade level to minimize the chance that your student will encounter peers who may perpetuate the challenging behavior. You can offer your classroom as a "buddy classroom" in return. |

## Planning for Practice

- Gather all the information you can about your student(s) with challenging behaviors. Find out what's worked in the past and what the triggers are so that you can create a supportive plan.

- Convene the team of supportive adults, including family members and the student him- or herself, to ensure a consistent approach across the various dimensions of the student's life.

- Create the systems and structures that will guide your interactions with this student and all students in your classroom. Write your scripts and do everything you can to feel prepared for an eventual meltdown.

## Scenario to Discuss with Colleagues:

A new student who moved into the district was just added to your class. You can already tell that his behavior is going to be challenging, and maybe even explosive. What steps can you take to prevent this behavior?

# Challenging Behavior, Part 1: Undermining Authority and Respect

**Maintain a positive classroom culture with transparency, consistency, and high expectations**

---

*Teryn had four sections of tenth-grade English; three of those classes usually went well, but one was a continual problem. In the latter, discussions of the novels they were reading as a class were disrupted almost daily in subtle ways that were difficult for her to address. One student—Isaiah—regularly asked questions that were inappropriate and provocative. When Teryn called him on it, Isaiah always feigned ignorance: "What? It's just a question. I didn't understand the reading." Occasionally she would catch him laughing at her or enticing others to do so.*

*Other students did not join in with these kinds of questions, but they sometimes laughed and enjoyed the disruption of the class and Isaiah's test of authority. Isaiah's game pushed Teryn out of balance. She was not only brittle and edgy with him, but with the whole class. She dreaded that class almost every day. And the more she was off her game, the more things escalated. She gave Isaiah detention regularly, and if anything, it just made things worse.*

*The cycle only broke when, by chance, she watched Isaiah play in a JV basketball game and saw a different side of him. He was not just a good player; he was team player. She talked to him after the game and explained how impressed she was, and later left a voice message for his parents saying the same thing. Without any direct mention of the problem, Isaiah's wise-guy attitude began to fade away.*

## What It Is

Even after all you've done to prevent challenging behaviors, they will still occur. There are many kinds of challenging behaviors, but for the purposes of this book, we have separated them into two basic types: the first focuses on behavior that undermines authority and respect but does not pose a safety risk to the student or others, and the second focuses on explosive behavior. We are assuming in our description of these paired practices that the challenging behavior is from an individual or small group. If the problem exists in the entire class, however, a systemic approach to improving the overall classroom culture is in order. That work should be guided by the full complement of practices in this book.

On typical days, most teachers won't experience explosive students and explosive situations (see Practice #21). Those events are much more episodic. Challenging behavior that undermines authority and respect, however, is much more common. It's the defiant walking away when you've given a direct instruction not to, the insults directed at you or other students, the inappropriate provocative questions, and the talking over you. No one is in danger in these circumstances, but the behavior must still be taken seriously. These violations of rules and norms in subtle and not-so-subtle ways can, when left unchecked, undermine your authority, erode the trust and respect within the classroom community, and create barriers to learning.

## What It Looks Like

For a wide variety of reasons, including deeply personal ones, individual students may feel the need to push back openly against the authority of the classroom and school. This may be directed at you, classmates, classroom norms, or at the school more broadly. In any of these cases, it is hard not take this behavior personally after all the work you have done trying to build a respectful and fair classroom. There are two main priorities for teachers in these situations. First, defusing the defiance and redirecting the student in a way that preserves your dignity and authority, the dignity of the student, and the focus on learning. And second, sending a clear message to the class that they are safe, the culture is intact, you are in charge—still confident, clear, and fair—and learning is the priority in your classroom.

There is no simple solution for these situations; the individual issues that cause challenging behaviors must be understood in order to address them well. However, there are general guidelines that may be helpful in any situation:

- **Remember the basics.** Your presence, your voice, and your actions are strongest when you are calm, clear, and confident. Manage your emotions. Don't take it personally. Every student, including the student who is acting out, wants you to be the leader of stability and order, even if his or her actions suggest otherwise.

- **Determine if you should temporarily ignore the behavior.** We don't generally advise ignoring challenging behavior, but there are specific times when it may be effective. If the behavioral challenge of the student is not particularly apparent to other students in a way that will undermine the authority of the classroom (e.g., the student is privately trying to get negative attention from you), ignoring may be a good first step. If the challenge is public but merely annoying (e.g., tapping a pencil, even when you have made eye contact that says "stop"), it may be worth ignoring it while giving directions to the class and then following up privately with the student. This private follow-up can help bypass any public negotiations the student may try to engage in with you. Importantly, if the challenge makes others feel unsafe or destabilizes the classroom culture, it cannot be ignored, even briefly.

*Challenging behaviors that undermine authority and respect require a clear and consistent response.*

**Deeper Support**

- **Use standard phrases or scripts to redirect students.** In the heat of the moment, when students question your authority, it is easy to say something that will escalate the situation or undermine your standing as a calm leader. As discussed in Practice #19, having prepared phrases can make things much easier. Use the language of choice to separate behavior from innate character (e.g., "Rohan, that was a poor choice. You'll need to see me after class"). Use reminders, rather than warnings, and describe the behavior you want to see (e.g., "Remember, when we line up for lunch, you need to show me a calm, quiet body so that I'll know you're ready"). Do not get into public verbal battle or negotiation.

- **Follow a consistent and transparent plan.** As discussed in Practice #19, you should have a protocol in place for responding when your students push on boundaries. For example: one reminder of the rules, followed by a hallway conversation, then a break in a "buddy teacher's" room, and a re-entry meeting the following day. Variations may include a second reminder, a call home, a detention, etc. There is no one right plan. But no matter the plan, you should follow it consistently and transparently because when students push on boundaries, they will often do so until they have figured out just how far they can go before meeting resistance. Ideally, the plan will be aligned across the school.

- **Ask questions privately after the challenge.** When students challenge you, their motivations can come from many places. Some do it to show off to their friends; some are angry about issues in their home lives; some lack impulse control. The reasons vary as much as the students themselves. Following a disruptive event, pulling students aside to ask questions can help them reflect on their choices and think about what they can do differently in the future. Importantly, restorative questions (discussed in depth in Practice #22) can help students identify who was harmed and how they can repair the damage.

For **elementary** level students, acting out is often an expression of frustration; defiance is often a need to know where the limits are. Simple, concrete language in a calm, caring, firm voice, and consistent follow-through is best for young students: "I see you doing x, and I need you to do y. If you can't do that in the next 30 seconds, we'll need to find you a new group. It's your choice." "I understand you are angry, but we use respectful language here. You need to come with me." "You are a good person, but you made a bad choice here. You chose not to follow directions. You need to leave the art area now."

At the **secondary** level, students displaying challenging, undermining behaviors are often doing so as a way to defy your authority. Despite this, it's not really about you—it's more about the position you hold. Defiant behavior is often to impress classmates—to save face, hide insecurities, or look tough—so it is especially important not to try to resolve it in a public confrontation. Students exhibiting that behavior are typically feeling bad about themselves already, and verbally humiliating them in public by berating them will deepen the problem. Don't take the bait of provocative comments. Be calm and confident, set clear limits, and resolve things in private. Practice your responses using scripts. Teacher Jillian, whom we met in Practice #19, had a simple, yet effective, favorite script: "Did I disrespect you?" "Almost always students would de-escalate when I asked them that question," she says, "and, often, they would apologize for their own disrespect toward me." With older students it is key to commit to following through with consequences that are respectful, relevant, and realistic. If you can get beyond your own frustration afterward to show compassion and ask questions, you may be able to break through the negative pattern that this student has built for him- or herself.

## Why It Matters

A commitment to self-management doesn't mean that preventative measures will always work. In real life, people try all sorts of things to prevent undesirable behavior and still make choices they regret later. Being prepared for when students make mistakes—and helping them see that making mistakes is an essential part of learning and growing—is how we teach them how to function not only in the classroom community, but in the wider community as well. It is this persistent, consistent approach that can help our students with the most challenging behaviors grow.

## Planning for Practice

- Work with a colleague to discuss or role-play situations in your classroom where a particular student undermines your authority. Brainstorm possible scripted phrases and actions that can help.

- If your school or classroom plan for challenging behavior—your "discipline ladder"—is not working, examine it with colleagues and figure out why. It may need changing, or you may need to recommit to using it consistently.

# Common Challenges:  Practice #20: Challenging Behavior, Part 1

| Challenges | Possible Solutions |
|---|---|
| I feel that when a student talks back to me, he needs a sharp response, not kindness. Showing understanding is like rewarding him for being rude. | Students who are rude do need a quick response that is clear and firm, though not necessarily "sharp." A sharp response often comes from a place of anger, meant to hurt a bit; it is not only unhelpful for the student, but can set a tone of disrespect for the whole class. Demonstrating some understanding is important for students to see because following up with questions and kindness later on can build a positive relationship that heals the bad pattern. |
| One student is derailing class just about every day. He's rude to me and he blatantly defies what I ask him to do. | Be consistent with your response to these behaviors. Follow your plan and follow through with any consequences you've promised. If you say, "One more time, Gabriel, and you're going to go spend some time with Mr. Cruz," it's important that you deliver on that promise if Gabriel continues. If the problem remains persistent, gather a team of adults, including Gabriel, his parent or guardian, a counselor, administrator, and others who may work with him to develop a behavior plan. Though we don't advocate the widespread use of rewards systems (i.e., sticker charts), when students exhibit ongoing and pervasive behavioral challenges, such systems can be effective. |
| I should have responded right away, but I didn't, and now I feel like I can't really hold students to the boundary I originally set. | It's never too late to re-establish the boundary. It's okay to say something like, "I let that one slip—my fault—but I'm not going to let another one slip." If your boundary keeps shifting and you let things slide, students will keep pushing. This might be a good time for a whole-class discussion about the classroom norms to "reset" the expectations for how the community will treat one another. |

## Scenario to Discuss with Colleagues:

Ariel, a leader in her social group of middle school girls, has been creating a quiet insurrection in your classroom. Following her lead, many of the girls routinely ignore you, rolling their eyes when you call them on it and blatantly disrespecting anyone not in their clique. What steps can you take to get these girls back on track and restore the positive classroom culture you have worked so hard to build?

# Challenging Behavior, Part 2: Explosive Students, Explosive Situations

**When crises happen, be prepared**

Deeper Support

*Patrick was a veteran sixth-grade teacher whose classroom was typically smooth and calm, but he knew this was not going to be that kind of year. One of his incoming students, Anthony, was a boy whose behavior was described as highly challenging, with regular explosive episodes. Up until fourth grade Anthony had had a full-time one-to-one aide, but in an effort to build his independence, that had been phased out as his self-control had improved.*

*Before the year began, the school's special education team worked with Patrick to provide history and to plan classroom modifications and structures. Because Anthony had an autism spectrum disorder and had issues with sensory input, those modifications included a tactile seat cushion, headphones, squeeze balls, a lead blanket, and a "safe place" in the classroom. They created protocols for crises that were aligned with school safety and behavioral policies and customized to address Anthony's challenges. Despite all of this preparation, Patrick knew things would not be easy, and they were not. This was a situation where Patrick understood that his own experience, heart, and skill as a teacher were not enough: it would take a team effort to make this a positive year for Anthony and the class.*

*Three things made a difference for Patrick in turning this around. First was an ongoing meeting structure among staff to build a consistent team approach. Second was regular meetings between Patrick and the school counselor—not just to discuss Anthony's needs, but also to discuss Patrick's own responses, which for the first time in his career were not always a model of self-control. With the help of the counselor, he created scripts of what he would say and do when outbursts occurred. Patrick, Anthony, and the whole class benefited from the predictability of the scripts.*

*Third, with Anthony's parents' permission, Patrick occasionally had meetings with the class when Anthony was absent. He was direct and compassionate with the class in describing many things that often go unspoken in these situations: Anthony was a good person who was trying hard, but he had some challenges that were not his fault; Anthony didn't always have control; it was scary for him and for everyone; they would have to work together as a class to handle those situations well. Students shared their feelings and brainstormed helpful strategies for when Anthony was in crisis and also to help him feel more appreciated and celebrated as a member of the class.*

*The year was never easy. But remarkably, Patrick, Anthony, and the whole class felt pride in the progress they made.*

## What It Is

Most teachers, even those whose classrooms are models of respectful behavior, experience situations when students become explosive—shouting, cursing, or verbally assaulting others, or physically hurting themselves, others, or the classroom. How you handle those situations makes a world of difference to the safety and growth of the student in crisis, to the class as a whole, and to your personal confidence as a teacher. There is no magic bullet for handling these situations. As teachers, we need to be equipped with general guidelines and strategies for how to react in crisis situations, as well as specific strategies that work best with individual students. Knowing students well is key to this practice. We also need to know when to enlist the support of our colleagues. Your individual efforts are important, but it's critical to remember that you can't do it alone. School safety procedures, legal mandates for students with special needs, and other supportive adults in the school and beyond, including family members, are all part of the web of support you must rely on when managing explosive behaviors.

## What It Looks Like

Helping students who are melting down is complex work. Not only do you have to respond to the student in crisis, but you also have to take care of the entire class. What follows are some key considerations when working with explosive students and explosive situations.

- **Remember the basics.** Your presence, your voice, and your actions are strongest when you are calm, clear, and confident. Manage your emotions. Don't take it personally. Every student, including the student who is acting out, wants you to be the leader of stability and order, even if his or her actions suggest otherwise.

- **Safety comes first.** If the student's behavior is posing a safety risk—either physically or emotionally—to himself or others, you must address this immediately. Ideally you will have a plan in place already for such situations, but even if not, stay calm, clear, and firm. This may require removing a student from class. Use vocal directions instead of physical contact if possible, although on some occasions physical intervention may be imperative for safety. Do not try to restrain a student if you have not been trained to do so; get help from others who are trained. Identify a classroom responsibility where one student is assigned to pick up the phone or get help in a crisis so things feel less chaotic for you and the students.

*Supporting students with explosive behaviors requires a team approach.*

- **Create scripted sentences and actions.** It is difficult to respond thoughtfully in crisis. As described in Practices #19 and #20, automatic phrases, scripts, and moves can protect you from getting into a personal battle with a student. Impersonal, short, standard statements (e.g., "Anthony, that is not the Lincoln School way. You need to step outside now." "Aleena, that was a poor choice of behavior. You need to stop right now") work better than what may be instinctual (e.g., "Don't you talk that way in my classroom!" "What are you thinking?"). You can narrate your actions to keep the class calm: "I need to step in the hallway with Aleena. You all should continue your work." Focus on de-escalation and safety.

- **When possible, keep students with you after the incident.** If possible—and other students will not be adversely affected as a result—try to respond to the student in such a way that he or she can stay in the classroom with you after the incident is over. Students who frequently exhibit challenging behaviors are used to being sent out of class, cutting them off from the classroom community and learning opportunities, and sending them into repeated cycles of disciplinary referrals and, often, shame. If you do have to send a student out of class for disruptive behavior, consider doing so without engaging a punitive disciplinary system. Identify a teacher who can offer his room as a "buddy classroom" if a student needs a break, or make a plan with case managers, nurses, counselors, or other adults whom the student trusts (e.g., secretaries, librarians) whom you can call upon to take the student from the room for a while. Plan ahead for a positive re-entry, including a chance to process the incident with the student.

- **When appropriate, address the entire class.** When students melt down, everyone notices. It can't be helped. Engaging students with scripts or actions plans of their own when it happens can be an effective form of "wrap around" response. When everyone is prepared with the right things to say and do in a time of crisis, everyone benefits. Using language that depersonalizes the challenges, as teacher Patrick did when speaking with his students about Anthony's struggles, can help students see the challenges for what they are—challenges—rather than character flaws.

When working with explosive students, the follow-up that happens after an incident is just as important that what happens in the heat of the moment. What follows are some guidelines to support students' growth:

- **Reteach.** Emotional intelligence is as important as content mastery. Once the crisis is over, give the student some coaching and the opportunity for a "do-over." A re-entry plan is an opportunity for growth.

- **Use positive feedback loops.** Occasionally students need behavior plans or contracts to help them break a cycle of explosive behavior. The concrete and immediate feedback that such plans can provide is more productive for some students than the kinds of reflective discussion adults tend to fall back on. These plans are best created by the team of adults who work with the student and with the student herself. We do not in general endorse reward systems for good behavior (e.g., stickers, prizes), as self-discipline is best built with internal rewards and praise from adults and peers, not external rewards. However, we acknowledge that for certain students with persistent behavioral challenges, plans that include behavioral tracking and external rewards can be the most effective strategy as the student builds internal capacity.

- **Determine a logical consequence.** Often, when students exhibit explosive behaviors, you won't be the only one in charge of determining consequences, but you can be an advocate for making them realistic, respectful, and relevant. Be a voice on the student's team for a consequence that promotes growth.

**Elementary**-level students may benefit from books, stories, and pictures that help them identify their feelings. Books such as Mary Hoffman's *The Great Big Book of Feelings* (2013) can be kept in the classroom and used as a tool for students to articulate their emotions. A resource like this may help you and your students identify code words or nonverbal signals they can use to signal that they need help with another student or a break from the classroom in order to stay in control. Young students may also benefit from sentence stems (e.g., "When you said that, it made me feel x"; "I feel x because y") posted prominently in the classroom.

Students at the **secondary** level may be frustrated and exhausted from years of grappling with the interface of their challenges and the school environment. They have likely felt singled out for their differences and may have been hurt by teachers' approaches in the past. Be sensitive to these potential issues as you work together with your students to come up with effective solutions. Teach them language to help them express their feelings. Also, work hard to build on their strengths. Adolescents desperately want to be seen for the whole people that they are, including their strengths. They may be angry at being defined by their differences or challenges (e.g., "the ADD kid" or "the diabetic") and may try to hide their challenges for these reasons. Find multiple ways to use and celebrate their strengths in class and among their peers.

# Common Challenges: Practice #21: Challenging Behavior, Part 2

| Challenges | Possible Solutions |
|---|---|
| I can't manage my own emotions when explosive situations happen. I lose my temper with students when they melt down. | Get help from colleagues. Discuss your emotions and responses with someone you trust. Create a plan ahead of time. Create scripted phrases and actions. Be ready to use your script. |
| I don't know how to handle the rest of the class when I need to tend to a student in crisis. | Prepare the whole class for such situations. Make a plan ahead with them. Use clear directions with them when you need them to be independent. |

## Why It Matters

When students exhibit explosive behaviors, it's natural to get frustrated, feel emotionally drained, or simply want the student out of your classroom. These challenging behaviors trigger all of us. But all students—even the toughest of them—deserve to be cared for in a supportive learning environment. The skills of self-control they learn with you may be the most important skills they learn for success in life.

## Planning for Practice

- Reflect on a particular student's chronic challenging behavior. Look at your classroom behavior plan or discipline ladder and any scripts you have created to determine what might need to be added, deleted, or tweaked to better support the student.

- Consider inviting a trusted colleague in to observe or record your interactions with the student. Are there identifiable antecedents to the student's explosive behavior? Can you identify ways that you can respond more consistently, positively, or clearly?

## Scenario to Discuss with Colleagues:

Twice in one week, second-grader Julian has refused to comply with very simple requests. The first time he wouldn't come to circle time, so you allowed him to stay at his desk. The second time he wouldn't go to math and when you tried to touch his shoulder to encourage him, he totally flipped out, yelling, "Don't touch me," and storming out. What should you do next?

# Restorative Practices, Part 1: Questions

**Solving problems through restoration and relationships**

*Fifth-graders Michael and Raul have been bickering all morning. Their teacher, Sasha, has overheard the occasional "shut up" or "jerk" being hissed from their desk group, where the two boys sit side by side. She has asked them to stop, and they will for a few minutes, but it doesn't take long for her to notice the temperature rising again. At one point during sustained silent reading, Raul put up a barricade around his desk with his books and binders and lowered his head behind this wall so that he wouldn't have to see Michael.*

*As Sasha dismisses the class for lunch, she catches out of the corner of her eye all of Raul's books and binders crash to the floor. Some other students' things have also been knocked off their desks, including Stacie's special nameplate, which is now ripped nearly in half. Michael is the only student standing nearby and immediately starts saying, "I didn't do it. It wasn't me!" with his hands in the air. Some of the other boys are laughing, and Michael's sly grin tells Sasha everything she needs to know about what happened. "Michael and Raul, stay here with me. The rest of you, I'll see you after lunch." Sasha quickly indicates that the two boys are to sit down and stay silent.*

*"I've noticed you two are having some issues with each other this morning. Damaging others' property and being disrespectful is a violation of our class norms. Michael, why don't you tell me, from your perspective, what's been going on today? Raul, I'll give you a chance to do the same in a moment."*

*Sasha learns from Michael and Raul that there was a conflict on the bus on the way to school. She then moves the discussion toward the most recent incident. "Michael, it looked to me like you knocked down those books. Can you tell me what you were thinking at that moment?" "I was just still mad because Raul was making fun of my sneakers on the bus," he says. "And how are you feeling now?" she asks. "I'm still kind of mad but not as much. I didn't mean to wreck Stacie's nameplate." Sasha goes on to tease out Michael's answers to questions about who was harmed by his actions. "What do you think you can do to make things right?" Before going to lunch, Michael apologizes to Raul and they come to some agreements. Raul agrees that making fun of Michael's shoes was disrespectful and agrees not to do it again to Michael or anyone. Michael agrees to clean up all of Raul's things and to use tape to repair Stacie's nameplate. He also writes her a note of apology, which he leaves on her desk. As they walk out the door, Sasha makes a note to herself to check in with the boys' bus driver after school.*

# What It Is

Traditionally, a classroom or school discipline plan focuses on individuals and consequences. A student breaks a rule; a student receives a consequence, which may or may not be relevant, respectful, or realistic. Restorative questions have a different aim: community and reparation. Through restorative questions, the student's actions are framed as choices that impact relationship. As a result, instead of simply "being punished," the student is given a chance to explain him- or herself and consider the impact of his or her actions. The student is then held accountable by taking actions that repair the harm that he or she has done. These actions strengthen the learning community and reintegrate the student.

| Traditional Approach | Restorative Approach |
| --- | --- |
| School rules are broken | People and relationships are harmed |
| Justice focuses on establishing guilt | Justice identifies need and responsibility |
| Accountability=Punishment | Accountability=Understanding impact; repairing harm |
| Rules and intent outweigh whether outcome is positive or negative | Offender is responsible for behavior, repairing harm, and working toward positive outcomes |
| Limited opportunity for expressing remorse and making amends | Opportunity is offered to make amends and express remorse |

Adapted from *Fix School Discipline Toolkit for Educators*, Public Counsel, 2015

The International Institute for Restorative Practices (2015) offers the following set of potential restorative questions to use to address challenging behavior: *What happened? What were you thinking at the time? What have your thoughts been since? Who has been affected by what you did? In what way have they been affected? What do you think you need to do to make things right?* We would also suggest an amendment to this list, which is to incorporate the language of choice (see Practice #14) whenever possible (e.g., "Who has been affected by the choice you made?" "What's a choice you can make

*Asking questions helps students frame their actions as choices that impact their community.*

Deeper Support

to make things right?"). Restorative questions can be used as an intervention in the moment or as a more formal means of reflecting with the student (or students) involved in challenging behavior after a short time has passed.

Restorative questions can serve as a framework for students to moderate their own discussions and conflicts before they ever get to you—posting them in the classroom will support students to repair the harm on their own. Restorative practices can be thought of as an ethic and a mindset, as well as a set of concrete classroom "moves." Teachers who engage in restorative questions must participate in a significant shift from belief in the efficacy of isolation and punitive consequences to the view that all students hold themselves responsible for their behaviors best when they are in healthy relationship with others and can see how their actions affect them.

## What It Looks Like

The beauty of restorative questions is that they mitigate the dynamic of teachers accusing students of misbehavior. By asking questions (instead of accusing), the power dynamic shifts. Students become less defensive, and teachers are more likely to remain calm and neutral. Don't hesitate to follow up on more general questions with context-specific questions to assist students in seeing the full range of their actions and their results. For example, if some verbal taunting was directed at a student who is new to the school, specific questions that help students relate to that situation can help: "Have you ever been the new kid? Can you remember what that felt like?"

The question "What do you think you need to do to make things right?" is an opportunity for students to decide on and agree to specific, actionable next steps. This "consequence" could range from a simple apology to replacing something that was broken to something more abstract, like giving time back that was "stolen" from you by a disruptive student. You could get that time back by having the student clean up the room after school or collate papers—something you would normally spend time doing.

On the **elementary** level, young children do not always possess the skills yet to accurately verbalize the antecedents to their behavior. "Reflecting" statements—rephrasing what was said and summarizing the student's feelings compassionately—are useful here. "So Jackie took your pencil without asking this morning and broke it. That must have made you feel really angry. Is that why you yelled at her at recess?"

On the **secondary** level, restorative questions appeal to an adolescent's well-developed sense of what is "fair" and engages and honors their desire to become autonomous adults with a say in how their behavior is treated. Be aware that restorative questions may seem odd to older students used to a system of punishment, and they may brag or comment later that they "got away with" something. Don't take a statement like this at face value. The only yardstick for success in restorative practice is whether the student stops the behavior and repairs the harm.

## Why It Matters

Initial evidence from American schools suggests that restorative practices can reduce suspensions, decrease recidivism, and help address issues of equity in school discipline systems. Beyond this, restorative practice strongly supports the goals of the self-managed classroom. It emphasizes respect and collaboration by grounding itself in community norms, and by connecting real people—classmates and teachers—to the choices students make. It is an active approach to discipline, requiring the student to be thoughtful and participatory instead of a passive recipient of disciplinary decisions. Finally, the approach prioritizes a growth mindset by offering students an open opportunity to make amends and try again.

## Planning for Practice

- Make sure you have a transparent, fully explained, and active set of classroom norms (see Practice #5 for more on norms). Create a set of restorative questions that bring in the language of your norms whenever possible.

- "Frontload" the restorative questions with your students. Make the questions transparent, accessible, and well-known to all students through anchor charts, handouts, reminder cards, and/or discussion.

- Be fully prepared. Put a laminated card with your classroom's restorative questions behind your school badge, taped inside your grade book, or in your bag so that you always have it with you. Memorize key phrases such as, "Let's decide how you can stay on track with the norms for the rest of the period."

# Common Challenges: Practice #21: Restorative Practices, Part 1

| Challenges | Possible Solutions |
|---|---|
| This approach is too "soft." My kids won't respect my authority if I use it and will continue to push the boundaries and misbehave. | If this is a new disciplinary approach for your students, there may be a "learning curve" where their feedback to you is negative or they do indeed attempt to test your new system. Don't let negative comments deter you from giving restorative questions a chance. Don't give up after a few attempts, and remember that consequences are a part of this system: they're just implemented in a different way. |
| My student will not answer the restorative questions, or is answering them in a disrespectful way. | Frame the student's choice in terms of your norms. "Alice, you're choosing not to cooperate with me here, and our norms emphasize cooperation. I need you to respond to my question in a respectful way." It may take some time for students to get comfortable with the system. Offer Alice a constrained choice: "You can either answer my questions sincerely now or I can come back to you in 15 minutes. What's your choice?" |
| I can't stop teaching to use restorative questions or my other kids will start going off task as well. | Consider how you might think creatively about gaining the two or three minutes you need for a typical round of restorative questions. Can you leave your students in an independent work period for that long? Can you have a para-professional, a co-teacher, aide, or an ally come in and watch the students for a few minutes? Can you step into the hall but keep your body in the doorway so you can also watch your class? |
| The behaviors I am dealing with are too severe to handle with restorative questions. | In a situation where there is a truly egregious violation of a norm (such as a student shouting and swearing at a teacher), a large power imbalance (such as bullying), or where safety is a major issue (such as throwing large items or physical contact), deeper support is required. See Practices #20 and #21 on Challenging Behavior or Practice #23 on Restorative Circles for more guidance. |

**Deeper Support**

## Scenario to Discuss with Colleagues:

You've introduced the restorative questions to your students, but they seem skeptical. "How are kids going to behave when you don't punish them? They have to know what they did was wrong," one of your students volunteers. How do you respond?

# Restorative Practices, Part 2: Circles

**Repairing communities through communication**

---

*Tension had been building in this small-town Vermont high school for months. The school draws students from many towns across the region, and the school population reflects this diversity. Some students show up at school after hours of chores starting in the pre-dawn hours on their family dairy farms and sit beside kids who grew up in town.*

*Following a dramatic and violent fight between an African-American student from town and a white student from one of the surrounding rural villages, a restorative circle was scheduled. Because the fight was emblematic of rising tension in the town, bystander involvement from many other students, and deeply entrenched views held by both sides in the conflict, the circle involved the students, selected friends, family members, selected school staff, and community leaders, including the head of a local civil rights group.*

*Facilitating the circle was Jonathan Chandler, the in-school suspension room supervisor. Chandler was trained in restorative practices, and he knew the students involved in the fight as "frequent fliers" in his room. As in all restorative circles, Chandler introduced the ground rules, including such things as only speaking in turn, using "I" statements, and what he called "deep listening." He asked questions and orchestrated the speaking opportunities, artfully focused on helping each student hear the impact of the fight (and its antecedents) on the other.*

*The power of the circle was in the white student, Chelsea, and her friends and family better understanding what it felt like for Monique to be one of a very few African-American students in the school, always expected to act a certain way, often a victim of racial slurs, and for Monique to hear what it felt like for Chelsea to be teased by Monique and others for the way she dressed, where she lived, and how she talked. Importantly, their friends and family members also heard these heartfelt revelations, and all left the meeting with agreements in place for how they would communicate with each other. They also committed to being "upstanders" in the school, speaking up when their peers were disrespecting others and seeking positive and proactive solutions to problems.*

*Taking part in the circle allowed the girls to avoid suspension. More importantly, however, it gave them a safe place, surrounded by people who cared about them and could support them, to hear each other's points of view. The school did not become a perfect place after this, but the tension died down and Chelsea and Monique never fought again.*

## What It Is

A restorative circle is a formal gathering of a student (or students) who has broken the norms or rules in place in the community, those harmed by the student (often involving other students, teachers, parents, law enforcement, or other community members), and a neutral facilitator. In most cases this facilitator is an adult, often formally trained in restorative practices; in others, with extensive training and the appropriate conditions, neutral peer facilitators may run the circle. Allies such as friends, mentors, or witnesses may also be included. During a typical restorative circle, the neutral facilitator uses a formal protocol to ensure equal participation. Together the group acknowledges the extent of the harm, giving equal weight to the victim's needs and the offender's responsibilities, and they collectively decide upon appropriate ways for the offender to repair the harm he or she has caused.

Restorative circles have come to be used by criminal justice systems in many communities as a way to repair harm, rather than just punish offenders. Restorative justice is new enough in the United States that there is a range of approaches to the work, and consensus on best practice is still evolving. However, currently there is encouraging evidence that restorative practices have a positive influence on schools (Fronius and Petrosino, 2014).

## What It Looks Like

A restorative circle can be a powerful but intensely draining experience, requiring the navigation of strong emotions and deep intentional preparation. Schools that wish to introduce the concept to their communities should move slowly to ensure proper training and to document the procedures and structures that will guide the work. In time, as students and staff become accustomed to the practice, the term "circle" tends to be used as a verb and students begin to value the practice of "circling up" as a way to address conflict.

At the Greene School in Greenwich, Rhode Island, restorative circles (called "conference circles") can be requested by anyone in the community by filling out a "peer conference request form." At Greene School, peers lead the circles. The conference must have no fewer than three young people and two adults. Each participant has time to speak, and restorative questions (see Practice #22) are used as a foundation for conversation. A resolution to the conflict is arrived upon collaboratively. The process tends to take about thirty minutes and can only take place if the requester and the participants agree to the process. Minutes are kept and shared with the participants. A sample restorative conference

*Whether run by a student or an adult, restorative circles require skillful facilitation.*

protocol, adapted from the Greene School's Restorative Student Leadership Peer Conferencing form, can be found in Appendix B.

On the **elementary** level, younger students can be provided with a simple restorative conference form that allows them to draw or write their responses. Jennifer Vanderschure, assistant principal of K-8 Springville School in Beaverton, Oregon, reports that such forms provide a structure that allows even her kindergartners to take part in a restorative conference with the support of an adult. A sample of their form can be found in Appendix C.

On the **secondary** level, circles can be more complex events, as illustrated in the opening vignette. Often an adolescent is deeply invested in "being right," and it can take time for a student to take responsibility for his or her behavior in the way demanded by a restorative circle. However, older students may also possess stronger skills at articulating themselves and reflecting upon their actions. Circles with older students are also more likely to involve more complex incidents off school grounds.

On all levels, the restorative circle is typically positioned as the heart of a schoolwide model. It requires support from all staff members and quality training for at least a subset of staff in order for the practices to truly take root and succeed. The circle is not a silver bullet; it will have the best chance of success in schools with a commitment to a positive schoolwide culture.

## Why It Matters

Students who have regular practice in restorative circles and other restorative approaches understand fully that apologies are only part of the solution to rectifying poor choices. And certainly detentions and suspensions don't usually make things better. To really succeed at repairing the harm from their choices and restoring trust, students must collaboratively determine steps to fix the problem and then see them through. Restorative practices have the power to rewrite the narrative of discipline in schools and reduce traditional punitive measures such as suspensions and expulsions. Insofar as schools commit honestly to furthering the vision of justice, equity, and community in which restorative practice grounds itself, these practices can be a powerful step in improving disciplinary practices for our students and their welfare as whole, self-managed human beings.

## Planning for Practice

- Build consensus among the school community. Widespread buy-in is critical to the success of restorative practices. Start early and often and talk with your staff honestly about their concerns. Reach out to families and inform them about restorative practices.

- Initiate formal training. Successful schoolwide restorative practices cannot be implemented "on the fly." Seek out the resources in your community that will allow you to partner with experts in the restorative approach, train faculty and staff, and/or support the implementation long-term.

- Emphasize that this is a long-term change, requiring patience and perseverance. Although restorative practices often result in immediate reduction in suspensions, other markers of success, such as student buy-in and ownership of the process, willing participation of the wider community, and hard data on recidivism, are going to take longer to acquire. Since the approach can be a radical departure from typical disciplinary procedures, setbacks and mistakes can be expected in the early stages.

## Scenario to Discuss with Colleagues:

You would like to bring a practice of restorative circles to your school, but no one is trained and there's not a lot of support from the administration. How can you begin?

# Common Challenges: Practice #21: Restorative Practices, Part 2

| Challenges | Possible Solutions |
|---|---|
| A sincere apology in a restorative circle can be tough to achieve, especially with older students. | Time is required to address this challenge. Scaffolding questions in such a way that students have time to really hear from each other about how they were impacted can go a long way. What seems like initial disinterest may actually be a defense mechanism against what can be a deeply challenging and personal process for students. |
| Some school staff members may feel that students are getting away with something and not being punished. Securing their buy-in is challenging. | It is essential that teachers' concerns are identified accurately and addressed openly and honestly while preparing to implement restorative practices. Questions such as "Is this strict enough? Will it prevent the behavior? Are students being held accountable?" need to be honored and answered with facts, evidence, and pragmatic actions that support teachers. Collecting data on detentions and suspensions or student and parent testimonials may be a good place to start. It is also important for all involved to understand that it is not necessarily easier for students to take part in a restorative circle. Often it is a deep and challenging process that elicits a more lasting kind of accountability from students. |
| Privacy and/or legal concerns surface when working with restorative circles. | Circles ask participants to move beyond a typical disciplinary structure in which the identities of the students and staff involved, and the penalties administered, are kept completely private. Explicit agreement from participants for this shift must be obtained, and each circle must be thoroughly and formally documented. If there are legal considerations involved in the circle, such as with a student with an IEP, the implications must be thoroughly investigated and prepared for prior to the circle. In some cases a circle will not be appropriate due to privacy concerns. |
| It is harder to use a restorative circle with challenging students who may have special needs. | Circles with students with special needs are not impossible, but as with instruction, the circle must be carefully differentiated to meet the needs of the student in question. An autistic student may need to have restorative questions couched in very specific, black and white terminology. A student with an emotional disturbance may need to have concrete advice consistent with his psychological diagnosis on how to make amends for his actions. A neutral ally of the student who is deeply familiar with his IEP and his needs should be included in the circle at all times. In some cases a circle may not be appropriate. |
| There is no research-based consensus on what constitutes best practice in schoolwide restorative approaches, so it's hard to know if it's being done correctly. | There is no one "right" way to approach restorative practices in a school. The strong emphasis on relationship naturally dictates an approach that is highly specific to the culture and community of the school and the neighborhoods surrounding it. While it is important to seek out all we know about restorative practice and secure high-quality training, schools must also be prepared to create and support a practice that is deeply informed by its specific circumstances and needs. Data about reduced rates of discipline can help assure you that you're on track. |

Deeper Support

# Part 1: References

Charney, R. S. (2002). Teaching children to care: Classroom management for ethical and academic growth, K-8 (2nd ed.). Greenfield, MA: Northeast Foundation for Children.

Deci, E. L., and Flaste, R. (1996). Why we do what we do: The dynamics of personal autonomy. New York: Penguin.

Emmer, E., Sabornie, E., Evertson, C. M., and Weinstein, C. S., eds. (2013). Handbook of classroom management: Research, practice, and contemporary issues. New York: Routledge.

Fronius, T. & Petrosino, A. (2014, December 26). What do we know about restorative justice in schools? Retrieved from http://www.wested.org/news-events/restorative-justice-in-schools/.

Glasser, W. (1998). Choice theory: A new psychology of personal freedom. Harper Collins Publishers.

Glasser, W. (1990). The quality school: Managing students without coercion. New York: Harper and Row Publishers, Inc.

Grossmann, T. (2010). The development of emotion perception in face and voice during infancy. Restorative Neurology and Neuroscience, 28(2), 219-236.

International Institute for Restorative Practices (2015). What is restorative practices? Retrieved from: http://www.iirp.edu/what-is-restorative-practices.php#restorative_conference.

Pink, D. H. (2011). Drive: The surprising truth about what motivates us. New York: Riverhead Books.

Public Counsel (2015). Fix school discipline toolkit for educators. Retrieved from: http://fixschooldiscipline.orgeducator-toolkit/.

Rodgers, C. R., & Raider-Roth, M. B. (2006). Presence in teaching. Teachers and Teaching: Theory and Practice, 12(3), 265-287.

Steele, C. M. (2010). Whistling Vivaldi: And other clues to how stereotypes affect us (issues of our time). New York: W.W. Norton and Co.

# Part 2:
# Protocols and Strategies to Build Engagement, Collaboration, and Responsibility

# Part 2: Contents

## Focus on Checking for Understanding and Ongoing Assessment

## Focus on Building Academic Vocabulary

# Part 2: Introduction

## What Is a Protocol?

A protocol consists of agreed-upon, detailed guidelines for reading, recording, discussing, or reporting that ensure equal participation and accountability in learning.

The basic structure of a protocol includes the following:

- Organized steps for the procedure (what students must do)

- Time frames for each step (when students do each step and for how long)

- Norms for students (who participates and how they treat each other)

Just as with other classroom routines, a protocol structure must be explicitly taught and rehearsed the first time it is used. During successive uses, it will likely need to be re-rehearsed and reinforced multiple times.

## What Are the Purposes of the Protocols and Strategies Described in This Book?

**Collaboration and Discussion:** Protocols and strategies for collaboration and discussion invite students to value different perspectives and new insights. They make room for listening as well as contributing to discussion: guidelines for timekeeping, turn taking, and focusing help students develop the skills they need for productive discussions. Sentence stems for academic conversation and asking questions, norms for honoring diverse perspectives, and procedures for synthesizing contributions to a discussion hold individuals and groups accountable for pushing their thinking further. Discussion protocols and strategies can be embedded into a workshop or daily lesson, or they can be the entire lesson.

**Consultation and Decision Making:** Protocols and strategies for consultation and decision making allow students to feel safe to ask challenging questions, take intellectual and emotional risks, and problem-solve difficult situations. Such protocols and strategies build trust as students learn from each other and devise strategies and solutions collaboratively. In groups facing difficult challenges or struggling with conflict, these protocols and strategies are an essential tool for mediation, embracing diversity, and overcoming fear.

**Sharing and Presenting:** Protocols and strategies for sharing and presenting focus on fairness and equity. They enable all members of a group to see or hear the work done by individuals or small groups in an efficient way. Timekeeping and turn-taking norms are emphasized in order to maximize equity of sharing.

**Reading, Writing, and Annotating:** Protocols and strategies for reading, writing, and annotating hold all students accountable for building background knowledge about a topic, and for analyzing what they read by annotating the text with questions, comments, or summary language. These protocols and strategies also allow the teacher to assess which students are struggling with the text and may need further support for comprehension. Finally, they allow students to gather and organize their thoughts prior to discussion or writing.

**Building Vocabulary:** Protocols and strategies for building vocabulary make domain-specific and general academic vocabulary come alive for students through creating meaningful context, connecting new words to previous schema, and repeating shared use of the words. Vocabulary protocols and strategies help students understand that acquiring new words is an active process requiring interaction and application.

**Checking for Understanding:** Through self-checks, visual cues, and written reflection, checking-for-understanding strategies allow teachers and students to monitor understanding and adjust instruction accordingly. The repeated nature of these strategies allows students to develop the in-the-moment habit of actively reflecting on their learning.

*Protocols help students communicate and collaborate productively.*

**Critique:** Protocols and strategies for peer critique are essential for teaching students how to offer and receive kind, helpful, and specific feedback on writing or problem solving. They allow students to navigate the tricky social terrain of giving constructive criticism, while keeping them focused on sharing and supporting rigorous content.

## How Do the Protocols and Strategies in This Book Support Diverse Learners?

The protocols and strategies described here are a powerful way to scaffold learning for students who need extra assistance and also "push" those who need academic challenge. The structured, consistent nature of the protocols and strategies removes unnecessary procedural mystery from the classroom experience, allowing students to relax and focus on what matters. The collaborative nature of many of the protocols and strategies also builds in a natural level of challenge for advanced students, asking them to share, teach, and build on their knowledge through the contributions of their peers.

We especially encourage using speaking and listening protocols to scaffold the learning experience for students with disabilities and English language learners. These students, who may struggle with reading grade-level texts, will likely be able to contribute to conversations and discussions when using an appropriately prepared discussion protocol. The repeated academic and procedural language of protocols and strategies also facilitates language acquisition.

## How Can I Begin to Implement the Protocols and Strategies in This Book?

This publication provides teachers with the purpose, materials, procedure, and possible variations for each protocol and strategy. We offer some suggestions for the timing of certain protocol steps, but in most cases you will need to determine the timing based on the length of your lesson. Unless otherwise stated for the purposes of the protocol or strategy, it is assumed that the protocols and strategies also use texts and academic materials appropriate to the lesson at hand. These are the "basics" that will launch any teacher successfully into using the protocols and strategies in the classroom.

Also, consider the following steps when introducing and implementing these protocols and strategies:

**Think small.** Teachers are often most successful when they choose three to five protocols and strategies that can focus and anchor their instruction.

**Be clear.** Providing table tents or an anchor chart with the bulleted steps of the protocol or strategy, or task cards that describe each person's role, will help students stay on task.

**Be consistent.** Having consistent routines for independent reading time, discussion, or collaboration will allow students to learn more effectively and, importantly, to develop the habit of taking responsibility for their own learning and for contributing to the collective understanding of the group.

**Always debrief.** The debrief is an essential conclusion to any protocol or strategy. It allows the purpose of the protocol or strategy to be completely transparent to the students, re-emphasizes the learning targets associated with the protocol or strategy, and formalizes both student and teacher reflection on whether and how the protocol or strategy was successful.

## What Do These Protocols and Strategies Look Like in Action?

The majority of the practices in Part 1 and some in Part 2 are accompanied by videos of the practice in action in schools across the United States. All videos can be accessed at: http://ELeducation.org/classroom-management-videos.

**Disclaimer:**

Protocols and strategies like those described in this book are used every day in classrooms all over the United States. In many cases, it's quite difficult to determine the origin of a particular protocol. We are not the creators of most of the protocols featured in this guide, but we have organized and modified a collection that we have found to be particularly useful based on our 20-plus years of working with teachers around the country.

We are grateful to other organizations and authors that have compiled protocols and strategies and made them available for educators to use: in particular, The School Reform Initiative, The National School Reform Faculty, The Reading Educator, and the authors of *The Power of Protocols: An Educator's Guide to Better Practice*.

# General Protocols
# and Strategies

**Protocols and strategies like those that follow have teamwork at their heart: they emphasize not only acquiring and refining knowledge, but the shared and social nature of constructing and applying that knowledge. These collaborative protocols and strategies span the content spectrum from science to ELA; most will work in any content area.**

# Admit and Exit Tickets

## Purpose

At the end of class, students write on 3x5 cards or slips of paper an important idea they learned, a question they have, a prediction about what will come next, a self-assessment of their own progress, or a thought about the lesson for the day. Alternatively, students turn in such a response at the start of the next day—based on either the learning from the day before or the previous night's homework. These quick writes can be used to assess students' knowledge or to make decisions about next teaching steps or points that need clarifying. This reflection helps students to focus as they enter the classroom or solidifies learning before they leave.

## Materials

- 3x5 cards, sticky notes, or half sheets of paper with teacher-chosen material copied onto them

- Writing utensils

## Procedure

1. For 3–5 minutes at the end of class (or at the start of the next one), have students jot responses to the reading or lesson on 3x5 cards or on a simple assessment you have designed.

2. Keep the response options simple, e.g., "Jot down one thing you learned and one question you have."

3. Don't let the cards become a grading burden. Glance over them for a quick assessment and to help you with planning for next learning needs. These are simple, quick writes, not final drafts.

4. After studying the "deck," you might pick out a few typical/unique/thought-provoking cards to spark discussion.

5. Cards could be typed up, anonymously if desired, to share with the whole group so they can help with summarizing, synthesizing, or looking for important ideas. It is a good idea to let students know ahead of time that this will be done, as they may put more effort into the write-up. When typing, edit for spelling and grammar.

## Variations

- 3-2-1: Have students write three of something, two of something, then one of something. For example, students might explain three things they learned, two areas in which they are confused, and one thing about which they'd like to know more or one way the topic can be applied. The criteria for listing items are up to the needs of the teacher and the lesson, but it's important to make the category for listing three items easier than the category for listing one.

# Anchor Charts:
# Making Thinking Visible

## Purpose

Anchor Charts build a culture of literacy in the classroom by making thinking visible: recording content, strategies, processes, cues, and guidelines during the learning process. Posting Anchor Charts keeps relevant and current learning accessible to students: to remind them of prior learning and to enable them to make connections as new learning happens. Students refer to the charts and use them as tools as they answer questions, expand ideas, or contribute to discussions and problem solving in class.

## Materials

- Poster or chart paper

- Dark, easily visible markers

## Procedure

1.  Build Anchor Charts with students to capture strategies and key ideas.

2.  Let students add ideas to Anchor Charts as they apply new learning, discover interesting ideas, or develop useful strategies for problem solving or skill application.

3.  Also add to Anchor Charts as you debrief student work time, recording important facts, useful strategies, steps in a process, or quality criteria.

4.  Anchor Charts should contain only the most relevant or important information.

5.  Post only those charts that reflect current learning and avoid distracting clutter—hang charts on clotheslines or set them up in distinct areas of the room; rotate the charts that are displayed to reflect the most useful content.

6.  Charts should be neat and organized, with simple icons and graphics to enhance their usefulness (avoid distracting, irrelevant details and stray marks).

7.  Organization should support ease of understanding and be varied based on purpose.

8.  Charts are best in simple, darker earth tones that are easily visible (dark blue, dark green, purple, black, and brown—use lighter colors for accents only).

## Variations

- Students can create Anchor Charts during small-group and independent work to share with the rest of the class.

- For a wide variety of other Anchor Charts, explore www.readinglady.com/mosaic/tools/AnchorChartPhotographsfromKellyandGinger/.

**Protocols and Strategies**

# Annotating Text

## Purpose

Annotating text goes beyond underlining, highlighting, or making symbolic notations or codes on a given text. Annotation includes adding purposeful notes, key words and phrases, definitions, and connections tied to specific sections of text. Annotating text promotes student interest in reading and gives learners a focused purpose for writing. It supports readers' ability to clarify and synthesize ideas, pose relevant questions, and capture analytical thinking about text. Annotation also gives students a clear purpose for actively engaging with text and is driven by the goals or learning targets of the lesson. It helps learners comprehend difficult material and engage in what Probst (1988) describes as "dialogue with the text."

## Materials

- Writing utensil (colored if desired)

- Optional: sticky notes

- Optional: Applications such as Notability, which allow you to annotate PDFs and electronic text

## Procedure

1.  Define the purpose for annotation based on learning target(s) and goals. Some examples include:

- Locating evidence in support of a claim

- Identifying main idea and supporting details

- Analyzing the validity of an argument or counterargument

- Determining author's purpose

- Giving an opinion, reacting, or reflecting

- Identifying character traits/motivations

- Summarizing and synthesizing

- Defining key vocabulary

- Identifying patterns and repetitions

- Making connections/making predictions

2.  Model how to annotate text:

- Select one paragraph of text from the reading and highlight or underline key word(s) or phrase(s) related to the lesson's purpose, using the "think aloud" strategy to share with students why you marked certain selections of the passage.

- Based on your "think aloud," model writing an annotated note in the margin, above underlined words and phrases, or to the side of text.

3.  Distribute the materials students will need, such as books, articles, highlighters, and pencils, or cue up the appropriate text and software on student-used technology (such as an iPad). *continued*

4. Practice annotating with students, choosing another paragraph/section of text and reminding them of the purpose. Have them highlight, underline, or circle relevant words and phrases in the reading and add annotations. Have students share what they selected and explain their annotations. Repeat over several classes or as necessary, working on gradual release toward student independence.

## Variations

- Annotations can look very different while accomplishing the same purpose—engaging deeply with text—depending on the focus of the lesson and the needs and preferences of the learners.

### References

Porter-O'Donnell, C. (2004, January 1). Beyond the yellow highlighter: Teaching annotation skills to improve reading comprehension. *English Journal*, 82-89.

Probst, R. (1988, January 1). Dialogue with a text. *English Journal*, 32-28.

Wolfe, J., & Neuwirth, C. (2001, January 1). From the margins to the center: The future of annotation. *Journal of Business and Technical Communication*, 333-371.

Protocols and Strategies

# Back-to-Back and Face-to-Face

## Purpose

This protocol provides a method for sharing information and gaining multiple perspectives on a topic through partner interaction. It can be used for reviewing and sharing academic material, as a personal "ice breaker," or as a means of engaging in critical thinking about a topic of debate.

## Materials

- Questions to be asked between student partners, prepared in advance

## Procedure

1. Have students find a partner and stand back-to-back with him or her, being respectful of space.

2. Give students a question or statement that they will share a response to with a partner.

3. Have students think about what they want to share and how they might best express themselves.

4. When you say, "Face-to-face," have students turn, face their partners, and decide who will share first if you have not indicated that a certain person should go first.

5. Have students listen carefully when their partner is speaking and be sure to make eye contact with him or her.

6. When given the signal, students should find a new partner, stand back-to-back, and wait for the new question, statement, etc.

7. This may be repeated for as many rounds as needed/appropriate.

## Variations

- Partners may be assigned.

- Partners may also stay together for the length of the protocol.

- The class may stand in two concentric circles with one circle rotating to a new back-to-back and face-to-face partner for each new question or prompt.

- The protocol may be repeated several times in a row with the same partners to give students multiple opportunities to check their understanding and receive information from their partners.

Protocols and Strategies

# Building Background Knowledge (BBK) Workshop

## Purpose

This protocol demonstrates how quickly people can become interested in a topic, build knowledge, and use that knowledge to become better and more informed readers of complex text. The protocol adapts easily to content in many disciplines, and the design ensures that all students read, think, and contribute. The protocol is particularly useful in introducing a topic because it fosters curiosity and builds in immediate feedback about learning. A BBK workshop, especially if it includes close reading of a common text, may comprise an entire class period or even multiple class periods (introducing different texts on successive days). When conducted and debriefed for educators, the protocol heightens awareness of key instructional and grouping practices.

## Materials

- Chart paper
- Colored markers
- Various texts on a related topic

## Procedure

1.  Choose a topic and find several texts as described in the following steps.

2.  Use a grouping strategy to shift students into groups of four or five.

3.  To each group, give a set of four different-colored markers, a piece of chart paper, texts, and loose-leaf paper.

4.  Share a "mystery text" with the whole class: Choose a relevant short text, poem, political cartoon, photograph, song, graph, map, etc., that sparks students' curiosity about the topic. Display or provide copies of the text (remove the title if it gives away the topic).

5.  Activate and share background knowledge:

    - Ask students to write down what they know about the topic of the mystery text.

    - Ask students, in their small groups, to number off, then share what they know about the topic, being sure that each person has a chance to speak.

    - Ask students to create a web or visualization of their collective knowledge/understanding of the topic on a piece of chart paper using just one of the colored markers. Number 1 in the group is the recorder for this part.

6.  Provide a "common text"—an article or essay on the topic that is interesting, offers a solid introduction to the topic, and provides multiple perspectives. All students read this article.                     *continued*

7. Ask students to text-code (use symbols, letters/numbers, and shorthand to annotate) the article with "N" for new information.

8. Ask students to add their new knowledge to their web using a different color of marker. Number 2 in the group is the recorder for this part.

9. Distribute "expert texts": Hand out a different text on the topic to each member of the group. This is an ideal time to differentiate texts if needed.

10. Again, ask students to text-code for new information.

11 After everyone has read, have each student share new knowledge with his or her group and capture key points on the chart paper using the third color. Number 3 is the recorder for this part.

12. Have on hand extra texts or additional media (drawings, maps, photos, graphs, etc.) for those who finish early.

13. Return to the mystery text. Reread the initial text or display it again.

14. Ask students to go back to where they had initially written about the mystery text in their journals; have students discuss what they now think about the mystery text, then record their new thinking on their web. Number 4 is the recorder for this part and uses a fourth color of marker.

15 Contrast the first and second reading/showing of the mystery text: "What was it like to hear the mystery text the second time?" "What made the experience so different?"

16. Ask a general question about what the process was like to read successive articles. Did they know much about the topic before? Had they been curious about the topic? What inspired their curiosity? If there is time, consider asking a question with four possible responses and having students with like responses group together in the four corners of the room. Ask follow-up questions for the groups to discuss together.

## Variations

- Boxing (see figure below): Draw a box to create a fairly wide frame for the poster. Draw a smaller box inside the first. The boxes will create three spaces for representing learning. In the frame, have the group write their prior knowledge, or possibly what they want to learn about the topic. Next, read and discuss to build knowledge. Inside the second box, write about new learning. Finally, in the middle, either write a summary of the learning or create a graphic illustration that synthesizes the group's understanding of the topic.

- Combine this protocol with a Poster Session to share webs or boxes among members of the class.

- Assign a "Roving Reporter" role to one or more students, having them view and report on group ideas to the rest of the class.

## Boxing

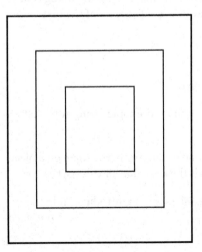

# Chalk Talk

## Purpose

A Chalk Talk is a written protocol in which students respond in writing, in a central place (such as a piece of chart paper), to an important, open-ended question—silently. It is a way to promote discussion and awareness of issues, perspectives, or academic challenges and to demonstrate knowledge of a topic. Chalk Talks bypass the social roadblocks that often impede classroom communication and ensure that all voices are heard. A Chalk Talk is also an excellent way to promote awareness of patterns and problems, as students reflect on the information they have shared.

## Materials

- Chart paper

- Markers (to write questions in bold letters on chart paper)

- Colored writing utensils, one per student

- Optional: sticky notes

- Anchor chart for protocol norms

## Procedure

1. Formulate one or more important, open-ended questions that will provoke comments and responses.

2. Write the questions or topics on separate pieces of chart paper in bold marker. Post the charts on the wall or on desks so that all students have ready access to them.

3. Give each student a different-colored pencil or marker.

4. Explain the Chalk Talk protocol and answer any student questions.

5. Set up norms for the Chalk Talk:

  - This technique works only if everyone is writing and responding throughout the designated time period and remains silent throughout.

  - Make it clear that everyone is responsible for writing a comment, reading others' comments, and responding to at least one to three comments on every chart paper.

  - No one should sit down until the time period is over.

  - Opinions must be freely expressed and honored. No personal attacks are allowed.

  - Comments should be thoughtful and further the discussion.

6. Allow 10 to 20 minutes for the Chalk Talk. It's helpful to walk around, read, and gently point students to interesting comments. All writing and responding is done in silence.

7. Search for patterns. In pairs, students should read through all the postings, search for patterns and themes (or "notice and wonder"), and record those patterns on a piece of paper. This part takes about 5 minutes and is not silent.

*continued*

8. Conduct a whole-group share. Pairs should report out patterns and themes, round-robin style, until all perceptions are shared.

## Variations

- Have students write on and post sticky notes instead of responding directly on the chart paper, so chart paper can be reused for multiple classes if needed.

- Adding an element of optional text coding (e.g., students placing a star next to comments they agree with or a question mark on comments they don't understand) can deepen the written discussion.

- Have students respond to the questions in collaborative groups, with each group using a different color marker. In this variation, students do not work silently—discussion among group members is key.

- Technological versions of Chalk Talk (such as commenting on a teacher-owned blog) may further students' interest and engagement. However, bear in mind that switching the format of Chalk Talk to a technological forum will require different guidelines, routines, and piloting to proactively plan for possible challenges.

### References

Adapted from: Original by Hilton Smith, Foxfire Fund; adapted by Marylyn Wentworth

# Dance Card

## Purpose

Dance Card sets up students with multiple, but consistent, partners for work across a unit, reducing the amount of energy and work it takes for the teacher to assign partners. It allows students autonomy and choice in whom they pick for partner work. Students of all ages are familiar with the idea of partnering off for dancing, although teachers may wish to explain the metaphor of the historical "dance card."

## Materials

- Three index cards per student, each in a different color, easily distinguishable from the others

- Recording sheet for Dance Card names, one per student, to be kept throughout the unit

## Procedure

1. Give the three colored index cards to each student. Students write their name on each card.

2. At your signal to "dance," students find one partner to trade their blue card with. This pair becomes blue "dance card" partners. Then direct students to do the same with their red card, green card, etc. (or whatever colors are being used). Optionally, for fun or to fill a need for movement, students can "dance" over to do their trade, do a quick dance after the trade (e.g., the chicken dance), or you can play music during this transition. Remind students that they can only pair up together for one of their colors. They must end up with as many different partners as they have colored index cards.

3. Once all rounds are complete, students fill in the recording sheet with the names of their three different partners.

4. At the end of the protocol, each student has different partners for discussion to be used repeatedly, but with variety, throughout the unit. When it is time for students to pair up, you can direct them to their "blue dance partner," "red dance partner," and so on.

## Variations

- This protocol can involve any number of partners. Colors are used for ease of repeating the protocol, but you may choose to add names to the dance cards (e.g., "Sudanese desert"; "the refugee camp"; "the box car") pertinent to the unit of study. If you wish to pre-assign a partnership for any reason, fill out two cards of matching color with the names you want matched and give them to the appropriate students before the dancing begins.

Protocols and Strategies

# Final Word

## Purpose

This protocol is designed to help students understand the meaning of a text, particularly to see how meaning can be constructed and supported by the ideas of others. This protocol is especially helpful when people struggle to understand their reading; the shared nature of the protocol allows students to not only present their ideas in a nonthreatening oral fashion, but also to benefit from the knowledge acquired by other members of their group. The roles of timekeeper and facilitator are especially important to this protocol and may require some training and practice for students: how to keep time politely but firmly; how to keep people on task respectfully; and so on.

## Materials

- Optional: recording form for purpose of reading text (e.g., main idea and details, "gist," answering a predetermined prompt)

## Procedure

1. Have each group select a timekeeper and facilitator.

2. Students then number off in the order that they will present.

3. All students may read the same text, or students may read different texts on a common topic for a jigsaw effect. Text selection is a critical step.

4. Students read silently and text-code, or fill out a recording form. They mark passages for discussion clearly so they can quickly locate them later.

5. The presenter shares a designated number of passages and his or her thinking about them. Be sure to indicate how long the presenter should speak so there will be enough time for each group member.

6. Each student comments on what was shared, in less than 1 minute each. Interesting similarities and differences in interpretations will arise as other students share their thinking without judgment or debate.

7. The presenter gets the final word, sharing how his or her thinking evolved after listening to others or re-emphasizing what was originally shared. The presenter may change his or her perspective, add to it, or stick with original ideas without criticism.

8. Follow steps 4-6 with each additional student taking the role of presenter.

## Variations

- Encourage students to write down their thoughts before speaking if needed, so their comments are focused and efficient.

- To promote critical thinking, design prompts for the discussion that ask students to include reasons for selecting a particular passage and evidence that supports a particular point.

### References

Adapted from: Original by Jennifer Fischer-Mueller and Gene Thompson-Grove

# Fishbowl

## Purpose

The Fishbowl is a peer-learning strategy in which some students are in an outer circle and one or more are in the center. In all Fishbowl activities, students in both the inner and outer circles have roles to fulfill. Students in the center model a particular practice or strategy. Students in the outer circle act as observers and may assess the interaction of the center group. Fishbowls can be used to assess comprehension, to assess group work, to encourage constructive peer assessment, to discuss issues in the classroom, or to model specific protocols such as literature circles or Socratic Seminars.

## Materials

- Chairs or desks for each student arranged in two concentric circles

- Checklist or reflection questions for the outer circle students, depending on the instructional need

## Procedure

1. Arrange chairs in the classroom in two concentric circles. The inner circle may be only a small group or even partners.

2. Explain the activity to the students and ensure that they understand the roles they will play.

3. You may either inform those who will be on the inside circle ahead of time, so they can be prepared, or just tell them as the activity begins. This way everyone will come better prepared.

4. The group in the inner circle interacts using a discussion protocol or the "script" of a role play.

5. Give each student in the outer circle a list of aspects of group interaction they should silently observe and comment on—for example, whether the group members use names to address each other, take turns, or let everyone's voice be heard.

6. Make sure all students have turns being in both the inside and the outside circle at some point, though they don't all have to be in both every time you do a Fishbowl activity.

## Variations

- Each person in the outside circle can have one opportunity during the Fishbowl to freeze or stop the inside students. This person can then ask a question or share an insight.

- Have each student in the outer circle observe one student in the inner circle (you may have to double, triple, or quadruple up)—for example, tallying how many times the student participates or asks a question.

# Idea Shop

## Purpose

Idea Shop allows students to create and share knowledge and meaning socially and collaboratively. It also encourages students to think critically about the quality of ideas. Students understand the metaphor of shopping, thinking critically about "purchases," and moving from store to store. This protocol allows them to enter into an "Idea Shop" to buy and sell ideas from their classmates.

## Materials

- Numbered or named Idea Shop signs/tent cards/posters/sticky notes

- Idea Shop recording form, one per student, labeled with Idea Shop numbers or names, and with large spaces for recording

- Criteria for a "strong" academic idea—to be determined by the subject matter at hand and the teacher

## Procedure

1. Set up physical spaces labeled as "Idea Shops," each one with a different number or name. The number of shops depends upon how many people you wish to work in a collaborative group.

2. Explain the protocol. Criteria for a strong idea—worthy of "buying"—are discussed. Sets limits for shoppers: 10 "shops" for pairs in a class of 20 students, for example.

3. Students are asked to enter a "shop" at random and share ("sell") two or more of their ideas on the topic at hand with their partner or group. Students then "buy" whatever idea they think works best or is strongest from the speaker by recording it on their recording form.

4. At your signal, students then move to a different shop and repeat the process until their recording form is filled.

## Variations

- In the case of quizzing or practice, correct answers may be used to "buy" some very small token of acknowledgement from the quizzing student: a written star on their paper, sticker, stamp, etc.

# Infer the Topic

## Purpose

This protocol offers students a chance to work together to uncover the heart of a larger concept before they begin to study a new topic. Students also get a chance to experience the ways an inference can change as they take in new information. The protocol allows students to draw on their own background knowledge and work in a fun, collaborative environment with new information from a variety of peers to uncover meaning.

## Materials

- Images and/or artifacts related to the topic of study

- Optional: recording form for each student to write down inferences

## Procedure

1. Locate images and/or artifacts with and without key words/quotes related to the concept. The goal is for students to infer what is happening in the image. Images can range from concrete to abstract.

2. Have students select an image and record their inference about the new topic of study.

3. Students mingle about the room and stop when prompted, facing a partner.

4. In one minute or less, students view each other's images, discuss, and record a new inference about the upcoming topic of study.

5. Students mingle about the room again, this time with the partner they were just sharing with. When prompted, partners stop, facing another set of partners.

6. All four students share their images/artifacts and inferences, discuss further, and make a new inference about what the new topic of study could be.

7. Students gather as a whole group, each displaying their image for all to see. The teacher invites a few to share their images/artifacts and their inferences about the upcoming topic.

8. After a few have shared, the teacher reveals the topic of study as well as the guiding questions and big ideas.

## Variations

- Vary partner instructions or adapt numbers of partners or rounds.

- To monitor understanding and support students struggling to infer the images/artifacts' meaning, teachers can circulate and give these students a "ticket" in the form of a colored card or sticky note. At an opportune time, call a meeting of an invitational group for anyone with tickets or anyone who is struggling.

# Interactive Word Wall

## Purpose

An Interactive Word Wall is an organized collection of words (and sometimes phrases) displayed on a wall or other space in the classroom. An Interactive Word Wall in a classroom is a powerful instructional tool: it makes words visible and easily referenced and manipulated; supports the teaching of key words and subject-specific terminology; and encourages independence in reading and writing.

## Materials

- Large index cards, strips of paper, or a tag board for writing and manipulating words

- Optional: an illustration, photograph, or object on or next to particular words, to support students' learning through the aid of visual cues

## Procedure

The "interactive" part is critical; actively engaging with the words will support student learning. There are many ways to interact with Word Walls. Some interactions are quick and can occur on a daily basis. Other interactions can constitute an entire lesson. Suggested activities include the following:

1. Categorize and classify: Have students classify the terms.

2. Compare and contrast: Create categories to compare and contrast.

3. Concept map: Use the words to create a concept map.

4. Conceptual model: Use the words to construct a conceptual model that represents student thinking or scientific phenomena.

5. Create descriptions: Use the words to describe concepts.

6. Contextualize use: Challenge the students to use some or all of the words in a short-answer quiz.

7. Label diagrams: Use the words on the wall to label student diagrams and illustrations.

## Variations

- Zoom In (Concept Map Approach): Pull cards from your Word Wall or write one word/phrase per card. Use a limited number of cards, perhaps ten to fifteen, or fewer for younger students. Also create cards with one-way and two-way arrows. Use the floor or magnets and a magnetic board to display the cards and group the students around the words. (Modification: Give each student his or her own set of word cards.) Ask a student or a pair of students to arrange two or three cards in a way that connects them or makes a model of the terms and to explain what they are doing as they place the words. Observers may ask questions once the connection or model is created. Repeat with another student or pair of students.

### References

Bear, D.R., Invernizzi, M., Templeton, S., & Johnston, R. (2000). *Words their way: Word Study for phonics, vocabulary, and spelling*. Upper Saddle River, NJ: Prentice-Hall.

Morris, D. (1981). Concept of word: A developmental phenomenon in the beginning reading and writing process. *Language Arts*, 58, 659-668.

Protocols and Strategies

# Jigsaw

## Purpose

This protocol allows small groups to engage in effective, time-efficient comprehension of a longer text. Having every student read every page or section may not be necessary. Students can divide up the text, become an expert in one section, hear oral summaries of the others, and still gain a summative understanding of the material.

## Materials

- Text divided into manageable sections, corresponding to the number of students in a group

- Optional: recording form for observations/thoughts and/or text-dependent questions

## Procedure

1. Divide the chosen text into manageable sections.

2. Arrange students into groups so that there is the same number of people in each group as there are sections to read. Assign the sections to each member.

3. Students read their section independently, looking for key points, new information, or answers to questions.

4. Each member in turn shares his or her important points or summaries of the text.

5. Have students independently write or reflect on their own understanding after the discussion.

## Variations

- Use Jigsaw to have students read several shorter texts, one per group.

- Jigsaw texts, if several are used, can be differentiated according to student need.

- Have students work with a single text in topic-alike groups first to become experts on a text. Then, redistribute the groups so that each student can serve as an expert on the text he or she read in the previous group.

### References

Aronson, E. (1978). *The Jigsaw classroom*. Beverly Hills, CA: Sage Publications.

McDonald, J., Mohr, N., Dichter, A., & McDonald, E.C. (2007). *The power of protocols: An educator's guide to better practice.* New York, NY: Teachers College Press.

**Protocols and Strategies**

# Mystery Quotes

## Purpose

This protocol offers students a chance to work together to uncover the meaning of a mystery quote/passage/image before they read more about it or work more deeply with inference as a critical thinking strategy. It allows students to work in a fun, collaborative environment to use new information from a partner and to draw on their own background knowledge to uncover meaning. This protocol also asks students to put things in their own words, to compare text to experience, and to work with a variety of partners.

## Materials

- Quotes, phrases, sentences, or words from the text copied onto strips or index cards, one per student

## Procedure

1. Decide on quotes, phrases, sentences, or words directly from the text to copy onto strips or index cards.

2. Don't paraphrase the text. You may omit words to shorten a sentence, but don't change the words.

3. Have students select a quote/passage and, without revealing it to a partner, tape it on his or her back. (Students may look for a partner who "fits" the quote, or selections can be randomly determined.)

4. Students mingle about the room and stop when prompted, facing a new partner.

5. In one minute or less, students read each other's quotes and think about one hint to give the partner about his or her quote.

6. In one minute total, each student shares a hint about the partner's quote.

7. Students mingle about the room again and stop when prompted, facing another partner.

8. Students take time to read the quote and think about a story that exemplifies or reminds them of it.

9. Each student shares the story related to the partner's quote in a set time frame.

10. Continue additional rounds as desired, offering a range of possible prompts, such as, "Create a metaphor or simile to describe the quote," "Give an example of the idea in the quote in action," etc.

11. Bring the whole group together to each share a final inference about the meaning of their quote.

12. Students then guess which quote has been taped to their back from a list of all quotes and share how their inferences about the quote compare to the actual text.

13. Discuss strategies students used for inferring and how the quotes deepened or introduced knowledge.

## Variations

- Students carry index cards with them, recording their current thinking about the essence of their quotes.

- Vary partner instructions or adapt numbers of partners or rounds.

- For nonreaders, use images with or without key words. The goal is to infer what is happening in the image on their back. Images can range from concrete to abstract. It is also possible to divide the class into readiness groups and have one group work separately with sentences while the other uses images.

# Poster Session

## Purpose

Poster sessions are a well-known, authentic means for researchers to share their work and knowledge at academic conferences. Poster sessions naturally involve elements of questioning and noticing, and can easily be adapted for both presenting and sharing student work and "launching" topics through observing and asking questions about artifacts and photographs. Critical thinking, dialogue, and individual responsibility for learning are given emphasis.

## Materials

- Chart paper
- Markers for each student
- Study and/or academic assignment materials
- Listener score cards

## Procedure

1. Divide students into groups—the size of the groups will vary depending on how the topic can be divided, size of class, age of students, and so on.

2. Assign each group a specific segment of a broad topic and/or a collaborative academic assignment (e.g., one group might be assigned the legislative branch of government, another the executive branch, and another the judicial branch).

3. Have students move into groups, provide each group with materials to further enhance their study of the topic and/or complete the academic assignment, and have each group research the topic and/or complete the assignment.

4. Explain the assignment or study.

5. Explain that each group will use their prior knowledge along with their new knowledge to create a poster or other visual with key points that each person in the group will use to teach others in the class. Be clear that each person has to understand the text and images on the poster in order to present the information effectively.

6. Students complete the assignment or study, and their posters.

7. Have student groups post the work around the room or in the hallway.

8. Regroup students so each new group has at least one member from the previously established groups.

9. Give specific directions: at which poster each group will start, that they will rotate through all the posters in their groups, and how much time they will have at each poster. Explain that the speaker at each poster is the person(s) who participated in its creation. Specify the kinds of information the speaker should present to the group—a summary, a synthesis, or an important question.

10. Explain what the listeners' jobs are as they rotate from poster to poster: to ask their presenters a certain number of questions and record the answers on their scorecards. The total number of questions expected is for the entire rotation, not for a single presenter (e.g., Listeners must ask three questions TOTAL throughout the rotation).

12. Groups rotate, listen to the presenter, and ask questions as specified on their scorecards.

*continued*

Protocols and Strategies

## Variations

- Use Poster Sessions to introduce and reflect on new material and build background knowledge, as in the beginning of a unit or lesson. For example, several quotes, photographs, or video clips can be set up around the room, while students rotate in groups and reflect on what they encounter. In this variation, "presenters" are students who have been introduced to the posters ahead of time and act as "experts" on the poster.

- Use Poster Sessions to display and share end products (writing, artwork, anchor charts, and so on) of group work.

# Praise, Question, Suggestion

Video Available

## Purpose

This protocol can be used to offer critique and feedback in preparation for revision of work. It should be used after a draft of what will become a finished product is completed. This process will help students see what is working and then ask questions and offer suggestions, leading to revision and improvement. It is important for students to understand that the focus should be on offering feedback that is beneficial to the author. Explicit modeling is necessary for this protocol to be used successfully.

## Materials

- Product descriptors and rubrics

- Revision checklist or questions

- Anchor chart for protocol norms (see Practice #15: Critique and Feedback in Part 1 for suggested norms)

## Procedure

1. Provide product descriptors and rubrics as clear guidelines of the expectations and criteria for the piece of work that will be critiqued. If the work is written, providing copies for the critique group is helpful.

2. As a whole group, create or refer to a list of revision questions based on the criteria for the piece of work.

3. Model the procedure with the whole group before allowing small independent feedback groups.

4. Have students work in groups of two to five.

5. The first student presents or reads the draft of her piece. She may ask peers to focus on a particular revision question or two that she is struggling with from the list.

6. Peers first focus on what is praiseworthy or working well. Praise needs to be specific. Simply saying, "This is good" doesn't help the author. Comments such as, "I notice that you used descriptive picture captions" or "You have a catchy title that makes me want to read your piece" are much more useful.

7. Next, ask questions and offer helpful suggestions: "This part is unclear. I wonder if it would be better to change the order of the steps?" or "I can't tell the setting. Maybe you could add some details that would show the reader where it is taking place?" or "I wonder if adding a graph to highlight your data would be effective."

8. Feedback should relate to the revision questions identified by the group or presenter.

9. After each member of the group has offered feedback, the presenter discusses which suggestions she wants to implement and thanks the group.

10. Others then present their work in turn and cycle through the feedback process.

## Variations

- Give time guidelines for each part of the protocol so students don't get "stuck" on a particular type of feedback.

- Feedback can be written on sticky notes and given to the author.

# Rank-Talk-Write

## Purpose

This protocol, adapted from Pause, Star, Rank in Himmele and Himmele's *Total Participation Techniques* (2011), allows students to actively review their notes about new concepts as well as analyze and discuss the importance of key ideas they identify.

## Materials

- White board/chart paper/poster paper

- Writing implements

- Notepaper

## Procedure

1.  During or after reading a text, students independently write a summary sentence for each key idea or concept they identify.

2.  Students then rank the summary sentences in order of importance ("1" next to most important, "2" and "3" next to the second and third most important summaries of each concept).

3.  In groups, students share out the concepts they ranked, explaining why they ranked each concept as they did in terms of importance.

4.  Each group determines which concept they think is most important and discusses the best summary sentence for that idea or concept.

5.  A scribe from the group writes the summary sentence of the idea or concept on a white board, piece of chart paper, or large blank page.

6.  Small groups share their summary sentence with the large group.

## Variations

- Provide the summary sentences to be ranked for the students.

- Provide the summary sentences to be ranked for the students, and include at least one that is inaccurate or off the mark as a formative assessment of how students respond to the erroneous information.

### References

Himmele, P., & Himmele, W. (2011). *Total participation techniques: Making every student an active learner.* Alexandria, VA: ASCD.

Protocols and Strategies

# Say Something

## Purpose

This is a paired reading strategy that provides students with a structure for reflecting on a portion of text. Students think out loud, listen closely to each other, and develop shared understanding of the text. The time frame for this protocol is intentionally brief.

## Materials

- A common text

## Procedure

1. For the portion of text students will read, choose the stopping point(s) or have partners decide together how far they will read silently before stopping to "say something."

2. Describe what students will say to each other when they reach the stopping point: it might be a question, a brief summary, a key point, an interesting idea, or a new connection.

3. Model. Provide one or two examples of what a student might say at each stopping point. Be sure that the modeled statements or questions are succinct, thoughtful, and related to the text.

4. Have students begin reading the text.

5. Once partners have reached the chosen stopping point, they each in turn "say something" to each other about the text.

6. Have partners continue the process, stopping at each chosen stopping point, until the selection is completed.

7. After a designated time, engage the whole group in a discussion of the text.

## Variations

- Post a public timer displaying the full time allotment so partners can determine how long to converse and how quickly to move on to the next reading.

- To focus the paired interactions or to stimulate a specific type of thinking, the teacher may want to provide a stem for completion. For example, "A question that comes to mind when I read this is ___." Use the same stem or provide variation for each stopping point.

### References

Egawa, K., & Harste, J. (2001, January 1). Balancing the literacy curriculum: A new vision. *School Talk*, 35-57.

Protocols and Strategies

# Science Talks

## Purpose

Science Talks are discussions about big questions. They are appropriate for any grade level, but they are particularly useful for elementary students. Like a Socratic Seminar, Science Talks deal with provocative questions, often posed by students themselves. Science Talks provide space for students to collectively theorize, to build on each other's ideas, to work out thoughts, and to learn about scientific discourse. Most importantly, they allow all students to do exactly what scientists do: think about, wonder about, and talk about how things work. These talks provide a window on student thinking that can help teachers figure out what students really know and what their misconceptions are. Armed with this insight, teachers can better plan hands-on activities and experiments.

## Materials

- Guiding question for the Science Talk, determined beforehand

## Procedure

1. Choose the question. The best questions are provocative and open-ended, so as to admit multiple answers and theories. Often, students generate great questions for Science Talks. Teachers can also generate questions based on their own wonderings.

2. Introduce Science Talks to students. Gather students into a circle on the floor. Introduce the first Science Talk by discussing what scientists do.

3. Then ask, "What will help us talk as scientists?" Record the students' comments, as these will become the norms for your Science Talks. If the students don't mention making sure that everyone has a chance to talk, introduce that idea, as well as how each person can ensure that they themselves don't monopolize the conversation. Stress how each student's voice is valued and integral to the success of a Science Talk.

4. Set the culture. Students direct their comments to one another, not to the teacher. In fact, the teacher stays quiet and out of the way, facilitating only to make sure that students respectfully address one another and to point out when monopolizing behavior occurs. In a good talk, you'll hear students saying, "I want to add to what Grace said..." or "I think Derek is right about one thing, but I'm not so sure about...."

5. Another good question to pose is "How will we know that what we've said has been heard?" Students will readily talk about how they can acknowledge what's been said by repeating it or rephrasing before they go on to add their comments. This is a great place to add (if the students don't) that talking together is one way scientists build theories.

6. A typical talk lasts about 30 minutes. Take notes during the talk about who is doing the talking and to record particularly intriguing comments.

*continued*

Protocols and Strategies

# Variations

- With young students, do a movement exercise that relates to the Science Talk. For a talk on how plants grow, students may be invited to show, with their bodies, how plants grow from bulbs. Not only does this give students a chance to move before more sitting, it also gives them a different modality in which to express themselves. Sometimes the shyer students also find acting something out first helps them to verbalize it.

- Have students prepare for a Science Talk by reading and annotating pertinent texts. Combining Science Talk with a Jigsaw or another text-based protocol could work well here.

- Pair a Science Talk with a writing activity on the same topic.

- Record the talks. Replaying the tapes later helps to make sense of what at first hearing can seem incomprehensible. Students also love hearing the tapes of Science Talks.

# Socratic Seminar

## Purpose

Socratic Seminars promote thinking, meaning-making, and the ability to debate, use evidence, and build on one another's thinking. When well designed and implemented, the seminar provides an active role for every student, engages students in complex thinking about rich content, and teaches students discussion skills.

## Materials

- Provocative question for discussion, chosen beforehand

- Associated text(s)

- Anchor Chart for protocol norms

## Procedure

1. Select a significant piece of text or collection of short texts related to the current focus of study. This may be an excerpt from a book or an article from a magazine, journal, or newspaper. It might also be a poem, short story, or personal memoir. The text needs to be rich with possibilities for diverse points of view.

2. Develop an open-ended, provocative question as the starting point for the seminar discussion. The question should be worded to elicit differing perspectives and complex thinking. Students may also generate questions to discuss.

3. Students prepare for the seminar by reading the chosen piece of text in an active manner that helps them build background knowledge for participation in the discussion. The completion of the pre-seminar task is the student's "ticket" to participate in the seminar. The pre-seminar task could easily incorporate work on reading strategies. For example, students might be asked to read the article in advance and to text-code by underlining important information, putting question marks by segments they wonder about and exclamation points next to parts that surprise them.

4. Once the seminar begins, all students should be involved and should make sure others in the group are drawn into the discussion.

5. Begin the discussion with the open-ended question designed to provoke inquiry and diverse perspectives. The teacher may pose follow-up questions.

6. The discussion proceeds until you call time. At that time, the group debriefs their process; if using a Fishbowl (see Fishbowl entry and variations that follow), the outer circle members give their feedback sheets to the inner group students.

7. Protocol norms: Students...

- Respect other students. (Exhibit open-mindedness and value others' contributions.)

- Are active listeners. (Build on one another's ideas by referring to them.)

- Stay focused on the topic.

- Make specific references to the text. (Use examples from the text to explain their points.)

- Give input. (Ensure participation.)

*continued*

- Ask questions. (Clarifying questions and probing questions that push the conversation further and deeper when appropriate.)

## Variations

- Combine with the Fishbowl protocol. When it is time for the seminar, students are divided into two groups. One group forms the inner circle (the "fish") that will be discussing the text. The other group forms the outer circle; they will give feedback on content, contributions, and group skills. (Note: "Fishbowls" may be used with other instructional practices such as peer critiques, literature circles, or group work. If the number of students in the seminar is small, a Fishbowl does not need to be used.) Each person in the outer circle is asked to observe one of the students in the inner circle. Criteria or a rubric for the observations should be developed by/shared with students in advance: see the following example.

| Did the student... | Consistently | Occasionally | Not This Time | Notes/Comments |
|---|---|---|---|---|
| Respond to other students' comments in a respectful way? | | | | |
| Listen attentively without interruption? | | | | |
| Make eye contact with peers? | | | | |
| Exhibit preparation for the seminar? | | | | |
| Reference the text to support response? | | | | |
| Participate in the discussion? | | | | |
| Ask clarifying or probing questions? | | | | |

- Provide sentence stems that allow students to interact positively and thoughtfully with one another: "I'd like to build on that thought..." "Could you tell me more?" "May I finish my thought?"

### References

Israel, E. (2002). Examining multiple perspectives in literature. In *Inquiry and the literary text: Constructing discussions in the English Classroom*. Urbana, IL: NCTE.

# Tea Party

## Purpose

As described by Kylene Beers in her book *When Kids Can't Read: What Teachers Can Do*, the Tea Party protocol offers students a chance to consider parts of the text before they actually read it. It encourages active participation and attentive listening with a chance to get up and move around the classroom. It allows students to predict what they think will happen in the text as they make inferences, see causal relationships, compare and contrast, practice sequencing, and draw on prior knowledge. This protocol is very similar to Mystery Quotes, but with a strong focus on pre-reading, hence its description as its own protocol.

## Materials

- Phrases, sentences, or words directly from the text copied onto strips or index cards, one per student

- Recording form for predictions and questions, one per student

## Procedure

1. Decide on phrases, sentences, or words directly from the text to copy onto strips or index cards.

2. Don't paraphrase the text. You may omit words to shorten a sentence, but don't change the words.

3. Have students organized into groups of four or five.

4. Hand out strips or cards with phrases from the text; two (or more) students will have the same phrases.

5. Each student independently reads his or her phrase and makes a prediction about what this article could be about. Then students write a quick statement on their prediction recording form.

6. Next, students mingle around the room, reading to each other and discussing possible predictions.

7. Return to the small groups and, as groups, write a prediction starting with "We think this article will be about..., because...." Also, list questions they have.

8. Now, read the selection. Students read independently or as a group, highlighting information that confirms or changes their predictions.

9. Write a statement about revised predictions. Also continue to list lingering questions.

## Variations

- Use this protocol as a kickoff to a larger unit or expedition on the topic in question.

- Have students remain in their groups for the protocol instead of mingling, or have them work in pairs.

### References

Adapted from: Original by Debbie Bambino adapted from: Beers, G. (2003). *When kids can't read, what teachers can do: A guide for teachers, 6-12*. Portsmouth, NH: Heinemann.

# The Three D's:
# Decide, Debate, Discuss

## Purpose

Students articulate and reflect on their opinions about controversial questions. This protocol not only provides practice in the social dimensions of debate, but encourages students to support, reflect on, and possibly change their opinions based on logic and evidence.

## Materials

- Large "Strongly Agree" and "Strongly Disagree" signs

## Procedure

1. Post a sign at each end of the classroom. At one end, post "Strongly Agree." At the other end, post "Strongly Disagree."

2. Tell students that today they will be using the Three Ds protocol, which will allow them to share and explain their opinions. After they hear a statement, they will **decide** on their position about the topic and move to one side of the room or the other, or along an imaginary line of "middle ground." They will have the opportunity to **debate** and **discuss** why they decided to stand where they did.

3. Explain the steps of the protocol:

- After you make a statement, you will pause for students to think and then ask all students to decide on their position and move to their spot. Point out that since one side of the room is labeled "Strongly Disagree" and the other side labeled "Strongly Agree," this means that the middle of the room is undecided, but students can position themselves relatively closer to one side or another depending on which direction they are leaning.

- Ask students to debate and discuss their opinions, making sure to hear from people on different sides of the room. If appropriate, students should use textual evidence.

- If a student hears an opinion that changes his mind, he can move to a different part of the room.

4. Model how the protocol will work. Make a statement (such as "Chocolate ice cream is delicious") and show students how you would move to reflect your opinion. The modeling helps students internalize how to position themselves.

5. As you use the protocol, repeat each statement twice.

## Variations

- Students may stand up or sit down in their places.

- Use the protocol to enhance the writing process for persuasive or argumentative pieces.

- Use the protocol as an effective formative assessment.

# Think-Pair-Share

## Purpose

This protocol ensures that all students simultaneously and collaboratively engage with a text or topic. It allows students to recognize and articulate their own ideas before considering the ideas of others; it also promotes synthesis and the social construction of knowledge.

## Materials

- Guiding questions, decided beforehand

- Optional: recording form with questions and answer spaces for students

## Procedure

1. Students are given a short and specific time frame (1 to 2 minutes) to independently and briefly process their understanding/opinion of a text selection, discussion question, or topic (this is the "thinking" part of Think-Pair-Share).

2. Students then pair up and share their thinking or writing with a peer for another short and specific time frame (e.g., 1 minute each).

3. Finally, the teacher leads a whole-class sharing of thoughts, often charting the diverse thinking and patterns in student ideas. This helps both students and the teacher assess understanding and clarify ideas.

## Variations

- Pair the Think-Pair-Share protocol with a close reading lesson to allow students time and space to collaboratively work on their answers to text-dependent questions.

- Allow students to facilitate the whole-class sharing.

### References

Lyman, F. (1981). The responsive classroom discussion: The inclusion of all students. In *Mainstreaming digest*. College Park, MD: University of Maryland College of Education.

# World Café

## Purpose

To discuss a topic or various topics, rotating the leadership role and mixing groups of students. This protocol is an extensive exercise in listening and speaking skills.

## Materials

- Chart/poster paper
- Marker for the leader/recorder

## Procedure

1. Form three groups of three or four and sit together at a table.

2. Each group should select a "leader." The leader's role is to record the major points of the conversation that takes place at the table and to then summarize the conversation using the recorded notes.

3. The group discusses the topic at hand until time is called. Groups can be discussing the same topic or related topics.

4. The leader stays put; the rest of the group rotates to the next table.

5. The leader (the one who didn't move) presents a summary of the conversation recorded from the former group to the new group.

6. Each table selects a new leader.

7. Again, the new leader's role is to record the major points of the conversation that takes place at the table and to then summarize the conversation using the recorded notes.

8. The group discusses the topic at hand until time is called.

9. Repeat the process, ideally until all students have had a chance to lead.

10. After the final round, the last group of leaders presents to the whole group rather than reporting out to a "next rotation."

## Variations

- Mix the Room: For large groups, begin with everyone in a circle. Number off around the circle, from one to five. The teacher provides a prompt, and at the teacher's signal, each group of five clusters into a small circle to discuss a topic for a designated amount of time. The teacher then signals for the ones to advance to the next cluster. Ones then provide a summary of the last group's discussion before the newly formed group discusses a second prompt. Each time a new prompt is given, the teacher asks a different number to move forward to the next cluster, thus "mixing the room" for each new prompt.

### References

Adapted from: www.theworldcafe.com

# Focus on Checking for Understanding and Ongoing Assessment

When we check all students' levels of understanding throughout each lesson, it sends the message that everyone's thinking is important and necessary, and furthers the learning and engagement of all. Using the checking for understanding and ongoing assessment strategies that follow allows us to track learning and adapt instruction on the spot.

# Catch and Release

## Purpose

When students are working on their own, they often need clarification or pointers so they do not struggle for too long or lose focus. Catch and Release allows them to retrain their attention on the learning and seek the answers or clarification they need for any questions that have come up during the preceding work time.

## Materials

- Optional: public timer

## Procedure

1. Set a small, manageable "chunk" of work time for students.

2. Circulate during the work time. Synthesize and take note of persistent questions or confusions.

3. Bring the class back together after the work time. Very briefly, answer or clarify as needed any questions students have had about the work.

4. Repeat the cycle.

## Variations

- A useful ratio of work time to checks for understanding or clarifying information is 7 minutes of work time (release), followed by 2 minutes of teacher-directed clarifications or use of quick-check strategies (catch).

Checking for Understanding

# Click It

## Purpose

Clickers allow for collective, instantaneous sharing of information or answers to academic questions and for an assessment of whether knowledge has been retained and learned correctly, both individually and in the class as a whole. Clickers are engaging and interactive and work especially well for vocabulary- and math-based questions.

## Materials

- Clickers, one for each student, and associated technology needed to display results

## Procedure

1. Students are given a question to answer. They use their clicker to respond to the questions.

2. All responses are immediately visible for the teacher and students to analyze and discuss.

## Variations

- Many tablet and computer applications also offer "clicker technology."

- If no technology is available, consider using white boards or blank paper for students to write on and hold up to reveal their answers.

# Cold Call

## Purpose

Cold Call serves as an engaging and challenging yet supportive way to hold students accountable for answering oral questions the teacher poses, regardless of whether a hand is raised. Cold Call requires students to think and interact with the question at hand, even if they're not sure of the answer. Cold Call also promotes equity in the classroom; students who normally dominate the discourse step back and allow other students to demonstrate their knowledge and expertise.

## Materials

- Optional: equity sticks, name cards, or tracking chart

## Procedure

1. Name a question before identifying students to answer it.

2. Call on students regardless of whether they have hands raised.

3. Scaffold questions from simple to increasingly complex, probing for deeper explanations.

4. Connect thinking threads by returning to previous comments and connecting them to current ones; model this for students and teach them to do it too.

## Variations

- Call on students using equity sticks, name cards, or a tracking chart to ensure that all students contribute.

- Pair Cold Call with No Opt Out to ensure that students have full access to the correct answers to the questions asked.

- Hot Seat: Place key reflection or probing questions on random seats throughout the room. When prompted, students check their seats and answer the questions. Students who do not have a hot seat question are asked to agree or disagree with the response and explain their thinking.

### References

Lemov, D. (2010). *Teach like a champion: 49 techniques that put students on the path to college.* San Francisco, CA: Jossey-Bass.

# Equity Sticks

## Purpose

Equity sticks are true to their name: they ensure academic equity by allowing teachers to physically track who they have called on or interacted with during the course of the class. This is especially useful during whole-class discussions or while working with large groups of students.

## Materials

- Wooden sticks (e.g., tongue depressors or popsicle sticks) or cards with a student's name on each

## Procedure

1. Pose a question to the class.

2. After giving students some think time, call on a student for an answer. As you do so, move the equity stick from one location to another, indicating that the student has participated in class that day.

## Variations

- Pair equity sticks with Cold Call by choosing a stick or card randomly for a student response.

- Color in one end of the equity stick. Instead of moving the whole stick, flip the stick upside down in its container to indicate via color that the student has been called on.

# Guided Practice

## Purpose

Teachers often provide Guided Practice in a lesson after students grapple with a concept or a text, before releasing them to independent application. Guided Practice provides a model for how the independent work will run as well as a concrete representation of the goal of the work.

## Materials

- Optional: Recording form to note which students need more individual attention after Guided Practice

## Procedure

1. During Guided Practice, students quickly try the task at hand in pairs or in a low-stakes environment.

2. Strategically circulate, monitoring students' readiness for the task and noting students who may need reteaching or would benefit from an extension or a more challenging independent application.

3. Use an appropriate quick-check strategy to determine needs for differentiation during independent application time. Be sure to check for understanding from all students before moving on from Guided Practice. Ensure that all students have an opportunity to respond to questions, receive feedback, and practice alongside the teacher until they are fluent in the content/task.

## Variations

- Break content into smaller "chunks" to scaffold understanding.

- Ask "fuzzier" questions that do not necessarily have discrete answers, and require students to explain their thinking.

- Make Guided Practice a game. Games increase engagement and focus.

- Combine Guided Practice with protocols that allow students to share their work during the practice session, such as Poster Session or Think-Pair-Share.

Checking for Understanding

# Human Bar Graph

## Purpose

A quick, visual, and engaging method of determining where students are in relation to a learning target. Like Thumb-O-Meter, the Human Bar Graph asks students to self-assess and share their impressions of their learning with their teacher and peers.

## Materials

- Signs or designations for the graph levels of mastery posted in the room

## Procedure

1. Identify a range of levels of understanding or mastery (e.g., beginning/developing/accomplished or confused/I'm okay/I'm rocking!) as labels for three to four adjacent lines.

2. Have students then form a human bar graph by standing in the line that best represents their current level of understanding.

## Variations

- Learning Line-Ups: Identify one end of the room with a descriptor such as "Novice" or "Beginning" and the other end as "Expert" or "Exemplary." Students place themselves on this continuum based on where they are with a learning target, skill, or task. Invite them to explain their thinking to the whole class or the people near them.

# No Opt Out

## Purpose

No Opt Out is a powerful method of supported accountability in a classroom. Any student who answers a question is responsible for giving the correct answer in that moment. Mistakes are not ignored, punished, or cause for embarrassment, but a part of the learning territory. By being provided with the correct answer from a peer, students feel challenged but safe.

## Materials

- Predetermined questions to pose to students

## Procedure

1. Require all students to correctly answer a question posed to them (in cases when questions actually have a "correct" answer).

2. Follow up on incorrect or partial answers by questioning other students until a correct answer is given by another student, through either Cold Call or calling on a volunteer.

3. Return to any student who gave an incorrect or partial answer. Have them give a complete and correct response, based on the correct response just given by their peer.

## Variations

- Give a student a "memory cue." "Who can tell Alisa where she can find the answer?" or "Who can tell Alex the first thing that he can do to find the answer?"

- As an extension, ask a more complex or difficult question to the same student: "Good. Let's try a harder one."

### References

Lemov, D. (2010). *Teach like a champion: 49 techniques that put students on the path to college.* San Francisco, CA: Jossey-Bass.

Checking for Understanding

# Presentation Quizzes

## Purpose

A summative assessment of a peer's presentation lends gravitas and importance to the material, and sends the message that all contributions to learning are important and valued. It also serves as a means of anchoring student accountability and engagement in the presentation.

## Materials

- Short summative quiz on information shared in a peer presentation (multiple choice, one or two short responses, true/false, etc.)

## Procedure

1. When peers present a project, speech, or other academic presentation, ensure that other students know they are responsible for learning the information.

2. Pair student presentations with short quizzes on the presentation material at the end of class.

3. Grade these as you would any other summative assessment.

## Variations

- Have the student presenting create and grade the quiz.

Checking for Understanding

# Red Light, Green Light

## Purpose

Red Light, Green Light, and other related strategies, help students and teachers visualize student comfort level or readiness in relation to a learning target using objects, colors, locations, or shared metaphors. Teachers can then adjust their instruction accordingly.

## Materials

- Popsicle sticks, cards, or poker chips in three colors (red, yellow, green)

## Procedure

1. Students have red, yellow, and green objects accessible (e.g., popsicle sticks, poker chips, cards).

2. When prompted to reflect on a learning target or readiness for a task, students place the color on their desk that describes their comfort level or readiness (red: stuck or not ready; yellow: need support soon; green: ready to start).

3. Teachers target their support to the reds first, then move to yellows and greens.

4. Students change their colors as needed to describe their status.

## Variations

- Table Tags: Place paper signs or table tents in three areas with colors, symbols, or descriptors that indicate possible student levels of understanding or readiness for a task or target. Students sit in the area that best describes them, moving to a new area when relevant.

- Glass, Bugs, Mud: After students try a task or review a learning target or assignment, they identify their understanding or readiness for application using the windshield metaphor for clear vision (glass: totally clear; bugs: a little fuzzy; mud: I can barely see).

# Thumb-O-Meter

## Purpose

To physically show degree of agreement, readiness for tasks, or comfort with a learning target/concept. Thumb-O-Meter creates a clear visual for teachers to use when checking for understanding.

## Materials

- None

## Procedure

1. Students show their agreement/disagreement, comfort level, or readiness by holding a thumb-up, thumb-sideways, or thumb-down (or some variation in between).

## Variations

- Get creative with other versions of "-O-Meters" that allow students to physically demonstrate where they are with a target or concept (e.g., Pinky-O-Meter; Eyelid-O-Meter).

# Tracking Progress

## Purpose

Tracking Progress allows students to see their cumulative and collaborative efforts toward mastery of a learning target. This visual representation not only stimulates self-reflection, but points to the social and accountable nature of the work. All students work together toward the goal.

## Materials

- Poster or individual charts of learning targets and levels of proficiency

## Procedure

1. Teachers post a chart on the wall or distribute individual charts displaying learning targets and levels of proficiency.

2. Students indicate their self-assessed level of proficiency by drawing a dot or making a mark on the chart, usually multiple times.

3. Students can use different-colored dots, ink stamps, or markers and dates to indicate progress over time.

## Variations

- Sticky Bars: Create a chart that describes levels of understanding, progress, or mastery. Have students write their names or use an identifying symbol on a sticky note and place their notes on the appropriate place on the chart.

# Turn and Talk

## Purpose

Turn and Talk is one of the easiest, quickest, and most efficient means of creating collaboration among students. It can be used practically at any time, anywhere, in a lesson in any content area.

## Materials

- None

## Procedure

1. When prompted, students turn to a shoulder buddy or neighbor.

2. In a set amount of time, students share their ideas about a prompt or question posed by the teacher or other students.

3. Depending on the goals of the lesson and the nature of the Turn and Talk, students may share some key ideas from their paired discussions with the whole class.

## Variations

- Students can use a written version of Turn and Talk, brainstorming their answers on paper very briefly and sharing them aloud, or switching papers.

Checking for Understanding

# Focus on Building Academic Vocabulary

Vocabulary is the foundational building block of reading comprehension, writing fluency, oral articulation, and content-based knowledge. Protocols and strategies for emphasizing vocabulary, like those that follow, play a large part in the active classroom, serve multiple academic purposes at once, and are appropriate for any grade level and content area.

# Contextual Redefinition

## Purpose

Contextual Redefinition gives students a point-by-point strategy for using the context of the text to find the meaning of unknown words. It asks students to find the unambiguous information in a text selection and synthesize it with the author's intent. Contextual Redefinition also asks students to pay attention to other "keys" to word meaning in the text, such as grammar and examples. This creates a platform from which students can make informed judgments about what a word might mean.

## Materials

- Optional: chart paper or digital camera

- Optional: vocabulary recording form

## Procedure

1.  Remind students that words have many meanings, and their context is a key component of determining that meaning.

2.  Choose words from a text that might be challenge for students to define. Write these words on the board, on chart paper, or under a digital camera.

3.  Have students predict definitions for these terms before reading the text. Students' predictions will be "loose" and possibly inaccurate, due to the fact that they are making these predictions independently of reading.

4.  Write all student predictions on the board, on chart paper, or under a digital camera.

5.  Have the students read the text, annotating where the vocabulary in question occurs.

6.  Ask students to revisit their previous definitions and see which reflect the use of these words in the context of the selection.

## Variations

- Use dictionaries, thesauri, or other vocabulary references to assist in making meanings clear to students.

- Combine Contextual Redefinition with other vocabulary strategies in this section, such as the Frayer model, to "zoom in" on particular words.

### References

Allen, J. (2007). *Inside words: Tools for teaching academic vocabulary, grades 4-12.* Portland, ME: Stenhouse.

Cunningham, J.W., Cunningham, P.M., & Arthur, S.V. (1981). *Middle and secondary school reading.* New York, NY: Longman.

Lenski, S., Wham, M., & Johns, J. (1999). *Reading and learning strategies for middle and high school students.* Dubuque, IA: Kendall Hunt.

# Frayer Model

## Purpose

The Frayer Model is a four-part graphic approach to analyzing and understanding vocabulary. For each word, the Frayer Model asks students to define the term, pinpointing its most important characteristics, and then provide both examples and non-examples of the word. The strength of the model lies in requiring students to both analyze the word's meaning, and then apply that meaning to the determination of examples and non-examples.

## Materials

- Frayer Model graphic organizer, one for each student

- List of key vocabulary from a reading selection

## Procedure

1. Choose key vocabulary from a reading selection and distribute/display the list to the class.

2. Explain the Frayer Model graphic organizer to the class, using a word of your choice to model the use of the graphic organizer.

3. Have the students break up into pairs.

4. Assign each pair one of the key vocabulary words and have these groups complete the organizer together.

5. Have student pairs present their models to the class.

## Frayer Model

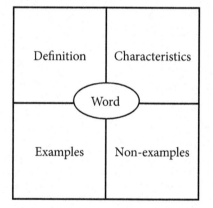

*continued*

## Variations

- Have students facilitate the summative discussion at the end of the protocol.

- Have students complete Frayer Models for particularly difficult words prior to a reading as a pre-teaching strategy.

- Combine this strategy with a Poster Session to share the information.

- Photocopy student work and distribute as a collated glossary.

**References**

Frayer, D., Frederick, W.C., & Klausmeier, H.J. (1969). *A schema for testing the level of cognitive mastery*. Madison, WI: Wisconsin Center for Education Research.

# List/Group/Label

## Purpose

The List/Group/Label strategy rests upon the critical thinking required to identify relationships between words. It uses three steps for organizing a general vocabulary list from a text selection into meaningful groups of words.

## Materials

- Optional: chart paper or digital camera
- Note-catcher for List/Group/Label, one for each student

## Procedure

1. Choose a main idea or concept from a text.
2. Have students brainstorm all the words they think relate to this concept.
3. Divide the class into groups of three or four students.
4. Teams take the brainstormed list and put the words into smaller, meaningful groups, providing evidence and reasoning behind the groupings.
5. Students create an overarching name or label for each of their groupings that reflects their reasoning.
6. Students read the text.
7. Students then revise their terms or groups so that they include only information that matches the concept's meaning in the context of the text.

## Variations

- New terms, groups, or labels can be added or revised as students increase their familiarity with the text.

### References

Lenski, S., Wham, M., & Johns, J. (1999). *Reading and learning strategies for middle and high school students.* Dubuque, IA: Kendall Hunt.

Taba, H. (1967). *Teacher's handbook for elementary social studies.* Reading, MA: Addison-Wesley.

Tierney, R.J. (2000). *Reading strategies and practices: A compendium (5th ed.).* Boston, MA: Allyn & Bacon.

# Semantic Webbing

## Purpose

Semantic Webbing builds upon students' background knowledge and experiences, allowing them to organize and synthesize that knowledge with that which they encounter from reading a text. Using a graphic organizer, students create a "map" of their knowledge about themes in a text both before and after reading.

## Materials

- Optional: chart paper or digital camera

- Note-catcher for semantic webbing, one for each student

## Procedure

1. Write a key word or phrase from the text on the board, on chart paper, or under a digital camera.

2. Have students think of as many words as they can that relate to this word or phrase and record them.

3. Students group the words meaningfully and label each group with a descriptive title.

4. Share the groupings and have students decide whether the groupings are appropriate or should be revised. Write the students' final decisions on the board, on chart paper, or under a digital camera.

5. Have the students read the text.

6. Repeat steps 1-4, revising the groups and terms again as indicated.

## Variations

- Identify several themes in a reading selection and have students share their background knowledge on these themes. Students should skim the text and then make predictions on how the themes will be treated. Record the most logical and strongly supported predictions. Then have the students read the text for the purpose of evaluating their predictions, revising their predictions accordingly.

### References

Maddux, C.D., Johnston, D.L., & Willis, J.W. (1997). *Educational computing: Learning with tomorrow's technologies.* Boston, MA: Allyn & Bacon.

Heimlich, J., & Pittelman, S. (1986). *Semantic mapping: Classroom applications.* Newark, DE: International Reading Association.

# SVES
# (Stephens Vocabulary Elaboration Strategy)

## Purpose

The Stephens Vocabulary Elaboration Strategy (SVES) requires that students keep a vocabulary notebook where they write and define any new terms they come across. Students should regularly review these words and work to use them in "real-world" contexts, in both their social and academic experiences. The use of a dictionary, electronic or otherwise, is critical to this strategy; students also study specific texts to decide upon the most context-appropriate definition of certain words.

## Materials

- Notebook, one per student

## Procedure

1. Ask students to write any new or unclear word in their notebook and record the context (advertisement, class reading, the sentence in which the word was found, and so on).

2. Students then write dictionary definitions (including the parts of speech) by any new word in their notebooks. Students should choose the most appropriate meaning for the context.

3. Students recast the dictionary definition in their own words and record it in their notebook.

4. Regularly review the notebooks. Provide opportunities for students to use their words in other reading assignments, oral class discussions, or writing pieces.

## Variations

- Combine vocabulary notebooks with Frayer Model graphic organizers for a rich interaction with new words.

- Have students create electronic notebooks using word processing software or free web-based applications (e.g., Evernote).

### References

Brown, J.E., Phillips, L.B., & Stephens, E.C. (1993). *Towards literacy: Theory and applications for teaching writing in the content areas.* Belmont, CA: Wadsworth.

# Vocabulary Squares

## Purpose

Vocabulary Squares is a strategy best used with texts that are at or slightly above a student's Lexile measure, and it is an effective strategy in cases where the semantic dimension of a text may impede reading fluency. The strategy helps students deepen their understanding of key words necessary to aid comprehension or make meaning.

## Materials

- Vocabulary Squares graphic organizer, one for each student

## Procedure

1. Vocabulary Squares consist of a four-part grid, each with a different label.

2. For each identified vocabulary word, the student fills in appropriate information in each section of the grid.

## Variations

- Some sample labels for the grid include the following:

    - Definition in your own words

    - Synonyms

    - Variations

    - Part of speech

    - Prefix/suffix/root

    - Sketch

    - Symbol

Vocabulary word: _____

| Definition | Synonyms |
|---|---|
| | |
| Parts of Speech | Sketch |
| | |

# Word Sort

## Purpose

Word Sorts allow students to find common roots, spellings, and phonemes; to use their background knowledge to sort words and set a purpose for reading; or to reflect on their learning after reading. Sorts can be used successfully throughout different content areas.

## Materials

- Word collection (on a note-catcher, 3x5 cards, paper strips, or the like)
- Note-catcher with listed word categories

## Procedure

1. In closed word sorts, the teacher defines the process for categorizing the words. Students engage in critical thinking to determine which words fit into which category.

### Closed Word Sort Example

| **Categories (provided by teacher):** metals, nonmetals **Words:** gold, silver, mercury, helium, potassium, quartz | |
| --- | --- |
| **Student Work Sample** | |
| *Metals* | *Nonmetals* |
| Gold | Helium |
| Mercury | Quartz |
| Silver | Potassium |

## Variations

- In open word sorts, the students determine how to categorize the words, using critical thinking to determine their own logical sorts (Vacca & Vacca, 1999).

### Open Word Sort Example

| Words: gold, silver, mercury, helium, potassium, quartz |
| --- |
| **Student Work Sample (categories chosen by students)** |
| *Metals with luster and malleability* Gold, silver, mercury |
| *Mineral* Quartz, Potassium |
| *Gas* Helium |

### References

Johns, J., & Berglund, R. (2002). *Fluency: Questions, answers, evidence-based strategies*. Dubuque: IA: Kendall Hunt.

Lenski, S., Wham, M., & Johns, J. (1999). *Reading and learning strategies for middle and high school students*. Dubuque, IA: Kendall Hunt.

Vacca, R., & Vacca, J. (1995). *Content area reading (5th ed.)*. Glenview, IL: Scott Foresman.

# Appendices

# Appendix A

---

## Transition Routines and Activities for Primary Students

Our youngest students often benefit from singing or listening to a song or verse, or moving in specific ways as they transition from one place or activity to the next. As with all transitions, those that follow must be taught and practiced in order to be most effective.

## Transitions with Song and Verse

- Play calming music as students first enter the classroom or as you start a new lesson or activity. When all students have arrived in the room or at a designated place have them watch you and copy your slow movements in silence. Breathe deeply, sway, lift arms, relax your body, etc.

- Play a clip of a well-known song that has an obvious ending that all students will recognize. When the music stops, all students must be at their seats.

- Sing together a simple transition song with words that match the actions you'd like to see. For example:

  > One, two, three, four, little feet cross the floor
  >
  > Five, six, seven, eight, little friends at their place
  >
  > Nine and 10... in our seats again!

- If you play an instrument and/or feel comfortable keeping a rhythm with clapping, snapping, or percussion, you can play a simple melody or put together clapping and snapping beats. Students do the rhythm as they move. Stop at the end of a set number of beats and have all students who are at their seats sit down. Continue the rhythm as the other students move to their seats, stopping after a set number of beats to have those at their seats sit down. Continue until all are seated.

- Have students recite a verse that gets quieter and quieter with each step they take so that the transition ends in silence. For example:

  > A wise old owl lived in an oak,
  >
  > The more he saw, the less he spoke.
  >
  > The less he spoke, the more he heard.
  >
  > Can we all be like that wise old bird?

## Transitions with Movement

- Begin with students in a circle holding hands or with hands on the shoulders of the student in front of them. Singing a song, chanting a verse, or moving like little mice as quietly as possible, lead the line to one seat or table at a time, dropping off students as you go.

- Divide students into animal groups. Birds, butterflies, mice, fish, and other small creatures that can move slowly, smoothly, and quietly are the best choices. Each group practices the movement of that animal. Then, on cue, the birds are asked to fly gently to their seats, the mice scamper off, and the fish swim along, etc. You may also choose to have the entire class do one movement all together.

- Play *Simon Says* starting in one place and eventually moving students to the next place you want them to be (e.g., Simon says, "stand up"; Simon says, "turn and face the tables"; Simon says, "take three small steps towards the tables").

# Appendix B

## Sample Restorative Circle/Conference Protocol

Adapted from the Greene School, Greenwich, Rhode Island

1.  Framing of Conference: the facilitator begins by explaining expectations, which include confidentiality, openness to process, and agreement to abide by the final resolution.

2.  Go-around 1: Introduce yourself—name, role/grade, and a favorite character from a book.

3.  Peer Facilitator reviews and reads the Conference Protocols:

    • One person talks at a time.

    • The person speaking uses "I" statements (e.g., I was angry: I wasn't thinking at the time).

    • The speaker sticks to the facts of the situation under discussion.

    • Strong feelings are fine, normal and even encouraged; aggression is not.

4.  Facilitator reads the Peer Conferencing Form and/or describes the situation that occurred.

5.  Peer Facilitator engages with the participant brought to the RSL Conferencing, and then all other participants/ "requester" using restorative questions. Before moving onto the next part, Peer Facilitator paraphrases what he or she heard and asks if there are any corrections that need to be made.

6.  Next, the Peer Facilitator asks/offers restorative questions to the "requester" or other party member. Before moving on to the next part, Peer Facilitator paraphrases what he or she heard and asks if there are any corrections that need to be made.

7.  Peer Facilitator now opens the floor for conversation, and closely monitors discussion for conferencing norms and following the protocols. Peer facilitator re-engages with restorative questioning when needed.

8.  Summary: Peer Facilitator tries to paraphrase and recapture main points.

9.  Go Around 2: What is the ideal resolution? What does restitution look like? Allow the participants to suggest resolutions first and then run the go-around to collaboratively come to the final resolution.

10. Facilitator summarizes the resolution(s) aloud, and the resolution(s) is recorded on the Request Form. Follow-up occurs at one week and two weeks.

11. (Optional) Go Around 3: Debrief the process with everyone, including the participants.

# Appendix C

## Sample Behavior Communication Grade K-2 Student Form

Adapted from Springville K-8 School, Beaverton, Oregon

Student_____    Date of incident_____

Teacher_____    Time of incident_____

Location of incident_____

What happened (draw or write):

What harm was caused?

       Person who was hurt:_____

       Community/Springville:_____

       Family:_____

       Other people:_____

What can be done to fix it? (Write or draw)

What will you do next time? (Write or draw)